Sustained Content Teaching in Academic ESL/EFL

Sustained Content Teaching in Academic ESL/EFL

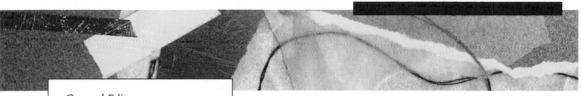

A Practical Approach

General Editor

Marcia Pally

New York University

Fordham University

Contributors

Nathalie Bailey

Rudolph W. Bernard

Paul J. Camhi

Joan G. Carson

Lynne Flowerdew

Charles S. Haynes

Loretta F. Kasper

Leila May-Landy

Gayle Nelson

Neil R. Williams

Houghton Mifflin Company   Boston   New York

Director of ESL Programs: Susan Maguire

Senior Associate Editor: Kathy Sands Boehmer

Editorial Assistant: Kevin M. Evans

Senior Project Editor: Janet Young

Editorial Assistant: Nasya Laymon

Senior Production/Design Coordinator: Jennifer Meyer Dare

Assistant Manufacturing Coordinator: Andrea Wagner

Associate Marketing Manager: Tina Crowley Desprez

Cover Design: Rebecca Fagan

Cover Image: Daniel Root/Photonica

CREDITS

Definition p. 2 used by permission. From *Merriam-Webster's Collegiate® Dictionary.* Tenth Edition. © 1999 by Merriam-Webster, Incorporated.

Excerpt in Chapter 3 reprinted with permission of Scribner, a Division of Simon & Schuster, Inc., from *The Old Man and the Sea* by Ernest Hemingway. Copyright 1952 by Ernest Hemingway. Copyright renewed © 1980 by Mary Hemingway.

Printed in the U.S.A.

Library of Congress Catalog Card Number: 99-71958

ISBN: 0-395-96076-2

123456789-DSG-03 02 01 00 99

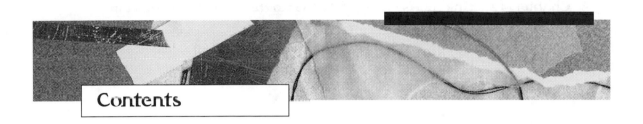

Contents

Preface   vii

Chapter 1   **Sustaining Interest/Advancing Learning:** Sustained Content-Based
Instruction in ESL/EFL—Theoretical Background and Rationale
Marcia Pally   1

Chapter 2   **Reading and Writing for Academic Purposes**   *Joan G. Carson*   19

Chapter 3   ***The Old Man and the Sea:*** A Data-Driven, Corpus-Based Grammar-
Reading Course   *Charles S. Haynes*   35

Chapter 4   **Sustained Content Study and the Internet:** Developing Functional
and Academic Literacies   *Loretta F. Kasper*   54

Chapter 5   **Frames for Reference:** Content-Based Instruction in the Context of
Speech   *Neil R. Williams*   74

Chapter 6   **Critical Thinking Development and Academic Writing for
Engineering Students**   *Lynne Flowerdew*   96

Chapter 7   **Well-Formedness Principles on Syntactic Structures**
Paul J. Camhi   117

Chapter 8   **Managing Information for Writing University Exams in
American History**   *Gayle Nelson with Jill Burns*   132

Chapter 9   **"Film & Society":** A Course for Analyzing Readings, Writing, and
Critical Thinking   *Marcia Pally*   158

Gratis

121508

Chapter 10   *E Pluribus Unum:* Health as Content for a Community of Learners
             Nathalie Bailey   179

Chapter 11   **Reflecting on Commentary:** Mind, Intellect, and a Use of Language
             Rudolph W. Bernard   200

Chapter 12   **Linking Assessment to the Content-Based Curriculum**
             Leila May-Landy   223

             Index   241

Contents

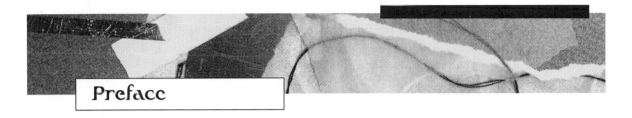

Preface

What Is Sustained Content? Who Should Use It and Why?

I became interested in content-based language teaching when I found I could not understand essays written in my native language, English. It was disturbing to read through grammatically and syntactically accurate passages and yet to lose the train of thought after three or so sentences. After several paragraphs, I was quite unsure as to what the essays were "about."

Many readers of this book will recognize this uncertainty from their own work with student papers. The book's readers may be ESL or EFL teachers in high school, college preparatory, technical, or adult education programs who focus on the needs of non-native speakers (NNS). Readers may also be teachers of writing classes in secondary schools, college, or continuing education programs; they may be guidance counselors, college advisors, or tutors, or staff the many writing and skills centers found in libraries, high schools, and colleges.

It is to these audiences that we bring our experiences of teaching English through **sustained content-based instruction (CBI).** These are classes in which students practice English language skills—reading, writing, speaking, listening, and grammatical forms—in the process of studying one subject area, usually for a semester. Students learn the skills because they need them for the immediate, pressing job of grasping the content. Their language teachers provide a "scaffold"—to borrow from Vygotsky—to help them do so. Although content-based instruction has been used extensively in language classes over the last 15 years, *sustained* content-based instruction is new. These are not language classes linked to "sister" content classes, but rather language classes which themselves follow a subject throughout the term. They simulate a college class but additionally provide explicit instruction in language and academic skills. It is our hope that the sustained content courses described here—our rationale for teaching them, methodology, assessment of student progress, and student feedback—will give readers a sense of the possible applications of sustained CBI and enable them to assess its effectiveness. To provide a brief introduction and a gloss of the book's chapters, I need to return to the papers above, which I could not understand.

These essays were written by NNS graduate students whose English language skills were advanced enough to gain them entrance into a prestigious urban university. They had high scores on TOEFL exams and were expected to perform alongside native speakers in their graduate programs. Some of the papers were written by master's degree students in TESOL, men and women who would be teaching their own ESL and EFL classes. And yet I could not follow their work. These student-writers were not for the most part lacking in vocabulary or sentence-level accuracy, nor did they fail to use appropriate cohering devices. In fact, they often overused them. But something, to my mind, did not "track."

That something turned out to be the way argumentation is made in English. The idea, for instance, of categorizing the components of argument into concept and proof was not evident in their writing—which meant either that these NNS were not classifying components of argument into "concept" and "proof" in the first place, or that they were but they did not use the same classification system as English speakers do. In other words, what counts as concept and proof for me did not count as such for them. Understandably, the arrangement of ideas into a thesis-and-support structure (be it inductive or deductive, for expository or persuasive purposes) was also something hard to discern in their writing, as were more complex tasks, such as abstracting an author's argument or synthesizing, comparing, and contrasting texts.

Listening to students' oral presentations, I found much the same. The exposition of claim-and-support was diffuse. Moreover, the use of emphasis, tone and emotion, appropriate register, pragmatic strategies such as time and conversation management, and other devices that roughly parallel the cohering and cohesive tactics of writing nevertheless did not make the presentations cohere (see Williams, this volume).

Reviewing many essays and oral presentations did not make me think that these students lacked claims or ways to make them. Just the opposite: they were clearly offering long sequences of ideas and employing many approaches to present them. But these approaches were not clear in English. As a result, students' ideas were not easily understood, and so not appreciated. Their academic/professional progress was being hobbled because, simply put, it was difficult to see how smart they were.

If graduate students already accepted into advanced degree programs were writing and speaking at odds with English language norms, how were younger students or those still in ESL programs communicating? Perhaps not as well as they could be. My exploration of student work in intermediate-advanced ESL classes supported research showing a gap between the skills taught in ESL programs and those needed by students headed for academic/professional settings (Chitrapu, 1996; Kasper, 1995/1996, 1997; Leki & Carson, 1994, 1997; Smoke, 1998; see Chapter 1, this volume, for an extended discussion). If language emanates from context, we were not providing the context for full development of this sort of English.

Students, like most other people, learn something when they have to. When something must get done, they learn what they need to do it. The question was, What context or situation could be created in the classroom in which students would "have to" do various academic/professional jobs and so learn the skills necessary to do them? Widdowson has persuasively argued (1990, 1998) that importing authentic English (even authentic academic English) to language classes misses the point, because it fails to create an authentic context where students use the language to do the real tasks from which the language emanated in the first place. The absence of authentic context produces "unrealistic uses of language," semantically meaningful and pragmatically meaningless (1998, p. 707).

> I would argue, on the contrary, against using authentic language in the classroom, on the fairly reasonable grounds that it is actually impossible to do so. The language cannot be authentic because the classroom cannot provide the contextual conditions for it to be authenticated by the learners. The authenticity or reality of language use in its normal pragmatic functioning depends on its being localised within a particular discourse community . . . But learners are outsiders, by definition, not members of user communities. So the language that is authentic for native speaker users cannot possibly be authentic for learners. (1998, p. 711)

In other words, reality can't be faked.

Widdowson goes some way toward explaining why widespread use of authentic material in language classes over the past 20 years has nevertheless left academic/professional skills underdeveloped, and why the oral and written presentations I observed did not "track." The students had not been using English as a real discourse community might. They were talking about articles they had read and were writing in reaction to them, but they were not grappling with the content in the rigorous ways that ideas are approached in English-speaking academic/professional settings. Because language classes generally cover readings on various topics and change topics often, students had no opportunity to stick with a subject and analyze a range of sources within a discipline—synthesizing, questioning, and evaluating them—nor were they writing from a position of some content-area expertise (which includes familiarity both with the subject and with the forms used to present it).

In what context would students in English classes "have to" do these academic tasks? What classroom setup would satisfy the requirement of Widdowson, and of communicative language teachers internationally, that students use language authentically? I agree with Widdowson that students—with their differing backgrounds, majors, and career goals—are not the discourse community, for instance, in which the words in this book make sense or provoke disagreement. They are not the discourse community of market analysts or radiology technicians, or any other academic/professional field. So authentic material from academic/professional disciplines will necessarily be inauthentic for them, and leave them outsiders producing pragmatically unrealistic English.

Yet those who find the use of authentic English insufficient as a method of language instruction are right by half. Bringing academic/professional English to the language classroom is inadequate—not because it imports too much academic/professional language (the language of a discourse community to which students do not belong), but because it brings in too little. The pragmatic context must be brought in as well. Students in language classes must do with authentic material what those in the discourse community do with it—the discourse community not of academic/professional experts but of academic/professional students.

Students in language classes are at bottom learners, who might be asked to do what learners in academic/professional programs do, and so they might compose a student discourse community. They might study a subject in which they are not yet expert, and thereby also learn what skills they need to study it—if they "had to" (that is, if they had to master, as students throughout colleges and professional training programs do, a subject over the course of a term or so). This is the reality that isn't faked, and what we call sustained CBI.

As in other academic/professional classes, students might be passionately or mildly interested in the subject of a course; others might be taking the class only because they have to. But students who learn a bit of the subject will also grasp something of the skills needed to learn it. Critically, *language teachers can help students acquire these skills before they must improvise on their own in content classes*. If the sustained content is a subject that college-educated people are generally familiar with, such as topics in introductory college courses, the information itself will be useful. But regardless of the subject matter, the skills needed to grapple with sustained content in language courses—from note-taking to report writing—will help students grapple with future academic/professional demands. (See Chapter 1 for a discussion of the "transferability" of academic language and skills.)

In any case, such was my hypothesis after pondering the essays I could not understand. But more than my own guesses, it was the frustrations of the students themselves that pointed me toward sustained CBI. They complained they had never been asked to do—or been helped to do—what their university classes now demanded of them. They were learning it on the fly, or using strategies from their academic work in other languages to complete assignments in English. A significant number had never before completed a book written in English (a finding also by Haynes and Bernard, Chapters 3 and 11). Though most had read ESL/EFL textbook material or newspaper articles, they had been asked only to answer general "reading comprehension" questions but not to extract the line of argumentation. Most had been asked to prepare personal reaction papers or oral presentations about such readings, but none had been required to master much of the content—its vocabulary, forms, registers, and methods of proof or persuasion. None had followed a subject long enough to synthesize information, question data, or present written or oral argumentation of his own. Given this lack of practice with academic/professional demands, it is little wonder that students were doing the best they could, but not well enough.

The Chapters

In an effort to help them do it better, the authors in this volume developed sustained CBI courses for advanced-beginner through advanced ESL/EFL students. We teach in public and private two- and four-year institutions in and outside the

United States, with students from a wide range of cultural and linguistic backgrounds with varying levels of preparedness for post-secondary programs. In the volume that follows, we describe why we came to teach sustained CBI courses in our particular programs, how we developed them, and what did and did not work as we went along.

The courses are described in detail, and though the subjects studied vary (from business to engineering to cinema), some characteristics prevail throughout, notably the recognition of declarative and procedural knowledge. *Declarative knowledge* is knowing about something, such as the effects of global warming or the factors leading to the development of atonal music. *Procedural knowledge* is knowing how to find this information. Each chapter describes both the declarative and procedural aspects of sustained CBI courses: **the subject taught** and **the skills** students practiced in order to grasp it. **Sample units, study aids** (charts, outlines, class and homework activities), **assignments**, and **assessment measures** are included. Chapters close with excerpts of student work and a discussion of achievement measures, such as fulfillment of course requirements, performance on school-wide exams, and student progress into "mainstream" classes.

Chapter 1 of this volume offers a review of the literature on content-based language teaching: types, purposes, benefits to students, and research on its effectiveness in ESL, EFL, and foreign-language settings. The chapter looks at how sustained CBI grew out of content-based ESL: at the needs of ESL/EFL students headed for academic/professional programs, at gaps remaining in their education, and at how sustained CBI might fill such gaps. The succeeding chapters are exemplars of sustained CBI courses.

Chapters 2 and 8 look at sustained CBI courses based on the procedural knowledge, or knowledge of tasks, that students need. For instance, students need to be able to take lecture notes in order to access information (in class), acquire it (outside class through studying), and display it (in exams or papers). The courses described in these chapters are part of a program at Georgia State University in which specific tasks are emphasized at each ESL level (beginner, intermediate, and advanced), and in which students practice these tasks in the authentic context of learning a "real" academic subject. In Chapter 2, students study introductory psychology and practice reading, listening and notetaking (from readings and lectures). In Chapter 8, students in an advanced ESL course study American history and practice the sorts of writing required on university exams, notably identification, short-answer, and essay questions.

The courses reviewed in Chapters 9 and 11, part of the University Preparatory Workshop at New York University, also focus on the humanities and social sciences. Chapter 9 describes a course called "Film & Society" in which intermediate through advanced students study how the assumptions, myths, and contradictions of a society appear in its cinema. While studying this subject, students practice a number of skills needed for academic/professional work: the close reading of texts in order to extract the line of argumentation; summarizing; questioning texts; and the organization of expository and persuasive academic writing, including strategies of comparison, contrast, and refuting opposing opinions. In Chapter 11, the subject is commentary—in this case, commentary on environmental issues—and the skills are a series of reflective practices that allows students to analyze, summarize, explore their reactions to, and question the purpose and argumentation of what they read, and present both a written and oral commentary of their own, in groups and individually.

Chapters 4, 6, and 10 rely on business and the sciences for their content. In Chapter 4, ESL students in an urban two-year community college are introduced to a number of subject areas during the term, such as marketing and biology, for which they must read, do research, and write papers as they would in college content classes. But additionally, each student must select one subject for "Focus Discipline Research," an extended research paper that synthesizes, analyzes, and evaluates material from a wide range of sources. Some of those sources must be Internet sites, and a key feature of this course is guiding students to use this new information technology for academic/professional purposes. The benefits of this Internet focus are twofold: first, it provides students with an important—but new and unfamiliar—research skill, and second, Internet searches give students practice in various analytic skills, such as classification, differentiation, and judging the importance, reliability, and validity of information.

Chapter 6 describes a technical communications course for engineering students in a university EFL setting. Skills taught include how to read discipline-specific material to improve vocabulary; how to use rhetorical forms; and how to use argumentation in a research setting, stating the research problem and its background, the need for the study, a hypothesis for a solution, and the implementation and assessment of the solution. With step-by-step support from the EFL teacher, students research and carry out a final project that mirrors the scientific procedures and rhetorical presentation of final projects in engineering classes.

Chapter 10 looks at physical and emotional health as the subject matter in a high-intermediate ESL course at a public urban college. Skills include analyzing and summarizing articles, an autobiography, and a film on AIDS, and writing descriptive, comparison/contrast, and persuasive essays. The final project of the course is oral and written analyses of chapters in an academic clinical-psychology text. Students then synthesize the information from all the chapters in a written final exam.

Chapter 5 further emphasizes oral skills by describing how students in a low-intermediate course at New York University study the Calvin and Hobbes humor book, *Yukon Ho!* The author reviews the differences between written and spoken language and discusses the advantages of teaching with a written text of dialogue (rather than live speech or TV, for example). From the "oral" dialogue in the text, students induce five categories of spoken English: lexical, referential, emotional, discourse, and attitudinal. By analyzing speech along these guidelines, students become familiar with the varying pragmatics, registers, and strategies of spoken language; moreover, they practice analytical skills such as inductive reasoning, classification, and comparison/contrast, useful in any academic/professional context.

Chapters 3 and 7 present two different approaches to teaching grammar forms with sustained CBI. Chapter 3 describes a course in which beginning and low-intermediate students at New York University induce form from an authentic text. In this case, the text is Ernest Hemingway's *The Old Man and the Sea,* and the forms are the basic blocks of English grammar: the noun phrase, the verb phrase, the participial phrase, the substitute, the clause, and the conjunction.

Overview of Chapters		
Chapter	**Content**	**Skills**
1	theoretical overview of sustained CBI	
2	psychology	reading, listening, notetaking
3	*The Old Man and the Sea* by Ernest Hemingway	grammar forms
4	business, sciences	Internet skills, research and synthesis of sources, reading and writing academic papers
5	humor writing: Calvin and Hobbes	oral presentation
6	engineering	research, reading and writing scientific papers
7	principles of English syntax	grammar forms
8	American history	university exam writing
9	film and society	text analysis, summarizing, synthesizing and questioning texts, writing academic papers
10	physical and emotional health	reading, summarizing, synthesizing, writing academic papers, oral presentation
11	commentary	text analysis, summarizing, exploring reactions to texts, questioning texts, oral presentation, writing commentary
12	assessment in sustained CBI courses	

While students read, discuss, and write about the novel, they analyze passages of it, identifying the grammar blocks (and their component parts) and learning how to combine these elements correctly in writing of their own. In other words, students analyze passages of the novel in order to understand and write about it; they learn the grammar to read and write. This goes to the heart of sustained CBI: students learn skills when they want to do something real with them.

Chapter 7 makes use of both inductive and deductive reasoning to teach form. Here, a body of metacognitive principles governing English syntactic structures is itself the sustained content of the course. Students at an urban two-year college study this content as though they were taking a class in "practical linguistics." They study a set of principles which allows them to analyze and correct writing of their own. (Background for the development of these principles and examples of their application are included.) Using these principles sharpens the analytic skills needed in academic/professional settings, such as the ability to induce patterns from language "data" (authentic texts), to apply principles to new data (one's own writing), to judge whether new data conforms to previously learned principles, and to revise principles to account for new information.

This volume closes with a chapter (Chapter 12) on assessment in sustained CBI courses that raises questions of methodology and purpose, notably, how to make assessment measures reflect the theories of language learning upon which our courses are based. The author discusses self- and peer-assessment, and the guiding role of formative and authentic assessment, which give students and teachers information not only on student achievement but on how well the course is accomplishing its goals. The author discusses practical issues such as balancing the assessment of content and language acquisition, and she offers hands-on models of appropriate assessment tools.

Acknowledgments

The courses described in this book have each been taught for several years, yielding snags and successes and prompting changes both in the theory of sustained CBI and its practice. I would like to thank all of the contributing teacher-researchers, who have been so dedicated to improving their students' education and so generous in sharing their work with me.

Additionally, I would like to thank my editor, Susan Maguire, who had faith in this project, whose energy and wit has seen it through its stages, and who has such a visionary approach to language pedagogy. Many thanks as well to all those at Houghton Mifflin whose ideas and talents contributed to this volume. I am indebted to Charles Haynes and Rudolph Bernard, who allowed me to observe their sustained content classes and taught me so much of how this approach works. I am grateful also to Miriam Eisenstein-Ebsworth, who guided my first explorations of sustained CBI and the earliest versions of the film and society course. I would not have been able to develop sustained content curricula without the help of Helen Harper, academic head of the American Language Institute at New York University; Christine Trotter, program coordinator of the University Preparatory Workshop there; Ines Modrcin; and Irene Badaracco, chair of the ESL Institute at Fordham University. I would like to thank Pam once again for her unending support and good humor over the years, and Ronnie for reading me so well.

M.P.

References

Chitrapu, D. (1996). Case studies of non-native graduate students' research writing in the disciplines. *Dissertation Abstracts International, 57* (10), 244A.

Kasper, L. (1995/1996). Using discipline-based text to boost college ESL reading instruction. *Journal of Adolescent and Adult Literacy, 39,* 298–206.

Kasper, L. (1997). The impact of content-based instructional programs on the academic progress of ESL students. *English for Specific Purposes 16* (4). 309–320.

Leki, I., & Carson, J. (1994). Students' perceptions of EAP writing instruction and writing needs across the disciplines. *TESOL Quarterly, 28* (1), 81–101.

Leki, I., & Carson, J. (1997). "Completely different worlds": EAP and the writing experiences of ESL students in university courses. *TESOL Quarterly, 31* (1), 39–69.

Smoke, T. (Ed.). (1998). *Adult ESL: Politics, pedagogy, and participation in classroom and community programs.* Mahwah, NJ: Lawrence Erlbaum.

Widdowson, H. (1998). Context, community, and authentic language. *TESOL Quarterly, 32* (2), 705–716.

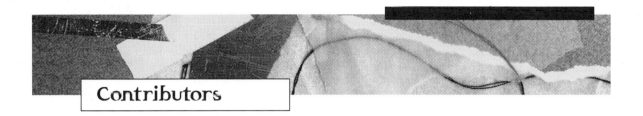

Contributors

Marcia Pally is adjunct assistant professor at New York University and teaches ESL at Fordham University. She is the author of a sustained content textbook, *Screening English: Studying Movies for Reading, Writing and Critical Thinking* (Burgess Press, 1997), as well as two books on censorship and free expression. Her work on ESL has appeared in *Journal of Second Language Writing, Journal of Adolescent & Adult Literacy, TESL-EJ,* and *TESOL Video News,* among other publications.

Nathalie H. Bailey is associate professor of English at Lehman College, City University of New York. She has edited one book and authored numerous articles, chapters, and presentations on second language reading, writing, and grammar learning.

Rudolph W. Bernard, master teacher, has for several decades been a full-time faculty member of the American Language Institute at New York University. His experience over the years as teacher, program developer, and curriculum consultant has served to focus his primary pedagogical interest in critical reflection on written commentary. His aim has been to give university students an experiential basis for using their continuing study experience to further develop their skill and confidence in handling sophisticated concepts of a relatively high degree of abstraction.

Paul J. Camhi is associate professor at the Borough of Manhattan Community College and teaches courses in linguistic theory to TESOL graduate students at the New York University School of Education. The 1997–1999 chair of the Higher Ed Special Interest Group of NYS TESOL, he has published numerous articles on metacognitive strategies for second-language acquisition.

Joan G. Carson is associate professor and chair of the Department of Applied Linguistics and ESL at Georgia State University. In addition to teaching TESL graduate courses, she has been involved in developing task-based curricula using sustained content. Her research interests include second-language reading-writing connections and academic literacy.

Lynne Flowerdew currently teaches in the Language Centre at the Hong Kong University of Science and Technology, where she coordinates technical communication skills courses for Science and Engineering students. She has publications in the areas of corpus linguistics, ESP, CALL, and learning styles.

Charles S. Haynes is associate professor of ESL at New York University. He has a Ph.D. in applied linguistics and has been an ESL/EFL teacher, teacher-trainer, curriculum developer, and administrator since 1961. He has been a Fulbright professor in Japan and Indonesia. He is a former director of ESL programs at Lehman College of the City University of New York and the American Language Center, University of California, Los Angeles.

Loretta F. Kasper is associate professor of English at Kingsborough Community College/City University of New York. She regularly teaches content-based ESL courses with an Internet component. Reports of her work have appeared in a number of national and international journals, among them *TESL-EJ, ITESL-J, English for Specific Purposes, Journal of Adolescent & Adult Literacy,* and *Teaching English in the Two-Year College.* She is the author of two content-based texts, *Teaching English through the Disciplines: Psychology,* Second Edition (Whittier, 1997) and *Interdisciplinary English,* Second Edition (McGraw-Hill, 1998). She is currently at work on the volume *Content-Based College ESL Instruction* for Lawrence Erlbaum Associates.

Leila May-Landy is a full-time lecturer in the American Language Program of Columbia University. Her interests in assessment began when she conducted a full-scale revision of the American Language Program English Placement Test. She was testing coordinator for five years and is currently coordinator of part-time programs.

Gayle Nelson, associate professor and director of graduate studies, Department of Applied Linguistics and ESL, Georgia State University, teaches graduate courses in L2 composition in the M.A. program and reading-writing courses in the ESL program. Her research interests include L2 composition pedagogy, the role of culture in second-language acquisition, and contrastive pragmatics. She has published in journals such as *The TESOL Quarterly, Journal of Second Language Writing, Applied Linguistics* and *International Journal of Intercultural Relations* and has published numerous book chapters.

Neil R. Williams has taught EFL and been a teacher trainer in France, Finland, and Italy. He is currently master teacher of ESL at the American Language Institute of New York University, where he teaches in the intensive ESL program and coordinates international teaching assistant training.

Sustained Content Teaching in Academic ESL/EFL

Chapter 1

Sustaining Interest/Advancing Learning

Sustained Content-Based Instruction in ESL/EFL— Theoretical Background and Rationale

Marcia Pally

New York University, Fordham University

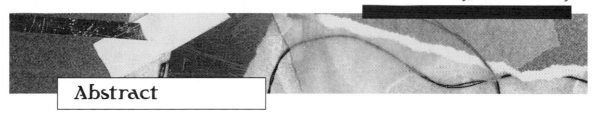

Abstract

This chapter provides a history and theoretical overview of content-based language instruction, and a rationale for using sustained content in teaching ESL/EFL students who are in or headed for college and professional/technical programs. After looking at the reading, writing, and critical thinking skills that these students need to succeed in academic/professional settings, I review the content-based instruction of the last 20 years: its development, types, and research on its benefits to students. Recent studies suggest that a gap exists between the skills students need and those taught (and learned) in ESL/EFL classes. I suggest a reason for this gap and propose that it might be filled by sustained content-based instruction (CBI), support for which comes from research in second-language acquisition, text analysis, and genre analysis. The chapter closes with a discussion of the challenges in using sustained CBI, notably selecting appropriate content, determining appropriate levels of technical information for the language classroom, and the acquisition of content-area expertise by language teachers. ■

Introduction

> [The] effectiveness of language teaching will depend on what is being taught, other than language, that will be recognized by the learners as a purposeful and relevant extension of their schematic horizons. (Widdowson, 1990, p. 103)

The role of content—how much belongs in language classes, what kind, who should teach it, and how language teachers might learn it—has been a subject of debate in ESL/EFL since the mid-1980s (Braine, 1988; Horowitz, 1986; Shih, 1986; Snow & Brinton, 1997; Spack, 1988). This book focuses on the academic needs of college and college-bound ESL/EFL students in undergraduate, graduate, and professional training programs, and investigates one kind of content-based instruction (CBI): **sustained CBI,** or studying one content area over time. This chapter describes student needs and the theoretical framework for using sustained CBI as a pedagogical approach.

The Academic Needs of College and College-Bound ESL/EFL Students: Critical Thinking Development

In addition to grammatical accuracy and appropriate ranges of vocabulary and idiomaticity, students in or headed for higher education in English need to master what counts, roughly speaking, as "a line of argumentation" in English written and oral presentation. They need to grasp the claims, positions, perspectives, or theses of what they read and hear; to appreciate the methods, descriptions, and evidence used to develop those positions; and to learn how to present their own descriptions, positions, or perspectives using appropriate academic/professional rhetorical conventions. These perspectives or positions and their development comprise *argumentation* in the broadest sense: "a coherent series of statements leading from a premise to a conclusion" and "the act or process of forming reasons and drawing conclusions, and applying them to a case in discussion" (*Webster's,* 1989). Argumentation is integral to the range of academic/professional tasks—from lecture comprehension to Internet research—and to all genres of written and oral presentation.

Yet argumentation and rhetorical conventions vary among languages, (sub)cultures, and discourse communities, easing communication within each community but impeding communication among them (Connor, 1996; Leki, 1991; Swales, 1990). The study of contrastive rhetoric and genre analysis finds that many cultures do not use the so-called linear analysis frequent in academic/expository English, with its distinctions between theses or perspectives and their proofs. They do not tend "to directness, to precise relationships between verbs and their subjects, to clear and relatively obvious transitions, to announcement of intent and summary statements" (Fox, 1994, p. 20; see also Fox, 1996). Rather, they rely on indirection, received wisdom, contextualization of issues (rather than under-a-microscope analysis), and collectivist notions of evidence. As a result, students from these traditions often see English texts as obvious, dull, or naive. Even advanced graduate students may find presentation of ideas in English distasteful or mysterious, either because they have not learned its conventions or because they require sizable (and undesirable) changes in worldview and identity.

As a step in guiding students to grasp and present ideas in English, educators in at least three areas of second-language acquisition (SLA) describe the critical thinking skills needed for academic/professional work. English for Academic Purpose (EAP) stresses that students grasp English-language criteria for cause and effect, description, categorization, and differentiation, specifically for comparison and contrast. EAP also stresses the skills of skimming, scanning, and using the rhetorical conventions of academic or professional disciplines (Carson & Leki, 1993; Horowitz, 1986; Johns, 1990; Swales, 1987). Cognitive psychology highlights understanding the principles of temporal sequence, cause and effect, judgment, and choice (Mohan, 1986, 1990; Vygotsky, 1962; Widdowson, 1990). Transformative pedagogy (or "critical pedagogy") focuses on examining "the deep meanings, personal implications, and social consequences of any knowledge, theme, technique, text, or material . . . its internal structure and its connections to self and society" (Shor, 1992, p. 169).

In academic/professional work, these skills are used sequentially and simultaneously. For example, to present (orally or in writing) an ecology project, one must skim, scan, and read extensively a range of material about ecological policies; understand the key points and supporting evidence of books, articles, and lectures; compare policies; understand their genesis and history; evaluate them; and present one's ideas within the rhetorical forms of English academic/professional writing or speaking. Rhetorical conventions themselves may be examined for their sociopolitical uses (Cope & Kalantzis, 1993). But this examination, if done in English, also makes use of these academic/analytical skills. In short, all academic study in English—including a critique of academic study in English—uses English critical thinking skills. Yet, "because some of our students do *not* share academic genre knowledge with their instructors, or with other readers and writers, they face considerable obstacles. It is these obstacles that we should attempt to face" (Johns, 1997, p. 37).

English-Language Academic Requirements and Student Populations

While these skills comprise preparation for academic/professional work in "mainstream" English cultures, students from other traditions arrive at different insights and express them differently. Teaching them English critical thinking procedures raises cultural, political, and psychosocial questions about English-language hegemony and its gatekeeper role in the advancement of ESL/EFL students (Al-Abed Al-Haq & Ahmed, 1994; Benesch, 1993a, 1993b; Freire, 1974; Freire & Macedo, 1987; Hornberger & Ricento, 1996; Tollefson, 1991). Yet, at least at present, ESL/EFL students who communicate with the "mainstream" English-speaking world—*to succeed in or challenge it*—benefit from command of these skills. These skills are arrows worth having in the quiver for students with a wide range of goals, and may raise students' awareness of the culture-bound nature of expression. In many complex ways, texts take their meanings from contexts. Students may more readily see that presenting ideas is a series of traditions, assumptions, and choices—an awareness that benefits students in all areas of study.

Critical thinking skills and awareness of cross-cultural variation are worth teaching not only to ESL/EFL students bound for college or professional work but to all students who want to understand the factors that affect their lives—from student loans to health insurance—and especially to students who did not learn Western protocols of power at home. "If you are not already a participant in the culture of power, being told explicitly the rules of that culture makes acquiring power easier" (Delpit, 1991, p. 486). Moreover, "to act as if power doesn't exist is to ensure that the power status quo remains the same" (p. 496). These issues are echoed in the debates on Black and standard English, notably in the work of Friere and Macedo (1987), who write, "The legitimization of Black English as an educational tool does not . . . preclude the need to acquire proficiency in the linguistic code of the dominant class" (p. 127; see also Aronowitz & Giroux, 1988). Indeed, students from non-mainstream traditions may have an advantage in learning mainstream critical thinking procedures and the assumptions behind them. Since these procedures are unnatural to them, they may more easily see the social/political functions of, for example, the passive-voiced, "authorless" style of much academic writing, lectures, and news reports. In some instances, this style signals group membership (rather than maverick invention) and the importance of showing that the writer/speaker is conforming to group procedures—in short, where achievement means executing agreed-on standards well: "Titrations were collected every third hour according to Doe's (19xx) taxonomy. . . ." In other instances, the passive voice obscures the causal agent: "The cavalry was dispatched into the village. . . ." (For a discussion of the sociopolitical functions of genre conventions, see Cope & Kalantzis, 1993.)

ESL/EFL students and teachers differ in their goals for language classes and the extent to which they wish to address sociopolitical issues that arise. Yet critical thinking skills—including questioning information and conventions—are used widely in academic/professional settings as a basis for comparing sources and formulating ideas. The power to question "the culture of power" is also the power to succeed within it.

The Development of CBI: History, Rationale, Types, and Research

History

Among the earliest CBI programs in the postwar period were those in English for Science and Technology (EST), where educators identified the lexical, grammatical, and sociolinguistic features of the sciences and math, and organized grammar-based curricula around them. EST methodologies were extended to other disciplines (English for Academic Purposes [EAP] and English for vocational training), and in the 1970s led to the investigation of "functions" and "notions." That is, educators identified the tasks and situations students might encounter in their careers (such as setting out a hypothesis) and taught the language needed to accomplish them (Tarone, Dwyer, Gillette, & Icke, 1981; Trimble, 1985).

In the 1980s, interest in CBI was broadened by the development of communicative approaches in language teaching, notably Krashen's proposal that meaningful, comprehensible input (i+1) is necessary for language acquisition, given a low affective filter and silent period (Krashen, 1981, 1985). Hymes (1971) developed the idea of communicative competence, which includes both linguistic and pragmatic knowledge—knowledge of both words and forms that are correct and those that are appropriate for the setting. The work of these researchers and others sent ESL/EFL teachers searching for what meaningful, communicative "input" might be—in short, for content. In addition, the Language Across the Curriculum and Whole Language movements helped to shift the focus in ESL/EFL from form (grammar, syntax, etc.) to communication. The work of the Soviet literary critic Bakhtin, advanced in the West by Cazden (1989), also lent weight to CBI. Bakhtin rejected Saussure's division of language into *langue* (formal organizational system) and *parole* (communication and social uses of language), and instead claimed that form is apprehended through communication. Researchers on schema (or "schemata," mental maps with which one organizes information) assumed CBI in their suggestion that ESL/EFL teachers provide students with organizers, diagrams, and other schema so that they more easily recognize L2 language forms and concepts (Carrell, 1984, 1987; Mohan, 1990; Tobias, 1994). Schema may draw students' attention to content or text organization, but both types of schema assume that students are not memorizing forms but reading texts.

While these developments supported content study, they left unclear what the content should be. A frequent choice was academic subjects, an idea that goes back to immersion programs beginning in 1946, when Malherbe studied 19,000 South African students from both British and Afrikaans backgrounds. He found that those who received CBI in their L2s made considerable language gains without loss of the L1. In 1965, Canada began a national immersion program teaching academic classes in French to Anglophones and academic classes in English to Francophones. Students in immersion classes showed higher L2 abilities (with no L1 loss) than students in traditional language classes (Cummins, 1983; Swain & Lapkin, 1982; for foreign language immersion programs, see Krueger & Ryan, 1993.) As a result of this and other programs, exploration into CBI increased, along with an understanding of its contributions to SLA and research on its effects. These are explored in the following sections.

Rationale for CBI

ESL/EFL educators identify four primary advantages of CBI: linguistic, psychological, pedagogical, and collegial (in relations among university staff). The linguistic benefits include the provision of meaningful input of both "everyday" communicative and academic language (Cummins, 1981; Mohan, 1990; Spanos, 1989) that exposes students to a wide range of vocabulary, forms, registers, and pragmatic functions (Snow, Met, & Genesee, 1989; Zuengler & Brinton, 1997). CBI recycles words and forms, easing memory and acquisition; calls on students' prior knowledge and schema; and builds schema through progressive units of content study. The psychological benefits include student interest and motivation (Short, 1991a; Snow & Brinton, 1988) and reduction of anxiety (Short, 1991b; Short, Crandall, & Christian, 1989). Students who are interested in what they study recall more information, synthesize it, and elaborate on it better than nonmotivated learners (Alexander, Kulikowich, & Jetton, 1994; Krapp, Hidi, & Renniger, 1992; Turner, 1993). The pedagogical advantages of CBI include the content-area learning that students accomplish while acquiring a new language (Short, 1993) and student engagement in activities earmarked by the educational psychologist Vygotsky (Grabe & Stoller, 1997; Lantolf & Pavlenko, 1995). CBI lends itself to the Vygotskian (1962) ideas of "scaffolding" (where a student works with the teacher or a more advanced student to grasp a challenging concept or skill) and "private speech" (inner-directed speech—a kind of "talking to oneself"—that helps students understand an idea or rehearse a presentation), both of which facilitate learning. Scaffolding occurs whenever students help one another. Although students do so in all language classes, CBI courses provide more varied opportunities for scaffolding because of the greater variety of projects and things to learn as students work not only with vocabulary and form but with concepts in the content area. Similarly, private speech occurs when students face challenges they must work through, and CBI presents students with a greater variety of challenges.

CBI may also enhance relations between content-area instructors and language teaching staff. "Our core values, which tend to place pedagogy and language acquisition above content, also separate us from the rest of the campus. . . . In the eyes of the 'academic' teachers, then, the literacy instructors appeared to be unconcerned with the 'real stuff' of the university" (Johns, 1997, p. 75). This is what Belcher and Braine (1995a) call the "professional diaspora" and what Benesch (1992) has called the "handmaid" status of ESL instruction, a status that affects students as well:

> As long as instruction in the [language] program is not integrated into the regular academic curriculum, no course in the program, however well designed and executed, is ever likely to rise above the status of an "exercise" in the minds of many students. (Ponder & Powell, 1989, p. 10)

Benesch suggests that ESL staff develop "a college curriculum that puts the ESL teacher on an equal footing with the cross-curricular partner and recognizes the role of all faculty in language teaching" (1992, p. 4). While ESL/EFL teachers vary in their approach to the politics of language teaching, CBI allows language faculty to act as "mediators between our students and other instructors and administrators, between what we know about teaching and learning and the academic cultures our students will enter" (Johns, 1997, p. 75).

Types of CBI

The four most popular types of CBI programs are theme-based, sheltered, adjunct, and based on academic tasks such as notetaking or lecture comprehension (Brinton, Snow, & Wesche, 1989; Carson, Taylor, & Fredella, 1997). Theme-based courses taught by ESL/EFL teachers are "structured around topics or themes, with the topics forming the backbone of the course curriculum" (Brinton, Snow, & Wesche, 1989, p. 14) such that reading, speaking, listening, writing, and sometimes grammar are based on the topic studied. In sheltered courses, the language used to teach content is adapted to suit ESL/EFL students. Taught by either content or ESL/EFL teachers, students are given instructional support in vocabulary development, reading comprehension, essay organization, and study skills. Chamot and O'Malley (1987) developed a variation on the sheltered model—the Cognitive Academic Language Learning Approach (CALLA)—aimed at training content teachers to incorporate language-teaching strategies into their classes. Drawing on the distinction between declarative knowledge (knowing about something, such as the Civil War) and procedural knowledge (knowing how to do something, such as how to use Internet research tools) (Anderson, 1985), Chamot and O'Malley analogized content as a kind of declarative knowledge and language skills as a kind of procedural knowledge, and developed a model to help content teachers teach both.

In the adjunct model, students enroll in two courses simultaneously: a content course and an ESL/EFL class in which they learn both subject matter and skills that help them with the coursework in the content class. In CBI organized by tasks, teachers identify tasks that students need for their academic work and choose content that allows students frequent practice in them (Carson, Taylor, & Fredella, 1997; Long & Crookes, 1993). The task-based approach derives from the work of Widdowson (1993), Prabhu (1987), and Ellis (1992), who recommend problem-solving activities (or "tasks") for the ESL/EFL classroom. To complete such tasks, Widdowson and colleagues claim, students must engage in a variety of research efforts, negotiations, and discussion, focusing on language to unravel the meaning of the material before them. In task-based CBI, students must also show they have understood the material (in reports, exams) and present ideas about it orally or in writing.

Research Findings on CBI

The complexities of language learning and the location of CBI in actual college settings make research factors numerous and difficult to isolate, presenting difficulties in evaluating CBI with controlled research protocols. Nevertheless, existing studies suggest that students completing CBI courses grasp both L2 and content better than at the start, and often better than students in traditional language classes. In interviews and course evaluations, they show greater satisfaction with language study and greater self-confidence in using their second language.

ESL Studies

Students in an adjunct ESL program at UCLA performed on exit criteria as well as nonparticipant controls, even though the participants began the term with lower English placement scores (Snow & Brinton, 1988). They showed improved study skills, reported heightened self-confidence, and believed they were better readers and writers of English. In an adjunct geography class at Macalaster College, "The NNS [non-native speaker] group with benefit of the study skills [adjunct] class was able to pass the NNS group with superior language proficiency and in some semesters to approach the average score for native speakers" (Guyer & Peterson, 1988, p. 104). Additionally, the adjunct language course dramatically reduced the dropout and failure rate in the content course. In an adjunct precourse for students not proficient enough for full-semester adjunct classes, participants wrote research papers, took exams, and participated in class discussion, though the course was far above their language abilities (Adamson, 1990). Students in a CBI tutoring program at Hostos Community College performed significantly better than those in the control group, with a mean final grade in content courses of 2.56 compared with 2.02 in the control group (Hirsch, 1988). Fifteen percent of the experimental group earned grades of A and 2 percent earned F's compared with 7 percent A's and 19 percent F's in the control group.

EFL and Foreign Language Studies

Two studies on EFL teaching methods spanning the last 25 years found that the number of years of CBI was a better predictor of L2 proficiency than years in traditional classes (Gradman & Hanania, 1991; Saegert, Scott, Perkins, & Tucker, 1974). In another study—one of the most thoroughly researched projects—students in sheltered and adjunct psychology classes in Ottawa did as well on their exams as they had done the previous semester when they took psychology in their mother tongue (Edwards, Wesche, Krashen, Clement, & Kruidenier, 1984; Hauptman, Wesche, & Ready, 1988; Wesche, 1993). These students did as well as or better than a control group taking L1 psychology from the same professors, and expressed significant satisfaction at having succeeded in a "real" second-language setting. The 1988 study showed that

> with only one exception, the experimental groups in both FSL [French as a second language] and ESL showed significant second-language gains on all measures, whereas the control groups did not. . . . The analysis of covariance results corroborates both the t-test results and our intuition that in terms of second-language learning, sheltered classes are at least as effective as are traditional classes and sometimes are even better. (p. 453)

Also in Canada, Francophone ESL teachers in Quebec made significant improvement in English after taking a content-based, teacher training course in linguistics (Buch & de Bagheera, 1978). Schleppegrel (1984) found that students improved significantly in essay writing and listening comprehension after taking a content-based course in economics. Students in CBI courses interviewed at Temple University in Japan reported improvement in reading and writing (at the college level), and that studying a subject rather than taking the traditional English class greatly increased their interest in the language (Mayer & Mayer, 1991).

In foreign language studies (see Krueger & Ryan, 1993, for overviews), Grandin (1993) reports strong student interest and successful job placement at a University of Rhode Island program in which students majoring in German and engineering intern at a German-speaking company. Also successful is Eastern Michigan University's Language and International Business Program, in which students take business classes in Spanish, French, Russian, German, or Japanese

(Palmer, 1993). Bilingual and ESL teachers at the University of Texas who took a summer teacher-training program in Spanish showed strong gains on Spanish language measures (Milk, 1990).

Academic Needs and CBI: "Sustained" Content Study

In the CBI courses just discussed, students advance their knowledge of two disciplines—the target language (the linguistic benefits of CBI) and the content area (the pedagogical benefits)—with greater motivation and less anxiety (the psychological benefits). Yet recent studies of college programs suggest that current pedagogical approaches may not be guiding students to the skills, or the level of skill, that they need for their academic/professional work (Chitrapu, 1996; Kasper, 1997; Leki & Carson, 1997). Higher-level reading, synthesis, research, and academic/professional presentation (written and oral) are among the skills that remain underdeveloped even after students leave ESL/EFL programs. In short, a gap exists between the skills provided by current methodology and the skills students need.

Students preparing for college or professional training need to learn in their L2s not only the "information" of content areas but how to gather, synthesize, and evaluate it, and organize ideas of their own—in other words, how to use the critical thinking skills of EAP, cognitive psychology, and transformative pedagogy. A cyclical, synergistic relationship exists between content and critical thinking skills: in order to grasp and manipulate content, students must learn critical thinking skills, but in order to learn these skills, students must study content that is complex enough and enduring enough that argumentation and rhetorical conventions can be identified, practiced, and questioned. This type of content can be thought of as *sustained CBI*. In his research on academic skills development, Cummins (1981) found that language learners cannot acquire from nonacademic language use what he calls *cognitive academic learning proficiency (CALPs)*. Students need to practice complex, synthetic reasoning in their L2s.

Cummins's idea and sustained CBI are worth considering for several reasons, among them content-class NS pedagogy and content-class expectations. It is in content classes that NS (native speakers) learn critical thinking skills. In order to acquire *content area expertise,* they develop the analytical abilities that they apply to future content areas. They gather information and opposing points of view from print, oral, and electronic sources; discuss, synthesize, and question that information; become familiar with the argumentations and rhetorical conventions of a discipline; and write over a long enough period of time to revise both ideas and prose. If NSs learn critical thinking through sustained study, ESL/EFL students may benefit from a similar approach. Second, since college and professional programs expect students to have these skills, ESL/EFL students may benefit from practicing them before they must perform commensurately with NS peers. In their survey of the requirements of 900 university classes, Ferris and Tagg (1996) found that ESL students benefited from learning in their ESL classes the skills specific to mainstream ones.

By studying a subject in a sustained way, listening to lectures and reading extensively in that subject, students acquire the content-area expertise that enables them to compare, synthesize, and judge what they read. Reading and listening extensively familiarizes students with the rhetorical conventions of a discipline, and academic presentations (oral and written) allow them to use those conventions to organize their ideas. English academic and professional presentation relies on certain claim-and-support strategies, in which the support includes concrete, specific information drawn from a range of sources. Without sustained study, there is little for students to accrue and little for them to synthesize into support for claims of their own.

Support for Sustained CBI:
Second-Language Acquisition Research and Pedagogy

Ironically, early research that pointed to the benefits of sustained CBI came from inadequacies in Canadian immersion courses, themselves sustained CBI programs. Although students learned more of the target language than in traditional language classes, certain grammatical forms, advanced oral fluency, and sociolinguistic tasks remained out of reach because, researchers found, *students did not use them* (Genesee, 1987; Swain, 1985, 1988). Swain suggested that these students lacked practice in form and "pushed output"—more varied and advanced speaking and writing. Because L2 listening tends to focus on meaning rather than form, students need activities beyond reading and lecture comprehension (meaningful, comprehensible input) to recognize and acquire a wide range of L2 forms (Schmidt, 1988; Van Patten, 1985, 1990). Following researchers who were reintroducing a focus on form into communicative language teaching (Long, 1983; Pica, 1987, 1992; Varonis & Gass, 1985a, 1985b), Swain suggested that two things be added to CBI classes: conversation in which the meaning is easily understood so that students are free to focus on form (such as negotiating tasks in a research project) and "pushed output" in speaking and writing:

> Negotiating meaning needs to incorporate the notion of being pushed to the delivery of a message that is not only conveyed but that is conveyed precisely, coherently and appropriately. Being "pushed" in output, it seems to me, is a concept parallel to that of the i+1 of comprehensible input. Indeed, one might call this the "comprehensible output" hypothesis. (Swain, 1985, pp. 248–249)

To move students to "comprehensible output," current SLA research recommends that ESL/EFL curricula avoid "the grab bag of supposedly high-interest readings with attendant assignments pulled from different topics every week or two" and that they focus instead on "in-depth treatments of subject matter" (Leki & Carson, 1997, p. 64). From their experience in developing EFL classes, Fredrickson, Hagedorn, and Reed (1991) suggest a paradigm for "in-depth treatment": (1) students study one subject through the term; (2) the language and content increases in sophistication such that comprehension of later material depends on a grasp of earlier material; (3) students become familiar with the vocabulary and rhetorical devices of the discipline; and (4) students are encouraged to develop theory by assessing how well existing theories account for data.

Other SLA research emphasizes that students read in the same rigorous ways that NS students do in order to grasp the linguistic and rhetorical aspects of the L2 (Kasper, 1995/1996; Leki, 1995; Leki & Carson, 1994; Schenke, 1996; Smoke, 1998):

> Reading at length and in depth about a single topic enhances the ability to deal with the linguistic elements of a novel text; as more and more texts on the topic are attempted, vocabulary and associated structures become increasingly familiar. Repeated reading on a topic also contributes to a store of information on the topic. . . . Schema research and psycholinguistic approaches to reading have emphasized that linguistic and cognitive structures are closely related in the process of comprehension. (Ponder & Powell, 1989, pp. 7–8)

SLA research recommends also that students write "text responsible" papers where "writers are responsible for demonstrating an understanding of the source text" (Leki & Carson, 1997, p. 41; see also Belcher & Braine, 1995a, 1995b). In addition, "a coherent framework of knowledge, focusing on a particular topic" (Kutz, Groden, & Zamel, 1993, p. 85) helps students develop a "voice" in their writing. Looking specifically at term paper writing, Mustafa (1995) found, interestingly, that teaching the conventions of L2 term papers improved students' ability to write papers in both L1 and L2. In sum, recent SLA research is compatible with sustained CBI in its recommendations that ESL/EFL students practice the in-depth investigation of subject matter and precise presentation of ideas that will be expected of them in college and professional settings.

Support from Research in Text Analysis and Genre Analysis

Text analysis studies in L1 (Connor, 1990) and L2 also recommend that ESL students study a discipline over time, long enough to practice the conventions and argumentation of academic/professional writing (Bardovi-Harlig, 1990; Connor, 1994; Connor & Farmer, 1990; Schneider & Connor, 1991). "In addition to treating style and mechanics . . . it may be advisable to emphasize argumentative structure and the use of persuasive appeals in the teaching of argumentative/persuasive writing" (Connor, 1990, p. 85). In principle, give students practice in what they need to do.

Similarly, genre studies suggests sustained CBI, as it directs students to many of the critical thinking skills flagged by EAP, cognitive psychology, and transformative pedagogy, such as learning and questioning the prominent vocabulary, modes of argumentation, and rhetorical conventions of a discipline, and understanding the sociopolitical structures they represent (Gosden, 1992; Hammond, Wickert, Burns, Joyce, & Miller, 1992; Strong & Candlin, 1993). Cope and Kalantzis (1993) describe conceptual, literate English as subordinative, analytical, minimally redundant, distancing, and either genuinely or disingenuously attempting balance and objectivity. To learn these rhetorical devices and question them, students need to "work their way through explicit analysis of genre features,"

(p. 85) and teachers need to organize their courses so that the various areas of study "build on each other to form an increasingly more sophisticated theory of language" (p. 89). Riazi (1997) found that graduate students engaged in "implicit genre analysis and research" in order "to conceptualize the texts they were aiming to produce" (p. 121), even though students were not instructed to use genre analysis techniques and did not refer to them by name in describing their writing strategies.

Summary

As a start, sustained CBI enhances the advantages of regular CBI: the provision of meaningful input of both daily communicative and academic English; the recycling of vocabulary and form, easing memory and language acquisition; the development of schema as students pursue a subject; increased motivation; decreased anxiety; and the learning of a subject while learning a new language. Sustained CBI brings still other advantages to the classroom, allowing students to participate in the cycle between content and critical thinking development—to learn critical thinking skills through acquiring content-area expertise, the way NS do. It gives students practice in precisely the academic activities expected of them by content classes, including extensive reading; lecture comprehension; synthesis and questioning of ideas; "pushed output" (Swain, 1985, 1988); and written and oral presentation appropriate to academic/professional settings, including "text responsible" writing (Leki & Carson, 1997). Text analysis research (in L1 and L2) and genre studies support CBI in recommending that students study a subject long enough to practice and question its conventions and argumentation.

Students come to the ESL/EFL classroom with a variety of critical thinking skills developed in their L1s, and they gain L2 critical thinking skills outside formal study. At least one job of ESL/EFL courses is to assist them. Absent adequate practice in L2 critical thinking, students lack a full "scaffold" (Vygotsky, 1962) to academic study and the workplace, to advance up its ladders or to challenge them. Those who have friends or family who can help with these skills (or who can pay for assistance) will learn them. Students who have less help—who often "are not already a participant in the culture of power" (Delpit, 1991, p. 486)—may find it harder to learn these skills or gain the leg-up into and over the "power" cultures that the skills introduce.

Challenges for the ESL/EFL Class

Sustained CBI presents a number of challenges to ESL/EFL teachers, among them selecting appropriate content; acquiring content-area expertise; and determining appropriate levels of technical information, discipline-specific vocabulary, and conventions.

Choosing appropriate content is a challenge in all classes where students do not share majors or career goals. Though some colleges have sheltered classes for subjects with high concentrations of ESL/EFL students, this approach often is not economically feasible and neglects ESL/EFL students interested in other disciplines or undecided about their career plans. ESL/EFL teachers facing students with wide-ranging goals must identify sustained CBI that nurtures the interest of many different students. In short, sustained CBI asks for "universal donors" of content.

Once a subject is chosen, teachers must determine how much technical information and discipline-specific language and rhetorical conventions should be included in course materials. An appropriate level is needed to work with the content; yet, except for students majoring in a particular discipline, the more specific details of the discipline are secondary to developing the critical thinking skills basic to English academic work. These are what Flowerdew (1993) and Widdowson (1993) call "transferable" language knowledge and the "elemental forms" (AMES, 1992) of English academic/expository presentation (oral and written). They are what NS with good college preparation learn throughout middle and secondary school. (Indeed, when secondary education fails NS, they are often placed in college remedial classes where they learn many of the tools NNS must learn.) In her analysis of articles and book reviews in 14 different fields of study, Belcher (1995) found that "there are differences as well as similarities across disciplines. . . . Nevertheless, there are also generic commonalities in the explicit critical writing in diverse fields" (p. 139). As they learn these "commonalities," students are on their way to working with a range of academic and professional requirements (Dudley-Evans, 1995). When they enter content classes, they will be in a position to polish both their skills and their knowledge of subject matter because they are building on a base of understanding about English (Cope, Kalantzis, Kress, & Martin, 1993; Hyon, 1996).

Finally, if students are to study content in a sustained way, ESL/EFL teachers must acquire sufficient content-area expertise and find the classroom time to teach it:

> Possible difficulties . . . include instructor hesitation about teaching in certain content areas and the need for staff time and expertise to select, adapt, and/or develop readings, minilectures, and study materials appropriate to student level. Topics with the greatest potential to hold students' interest may not also be areas in which ESL instructors are knowledgeable. (Shih, 1986, p. 635)

In 1997, Goldstein, Campbell, and Cummings wrote, "they [ESL and writing instructors] will never understand the content to the same degree as the content instructors. . . . Nor should they" (p. 336). Instead, they suggest, language teachers should take on the role of "discourse analysts," helping students to identify and use the assumptions, rhetorical conventions, and argumentation of English.

The rest of this book discusses ESL/EFL sustained CBI classes taught and developed over several semesters. Authors describe "universal donors" of content that have engaged students with varying goals, including materials used, how teachers learned them, and the level of technical information and discipline-specific vocabulary and conventions. Authors outline the skills they focused on and the integration of skills and content—how they balanced class activities in the cycle of content and critical thinking development. It is our hope that descriptions of these courses, including stumbling blocks and disappointments, will answer at least some of the questions about content in the language classroom and convey student achievement.

References

Adamson, D. (1990). ESL students' use of academic skills in content courses. *English for Specific Purposes, 9,* 67–87.

Al-Abed Al-Haq, F., & Ahmed, A. (1994). Discourse problems in argumentative writing. *World Englishes, 13*(3), 307–323.

Alexander, P., Kulikowich, J., & Jetton, T. (1994). The role of subject-matter knowledge and interest in the processing of linear and nonlinear texts. *Review of Educational Research, 64*(2), 201–252.

AMES (Adult Migrant Education Service). (1992). *Literacy for further studies. Project report.* Queensland, Australia: Author.

Anderson, J. (1985). *Cognitive psychology and its implications* (2nd ed.). New York: W. H. Freeman.

Aronowitz, S., & Giroux, H. (1988). Schooling, culture, and literacy in the age of broken dreams: A review of Bloom and Hirsch. *Harvard Educational Review, 58*(2), 172–194.

Bardovi-Harlig, K. (1990). Pragmatic word order in English composition. In U. Connor & A. M. Johns (Eds.), *Coherence: Research and pedagogical perspectives* (pp. 43–66). Alexandria, VA: TESOL.

Belcher, D. (1995). Writing critically across the curriculum. In D. Belcher & G. Braine (Eds.), *Academic writing in a second language: Essays on research and pedagogy* (pp. 135–154). Norwood, NJ: Ablex.

Belcher, D., & Braine, G. (1995a). Introduction. In D. Belcher & G. Braine (Eds.), *Academic writing in a second language: Essays on research and pedagogy* (pp. xiii–xxxi). Norwood, NJ: Ablex.

Belcher, D., & Braine, G. (Eds.). (1995b). *Academic writing in a second language: Essays on research and pedagogy.* Norwood, NJ: Ablex.

Benesch, S. (1992). Sharing responsibilities: An alternative to the adjunct model. *College ESL, 2,* 1–10.

Benesch, S. (1993a). Critical thinking: A learning process for democracy. *TESOL Quarterly, 27*(3), 545–548.

Benesch, S. (1993b). ESL, ideology, and the politics of pragmatism. *TESOL Quarterly, 27*(4), 705–717.

Braine, G. (1988). Comments on Ruth Spack's "Initiating ESL students into the academic discourse community: How far should we go?" *TESOL Quarterly, 22*(4), 700–702.

Brinton, D., Snow, M., & Wesche, M. (1989). *Content-based second language instruction.* Boston: Heinle & Heinle.

Buch, G., & de Bagheera, I. (1978). An immersion program for the professional improvement of non-native teachers of ESL. In C. Blatchford & J. Schachter (Eds.), *On TESOL '78* (pp. 106–117). Washington, DC: TESOL.

Carrell, P. (1984). The effects of rhetorical organization on ESL readers. *TESOL Quarterly, 18*(2), 441–469.

Carrell, P. (1987). Content and formal schemata in ESL reading. *TESOL Quarterly, 21*(3), 461–481.

Carson, J., & Leki, I. (1993). *Reading in the composition classroom.* Boston: Heinle & Heinle.

Carson, J., Taylor, J., & Fredella, L. (1997). The role of content in task-based instruction: What is the relationship? In M. Snow & D. Brinton (Eds.), *The content-based classroom: Perspectives on integrating language and content* (pp. 367–370). White Plains, NY: Addison Wesley Longman.

Cazden, C. (1989). Contributions of the Bakhtin circle to "Communicative competence." *Applied Linguistics, 10,* 116–127.

Chamot, A., & O'Malley, J. (1987). The cognitive academic language learning approach. *TESOL Quarterly, 21,* 227–247.

Chitrapu, D. (1996). Case studies of non-native graduate students' research writing in the disciplines. *Dissertation Abstracts International, 57*(10), 244A.

Connor, U. (1990). Linguistic/rhetorical measures for international persuasive student writing. *Research in Teaching English, 24,* 67–87.

Connor, U. (1994). Text analysis. In A. Cumming (Ed.), Alternatives in TESOL research: Descriptive, interpretive, and ideological orientations (pp. 682–684). *TESOL Quarterly, 28*(4), 673–703.

Connor, U. (1996). *Contrastive rhetoric.* Cambridge, UK: Cambridge University Press.

Connor, U., & Farmer, M. (1990). Teaching topical structure analysis as a revision strategy. In B. Kroll (Ed.), *Second language writing: Research insights for the classroom* (pp. 129–135). New York: Cambridge University Press.

Cope, B., & Kalantzis, M. (1993). The power of literacy and the literacy of power. In B. Cope & M. Kalantzis (Eds.), *The powers of literacy: A genre approach to teaching writing* (pp. 63–89). Pittsburgh: Pittsburgh University Press.

Cope, B., Kalantzis, M., Kress, G., & Martin, J. (1993). Bibliographical essay: Developing the theory and practice of genre-based literacy. In B. Cope & M. Kalantzis (Eds.), *The powers of literacy: A genre approach to teaching writing* (pp. 231–247). Pittsburgh: Pittsburgh University Press.

Cummins, J. (1981). The role of primary language development in promoting educational success for language minority students. In California State Department of Education (Ed.), *Schooling and language minority students.* Los Angeles: Evaluation, Dissemination, and Assessment Center.

Cummins, J. (1983). *Heritage language education: A literature review.* Toronto: Ontario Ministry of Education.

Delpit, L. (1991). The silenced dialogue: Power and pedagogy in educating other people's children. In M. Minami & B. Kennedy (Eds.), *Language issues in literacy and bilingual/multicultural education* (pp. 483–502). Cambridge, MA: Harvard Educational Review.

Dudley-Evans, T. (1995). Common-core and specific approaches to the teaching of academic writing. In D. Belcher & G. Braine (Eds.), *Academic writing in a second language: Essays on research and pedagogy* (pp. 293–312). Norwood, NJ: Ablex.

Edwards, H., Wesche, M., Krashen, S., Clement, R., & Kruidenier, B. (1984). Second language acquisition through subject-matter learning: A study of sheltered psychology classes at the University of Ottawa. *Canadian Modern Language Review, 41,* 286–292.

Ellis, R. (1992). The classroom context: An acquisition-rich or an acquisition-poor environment? In C. Kramsch & S. McConnell-Ginet (Eds.), *Text and context: Cross-disciplinary perspectives on language study* (pp. 171–186). Lexington, MA: D. C. Heath.

Ferris, D., & Tagg, T. (1996). Academic oral communication needs of ESL learners: What subject-matter instructors actually require. *TESOL Quarterly, 30*(1), 31–58.

Flowerdew, J. (1993). An educational, or process, approach to the teaching of professional genres. *ELT Journal, 47,* 305–316.

Fox, H. (1994). *Listening to the world: Cultural issues in academic writing.* Urbana, IL: National Council of Teachers of English.

Fox, H. (1996). "And never the twain shall meet": International students writing for a U.S. university audience. *ERIC Document* 300540.

Fredrickson, T., Hagedorn, J., & Reed, H. (1991). The content-based curriculum at ITM/MUCIA. *Cross Currents, 18*(2), 200–205.

Freire, P. (1974). *Pedagogy of the oppressed.* New York: Scabury.

Freire, P., & Macedo, D. (1987). *Literacy: Reading the word and the world.* South Hadley, MA: Bergin and Garvey.

Genesee, F. (1987). *Learning through two languages.* Rowley, MA: Newbury House.

Goldstein, L., Campbell, C., & Cummings, M. (1997). Smiling through the turbulence: The flight attendant syndrome and writing instructor status in the adjunct model. In M. Snow & D. Brinton (Eds.), *The content-based classroom: Perspectives on integrating language and content* (pp. 331–339). White Plains, NY: Addison Wesley Longman.

Gosden, H. (1992). Discourse functions of marked theme in scientific research articles. *English for Specific Purposes, 11,* 207–224.

Grabe, W., & Stoller, F. (1997). Content-based instruction: Research foundations. In M. Snow & D. Brinton (Eds.), *The content-based classroom: Perspectives on integrating language and content* (pp. 5–21). White Plains, NY: Addison Wesley Longman.

Gradman, H., & Hanania, E. (1991). Language learning background factors and ESL proficiency. *Modern Language Journal, 75,* 39–51.

Grandin, J. (1993). The University of Rhode Island's international engineering program. In M. Krueger & F. Ryan (Eds.), *Language and content: Discipline- and content-based approaches to language study* (pp. 130–137). Lexington, MA: D. C. Heath.

Guyer, E., & Peterson, P. (1988). Language and/or content? Principles and procedures for materials development in an adjunct course. In S. Benesch (Ed.), *Ending remediation: Linking ESL and content in higher education* (pp. 91–111). Washington, DC: TESOL.

Hammond, J., Wickert, R., Burns, A., Joyce, H., & Miller, A. (1992). *The pedagogical relations between adult ESL and adult literacy.* Canberra: Commonwealth of Australia.

Hauptman, P., Wesche, M., & Ready, D. (1988). Second-language acquisition through subject-matter learning: A follow-up study at the University of Ottawa. *Language Learning, 38*(3), 433–466.

Hirsch, L. (1988). Language across the curriculum: A model for ESL students in content courses. In S. Benesch (Ed.), *Ending remediation: Linking ESL and content in higher education* (pp. 67–89). Washington, DC: TESOL.

Hornberger, N., & Ricento, T. (Eds.). (1996). Language planning and policy [Special issue]. *TESOL Quarterly, 30*(3).

Horowitz, D. (1986). What professors actually require: Academic tasks for the ESL classroom. *TESOL Quarterly, 20*(3), 445–462.

Hymes, D. (1971). *On communicative competence.* Philadelphia: University of Pennsylvania Press.

Hyon, S. (1996). Genre in three traditions: Implications for ESL. *TESOL Quarterly, 30*(4), 693–722.

Johns, A. (1990, March). *Process, literature, and academic realities: Dan Horowitz and beyond.* Handout for paper presented at the 24th Annual TESOL Convention, San Francisco, CA.

Johns, A. (1997). *Text, role, and context: Developing academic literacies.* New York: Cambridge University Press.

Kasper, L. (1995/1996). Using discipline-based texts to boost college ESL reading instruction. *Journal of Adolescent and Adult Literacy, 39,* 298–306.

Kasper, L. 1997. The impact of content-based instructional programs on the academic progress of ESL students. *English for Specific Purposes, 16*(4), 309–320.

Krapp, A., Hidi, S., & Renninger, K. (1992). Interest, learning, and development. In K. Renninger, S. Hidi, & A. Krapp (Eds.), *The role of interest in learning and development* (pp. 3–25). Hillsdale, NJ: Erlbaum.

Krashen, S. (1981). *Second language acquisition and second language learning.* New York: Prentice Hall.

Krashen, S. (1985). *The input hypothesis: Issues and implications.* New York: Longman.

Krueger, M., & Ryan, F. (Eds.). (1993). *Language and content: Discipline- and content-based approaches to language study.* Lexington, MA: D. C. Heath.

Kutz, E., Groden, S., & Zamel, V. (1993). *The discovery of competence: Teaching and learning with diverse student writers.* Portsmouth, NH: Boynton/Cook.

Lantolf, J., & Pavlenko, A. (1995). Sociological approaches to second language acquisition. In W. Grabe, C. Ferguson, R. Kaplan, G. Tucker, & H. Widdowson (Eds.), *Annual Review of Applied Linguistics, 15* (pp. 125–150). New York: Cambridge University Press.

Leki, I. (1991). Twenty-five years of contrastive rhetoric: Text analysis and writing pedagogies. *TESOL Quarterly, 25*(1), 123–143.

Leki, I. (1995). Good writing: I know it when I see it. In D. Belcher & G. Braine (Eds.), *Academic writing in a second language: Essays on research and pedagogy* (pp. 23–46). Norwood, NJ: Ablex.

Leki, I., & Carson, J. (1994). Students' perceptions of EAP writing instruction and writing needs across the disciplines. *TESOL Quarterly, 28*(1), 81–101.

Leki, I., & Carson, J. (1997), Completely different worlds: EAP and the writing experiences of ESL students in university courses. *TESOL Quarterly, 31*(1), 39–69.

Long, M. (1983). Native speaker/non-native speaker conversation in the second language classroom. In M. Clarke & J. Handscombe (Eds.), *On TESOL '82: Pacific perspectives on language learning and teaching* (pp. 207–225). Washington, DC: TESOL.

Long, M., & Crookes, G. (1993). Units of analysis in syllabus design: The case for task. In G. Crookes & M. Gass (Eds.), *Tasks in a pedagogical context: Integrating theory and practice* (pp. 9–54). Clevedon, Avon: Multilingual Matters.

Malherbe, E. (1946). *The bilingual school.* Johannesburg, South Africa: Bilingual School Association.

Mayer, L., & Mayer, M. (1991). 4 years later—Are we content with content? *Cross Currents, 18*(2), 206–209.

Milk, R. (1990). Preparing ESL and bilingual teachers for changing roles: Immersion for teachers of LEP children. *TESOL Quarterly, 24*(3), 407–426.

Mohan, B. (1986). *Language and content.* Reading, MA: Addison-Wesley.

Mohan, B. (1990, September). LEP students and the integration of language and content: Knowledge structures and tasks. In *Proceedings of the Research Symposium on Limited English Proficient Students' Issues* (pp. 113–160). Washington, DC: Office of Bilingual Education and Minority Language Affairs.

Mustafa, Z. (1995). The effect of genre awareness on linguistic transfer. *English for Specific Purposes, 14*(3), 247–256.

Palmer, B. (1993). Eastern Michigan University's programs in language and international business: Disciplines with content. In M. Krueger & F. Ryan (Eds.), *Language and content: Discipline- and content-based approaches to language study* (pp. 138–147). Lexington, MA: D. C. Heath.

Pica, T. (1987). Interlanguage adjustments as an outcome of NS NNS negotiated interaction. *Language Learning, 38*(1), 45–73.

Pica, T. (1992). The textual outcomes of native speaker–non-native speaker negotiation: What do they reveal about second language learning? In C. Kramsch & S. McConnell-Ginet (Eds.), *Text and context: Cross disciplinary perspectives on language study* (pp. 198–237). Lexington, MA: D. C. Heath.

Ponder, R., & Powell, W. (1989). *Sourcebooks as content-bearing instruction in intensive ESL programs.* Tallahassee, FL: Florida State University, Center for Intensive English Studies. (ERIC Document Reproduction Service No. ED 307 805).

Prabhu, N. (1987). *Second language pedagogy.* Oxford, UK: Oxford University Press.

Riazi, A. (1997). Acquiring disciplinary literacy: A social cognitive analysis of text production and learning among Iranian graduate students of education. *Journal of Second Language Writing, 6*(2), 105–138.

Saegert, J., Scott, M., Perkins, J., & Tucker, G. (1974). A note on the relationship between English proficiency, years of language study and medium of instruction. *Language Learning, 24,* 99–104.

Schenke, A. (1996). Not just a "social issue": Teaching feminism in ESL. *TESOL Quarterly, 30*(1), 155–159.

Schleppegrel, M. (1984). Using input methods to improve writing skills. *System, 12,* 287–292.

Schmidt, R. (1988). *The role of consciousness in second language acquisition.* Paper presented at the Eighth Second Language Forum, University of Hawaii at Manoa, Honolulu.

Schneider, M., & Connor, U. (1991). Topical structure in ESL essays: Not all topics are equal. *Studies in Second Language Acquisition, 12,* 411–427.

Shih, M. (1986). Content-based approaches to teaching academic writing. *TESOL Quarterly, 20*(4), 617–648.

Shor, I. (1992). *Empowering education: Critical teaching for social change.* Chicago: University of Chicago Press.

Short, D. (1991a). Content-based English language teaching: A focus on teacher training. *Cross Currents, 18*(2),167–173.

Short, D. (1991b). *How to integrate language and content instruction: A training manual.* Washington, DC: Center for Applied Linguistics.

Short, D. (1993). Assessing integrated language and content instruction. *TESOL Quarterly, 27*(4), 627–656.

Short, D., Crandall, J., & Christian, D. (1989). *How to integrate language and content instruction: A training manual.* (Report No. CLEAR-ER15). Los Angeles: California University, Center for Language Education and Research. (ERIC Document Reproduction Service No. ED 305 842).

Smoke, T. (Ed.). (1998). *Adult ESL: Politics, pedagogy, and participation in classroom and community programs.* Mahwah, NJ: Erlbaum.

Snow, M., & Brinton, D. (1988). Content-based language instruction: Investigating the effectiveness of the adjunct model. *TESOL Quarterly, 22*(4), 553–574.

Snow, M., & Brinton, D. (Eds.) (1997). *The content-based classroom: Perspectives on integrating language and content.* White Plains, NY: Addison Wesley Longman.

Snow, M., Met, M., & Genesee, F. (1989). A conceptual framework for the integration of language and content in second/foreign language instruction. *TESOL Quarterly, 23*(2), 201–217.

Spack, R. (1988). Initiating ESL students into the academic discourse community: How far should we go?" *TESOL Quarterly, 22*(1), 29–51.

Spanos, G. (1989). On the integration of language and content instruction. *Annual Review of Applied Linguistics, 10,* 227–240.

Strong, R., & Candlin, C. (1993). Forward. In P. Hagan, S. Hood, E. Jackson, M. Jones, H. Joyce, & M. Manidis (Eds.), *Certificate in spoken and written English* (2nd. ed.). Syndey, Australia: New South Wales Adult Migrant English Service & National Centre for English Language Teaching and Research.

Swain, M. (1985). Communicative competence: Some roles of comprehensible input and comprehensible output in its development. In S. Gass & C. Madden (Eds.), *Input in second language acquisition* (pp. 235–253). Rowley, MA: Newbury House.

Swain, M. (1988). Manipulating and complementing content teaching to maximize second language learning. *TESL Canada Journal, 6*(1), 68–83.

Swain, M., & Lapkin, S. (1982). *Evaluating bilingual education: A Canadian case study.* Clevedon, Avon: Multilingual Matters Limited.

Swales, J. (1987). Utilizing the literatures in teaching the research paper. *TESOL Quarterly, 21*(1), 41–68.

Swales, J. (1990). *Genre analysis: English in academic and research settings.* Cambridge, UK: Cambridge University Press.

Tarone, E., Dwyer, S., Gillette, S., & Icke, V. (1981). On the use of the passive in two astrophysics journal papers. *ESP Journal, 1*(2), 123–140.

Tobias, S. (1994). Interest, prior knowledge, and learning. *Review of Educational Research, 64*(1), 37–54.

Tollefson, J. (1991). *Planning language, planning inequality: Language policy in the community.* New York: Longman.

Trimble, L. (1985). *EST: A discourse approach.* Cambridge, UK: Cambridge University Press.

Turner, J. (1993). A motivational perspective on literacy instruction. In D. J. Leu & C. K. Kinzer (Eds.), *Examining central issues in literacy research, theory and practice* (pp. 153–161). Chicago: National Reading Conference.

Van Patten, B. (1985). Communicative values and information processing in L2 acquisition. In P. Larson, E. Judd, & D. Messerschmitt (Eds.), *On TESOL '84: A brave new world for TESOL* (pp. 89–99). Washington, DC: TESOL.

Van Patten, B. (1990). Attending to form and content in the input. *Studies in Second Language Acquisition, 12,* 287–301.

Varonis, E., & Gass, S. (1985a). Miscommunication in NS/NNS interactions. *Language in Society, 14.2.*

Varonis, E., & Gass, S. (1985b). Non-native/non-native conversations: A model for negotiation of meaning. *Applied Linguistics, 6.1,* 71–90.

Vygotsky, L. (1962). *Thought and language.* Cambridge, MA: MIT Press.

Webster's Ninth New Collegiate Dictionary. (1989). Springfield, MA: Merriam-Webster.

Wesche, M. (1993). Discipline-based approaches to language study: Research issues and outcomes. In M. Krueger & F. Ryan (Eds.), *Language and content: Discipline- and content-based approaches to language study* (pp. 57–82). Lexington, MA: D. C. Heath.

Widdowson, H. (1990). *Aspects of language teaching.* Oxford, UK: Oxford University Press.

Widdowson, H. (1993). The relevant conditions of language use and learning. In M. Krueger & F. Ryan (Eds.), *Language and content: Discipline- and content-based approaches to language study* (pp. 27–36). Lexington, MA: D. C. Heath.

Zuengler, J., & Brinton, D. (1997). Linguistic form, pragmatic function: Relevant research from content-based instruction. In M. Snow & D. Brinton (Eds.), *The content-based classroom: Perspectives on integrating language and content* (pp. 263–273). White Plains, NY: Addison Wesley Longman.

Chapter 2

Reading and Writing for Academic Purposes

Joan G. Carson
Georgia State University

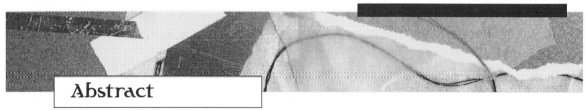

Abstract

ESL students preparing for academic coursework need to develop academic language abilities that will enable them to succeed in their entry-level undergraduate classes. This chapter describes a general model for a task-based English for Academic Purposes curriculum and focuses on one course in the curriculum: Reading and Listening for Academic Purposes.[1] In this course, sustained content is necessary to support the academic tasks (multiple-choice, true/false, fill-in-the-blank, and short-answer tests; book reviews) being taught as students learn to access content, acquire content knowledge, and display that knowledge. The chapter provides descriptions of the pedagogical tasks, which include vocabulary building, study skills, and test-taking skills. ∎

[1] I would like to thank Laureen Fredella and Jo Taylor, who contributed much to the development of this curriculum.

Introduction

The reasons for connecting reading and writing in second-language learning constitute a compelling argument for practitioners and theorists, and nowhere are they more compelling than in academic settings for the simple reason that in these settings, reading and writing co-occur in persistent and nontrivial ways. For the most part, students in undergraduate courses read to write: reading notes, lecture notes, study notes, and exam questions (short answer, short essay, long essay). They also write to read: their own writing, writing as guides to ongoing research, and questions to be answered by further reading. All of these activities comprise reading and writing to learn, of course, since that is the goal of all education, including undergraduate courses (if not of undergraduates themselves). Reading and writing to learn also implies displaying one's learning for the purpose of earning a grade.

At Georgia State University, we have found that the best approach to English for Academic Purposes (EAP) is a task-based curriculum in which students are required to do the real-world tasks of undergraduate coursework to acquire the academic reading and writing skills they will need to support the tasks needed for success in their entry-level content classes. We focus on tasks in entry-level courses only as determined by our needs analysis, since other skills, such as research papers and essay writing, are taught in freshman composition courses and are neither expected nor assigned in freshman content courses.

We have chosen to develop this task-based curriculum for two reasons: face validity and transferability. We have found that students in EAP classes are more motivated to learn when they recognize that what they are doing in these classes are tasks they will actually engage in when they begin their university studies. **Face validity** results from students' understanding of their need to acquire the language, study skills, test-taking abilities, and content that they are learning in their EAP courses. Furthermore, the language they are learning is embedded in contexts that they will recognize once they begin academic courses, and thus the situated skills they acquire are more readily available for **transfer** to similar situations. Tasks, in other words, provide a focus and a rationale for the language learning that L2 students do in their EAP classes such that all the subskills that they learn fit into their overall picture of developing academic language proficiency.

Task-Based EAP Model

A task-based EAP curriculum is based on the actual tasks that entry-level university students must perform to do well in their academic coursework. We define these tasks at the level of graded products (e.g., exams, papers) rather than at the level of skills and subskills (reading, summary writing, etc.), since we have found, based on student interviews, that students' understanding of "what the professor wants on the test" is what drives their study habits and learning (Carson, Chase, & Gibson, 1993). This is not as "grade-grubbing" as it might appear at first glance. Rather, students understand that what is important in a course is what the professor is likely to be testing, and they use the tests to help them figure out the course focus.

A needs analysis of entry-level courses will show what tasks are important, and these tasks are likely to vary with the setting. For example, our needs analysis (Carson, Chase, & Gibson, 1993) was done at a large, urban research university, where entry-level courses typically are large lecture settings with little student interaction and few major writing assignments. In this setting, students are often tested with multiple-choice and objective exams since large lecture classes do not lend themselves to labor-intensive (for the professor) essay exams and papers. However, the predominance of large lecture classes does not mean that students need only reading and listening skills. In some departments—history, for example—writing is considered an important skill, and students are required to write essay exams and papers. Freshman composition, too, will focus on essayist prose, and students will need to do this type of writing when they begin their university coursework. In addition, speaking skills are important in lab classes, in discussion sections, for interacting with professors in office hour conversations, and for contributing to various group activities such as peer editing and study sessions.

Thus, we find a picture of integrated language abilities in which reading, writing, speaking, and listening must co-occur, in the context of a focus on a particular content area, with professors' varying expectations of grammatical accuracy. Interviews with professors in our institution (Carson, Chase, and Gibson, 1993), as well as a number of research studies, have shown that instructors tend to be more tolerant of NNSs' grammatical errors in in-class/timed writing, such as exams, than of such errors in out-of-class writing, such as papers and reports. In all cases, of course, what the student is trying to say must be comprehensible, if not syntactically perfect.

Our challenge as EAP instructors, then, is to help students develop the language necessary for (1) *accessing* the necessary content, (2) *acquiring* knowledge of that content, and (3) *displaying* that knowledge in various ways (see Figure 2.1). Obviously, reading and writing play a major role in accessing content from what I call the course text: the textbook itself and the material presented in the lecture (and, at times, in labs). Simply put, students must deal with two main sources of content input—the text and the oral information—and in this context, reading and writing (in the form of notetaking) are the critical tasks. I want to clarify here that I consider notetaking, whether from reading or listening, to be primarily a writing task, because it is a form of summary writing (i.e., students write summaries of material they have either read or heard). Taking reading notes based on static texts can be thought of as a somewhat less difficult language task, since students have access to dictionaries and can reread material they have not understood well. Taking lecture notes, on the other hand, is an on-line writing task, and thus is somewhat more difficult because the lecture setting allows neither dictionary look-up time nor the opportunity to go back to material that was missed. Nevertheless, the summary writing task is more or less similar; what differs is the source of input.

In an EAP curriculum, then, students acquire content by integrating material they have accessed through reading (reading notes, marginal notes, highlighting) and through writing based on listening (lecture notes). From these integrated notes comes the students' study text, the text they use to acquire the content

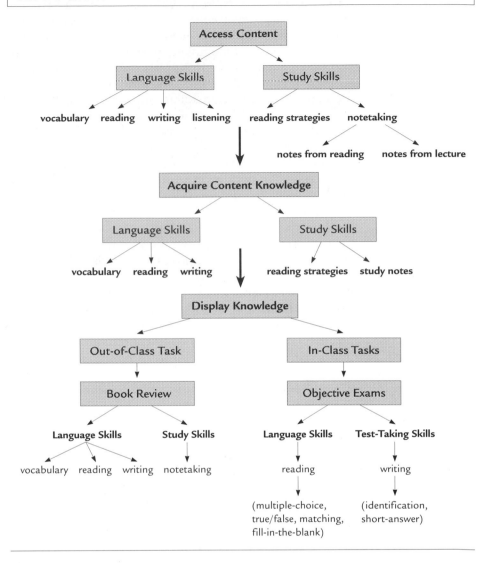

Figure 2.1 A Model of Undergraduate Language Needs Taught in One EAP Course

Access Content

Language Skills
vocabulary   reading   writing   listening

Study Skills
reading strategies   notetaking
notes from reading   notes from lecture

Acquire Content Knowledge

Language Skills
vocabulary   reading   writing

Study Skills
reading strategies   study notes

Display Knowledge

Out-of-Class Task

In-Class Tasks

Book Review

Objective Exams

Language Skills
vocabulary   reading   writing

Study Skills
notetaking

Language Skills
reading

(multiple-choice,
true/false, matching,
fill-in-the-blank)

Test-Taking Skills
writing

(identification,
short-answer)

information and to prepare for graded display tasks—papers, exams, and so forth. I realize, of course, that this is not what all students do. (We interviewed one NNS in a freshman history course who was confident in his ability to sit back and understand the professor's lecture without taking notes. He was a little taken aback when we asked how he planned to review for the final exam: he had focused on access and seemed to have forgotten about acquisition and display.) But our job as EAP instructors is to prepare students to be able to do what they need to do, even if individual students choose not to do it in the end!

What are these display tasks? Our needs analysis of entry-level undergraduate courses showed two major categories of graded products: in-class assignments and out-of-class assignments. In-class assignments were primarily objective test items (multiple-choice, true/false, matching, and fill-in-the-blank) and constructed response test items (identification, short answer, and essays). Out-of-class assignments were primarily essays and reports, including book reviews that required students to integrate the book's content with the course content. Most writing assignments, except for some freshman composition essays, were what Leki and I have called "text responsible" writing (Leki & Carson, 1997) in that students were required to represent text content accurately with, at times, critical interpretation. Although these tasks do not appear to be unusual in any significant way, they represent the graded products at our institution and are not meant to be generalizable to other institutions.

These display tasks imply various subtasks that are necessary for accessing and acquiring the content to be displayed. In other words, students must be able to perform various subtasks in the process of writing a report, responding to an essay question under timed conditions, or taking a multiple-choice exam. Subtasks in one course, History 113, include the ability to read extensively, take lecture and reading notes, synthesize these notes, and write concisely under time constraints, among others (Carson, Chase, Gibson, & Hargrove, 1992). These subtasks become the ongoing daily work of the task-based EAP curriculum, and are always done in the context of the display task. In other words, students work on taking lecture notes, for example, which become part of their study texts, which in turn are used to prepare for the exam or paper that they will be required to do.

The pedagogical tasks, then, of the EAP instructor are tasks that provide students with the opportunity to develop the language, study, and test-taking skills they will need to perform the display tasks and the subtasks necessary to support that display. Because the academic language tasks involved in undergraduate study assume the need for displaying knowledge in a single content area, our courses rely on sustained content; they do not mix different content areas or use/teach a single content from sources other than those encountered in academic courses. If we didn't use sustained content, it would not be possible, for example, to prepare students for display tasks such as cumulative exams that require them to integrate information across course chapters—a task that is simply unavailable when course content changes from topic to topic. Furthermore, the content focus is that of typical entry-level courses: history, psychology, sociology, anthropology, biology, and so on. In the most advanced levels of our curriculum, we use the actual texts that students will be assigned in their entry-level courses. The advantages of sustained content are that it allows students to develop (1) the vocabulary associated with that specific content, (2) the syntactic patterns that are likely to recur in continuing text, (3) the background knowledge students will actually need when they take these courses, and (4) the opportunity to work with cumulative knowledge/concept building throughout the course. Thus, students find the material more and more accessible as the course progresses because they are building on language and content to which they are continually exposed.

Principles and Parameters of the EAP Curriculum

Our EAP curriculum is based on a few principles and parameters that seem to me to be general statements about preacademic EAP curricula:

General Principles

1. Emphasize integration—of reading with writing, of oral exposition with written texts, of in-class with out-of-class learning.

2. In general, construct tasks that require students to manage content in "text responsible" ways rather than to generate it (as is the case with expressive writing).

3. Distinguish between what is possible to do in EAP courses and what is feasible. It would be possible, but not feasible, to become experts in various content fields. Our expectation is that ESL instructors need to understand what is in the freshman-level text and nothing more. Because the texts we use are entry-level texts, ESL teachers have experienced no difficulties in understanding and explaining the content.

4. Whenever possible, translate pedagogical metalanguage into task-based language (e.g., thesis/topic sentence/main idea = the point of the reading/writing/lecture).

General Parameters

1. Task

   a. Identify tasks by display task (essay exam, report, short ID question) and by subtask (notetaking, synthesizing, summarizing, etc.).

   b. Contextualize subtasks so that they are goal directed, that is, embedded in the display tasks (e.g., summarize readings and synthesize with lecture notes to create study notes to use on an essay exam).

   c. Develop pedagogical tasks to directly teach display tasks and subtasks.

2. Content

   a. Length of materials

      (1) For reading, longer texts are better than shorter texts.

      (2) In general, writing should be specified in length rather than in structural units (e.g., your answer should be about a page long rather than three paragraphs.) The structure will emerge from ways in which students develop the task.

   b. Types of materials can be anything that provides academic content in academic language.

   c. Students' ideas and opinions are relevant for journal entries related to text or metacognitive issues (e.g., strategies), but are not themselves the content of the course.

3. Language

   a. Linguistic proficiency is developed as a function of assigned tasks.

   b. Because academic register is often a function of the lexicon, academic vocabulary needs to be expressly taught and emphasized.

   c. Discourse-level grammar is taught to enable students to express concepts and relationships among concepts.

d. Paraphrasing is an extremely difficult skill requiring an extensive vocabulary and sophisticated syntax, and is best emphasized with more advanced students. (In fact, for in-class writing, the professors we interviewed did not object to students' using phrases, sentences, or longer stretches of material directly from the course text. One professor remarked that it was fine if students used her words exactly—she thought she said it best, anyway!)

4. Testing

a. Test both language skills and integration of language skills (e.g., use writing to test reading where the lecture or reading notes are part of the test [see discussion below]).

b. The test format and evaluation need to balance issues of content (have they answered correctly?), task (did they do what the question specified—analyze, compare and contrast, etc.?), and language proficiency (did they say it such that it was comprehensible?).

c. The test should test the content that students have learned through various activities, since this is the real-world task of the content classroom (e.g., a reading test should never include a passage that students have not seen prior to the test).

d. The test should be designed to familiarize students with typical classroom test formats and to facilitate the development of test-taking strategies.

The task-based EAP curriculum that we have developed at GSU is based, then, on these principles and parameters, as well as on the needs analysis we have conducted of entry-level undergraduate courses.

Core Courses

In addition to oral communication labs, vocabulary-building labs, and computer workshops, the curriculum is composed of four core courses.

The first course targets the oral communication skills that students will need in their academic coursework, including improving conversation skills, developing basic vocabulary, improving listening comprehension, and improving pronunciation. Students learn basic notetaking skills, as well as how to ask questions in class, respond to instructors' questions, contribute during group-work activities, interact with instructors during office hours, and converse with classmates outside of class for study purposes.

The second course focuses on untimed, out-of-class writing tasks such as papers, essays, memos, and reports. In these types of writing, organization, development, and grammatical accuracy play important roles, and it is in these classes that students work on discourse-level grammar (the only kind of grammar that we teach). Academic formats (e.g., comparing, defining, classifying) are taught here, and the course focuses on revision and editing skills as well as on accuracy in grammar. Grammatical accuracy is an appropriate focus in the context of out-of-class assignments, where students have the time and resources (books, tutors, etc.) to monitor for accuracy.

The third course, Academic Writing, targets timed, in-class writing tasks, primarily written exams. In this course, students learn how to manage academic reading, take reading notes, and understand and answer test questions requiring a constructed response—identification, short-answer, and essay questions (see Chapter 8). Vocabulary is important in this course as well, and instruction includes helping students organize information in ways specified by various test questions: citation, comparison, classification, definition, exemplification, and cause and effect.

The fourth course, Reading and Listening for Academic Purposes, is the focus of this chapter and exemplifies the ways in which reading and writing (in spite of the course name!) work together to help students access, acquire, and display their knowledge of course content. The graded-task focus of this course includes answering matching, true/false, multiple-choice, and short-answer test questions. This is also the course where we focus on extensive reading, since our needs analysis has identified the importance of critical reviews of books related to course content. Each of these tasks presents its own reading/writing challenge, even in cases where writing is not a part of the actual final task (matching, true/false, multiple-choice, etc.).

Reading and Listening for Academic Purposes

We call this course Reading and Listening for Academic Purposes because reading and listening highlight the sources of input students will use to access the content, whereas integrated reading/writing skills are needed to acquire and display content knowledge. This is our advanced-level course in which the content is the text from Psychology 101, *Psychology* (Myers, 1995). From the required text, we reproduced the following:

1. the table of contents, which we included to help students develop the reading strategy of using this material to gain an overview of the organizational pieces of a chapter and of the relationship among chapters

2. the introductory chapter, which we included to provide an overview of the subject matter

3. three text chapters ("Adolescence and Adulthood," "Intelligence," and "Personality"), selected for student interest, for the presentation formats (chronological order, analysis, and cause and effect), and for the fact that they are topics that could be interrelated in cumulative assignments and exams

4. the glossary, selected to provide students with discipline-specific word meanings

5. the name index and the subject index, which we included to help students develop study strategies using these guides

This textbook material was bound in a reading packet for the students. They were also required to purchase a study guide packet that included materials, explanations, and exercises we developed to accompany the reading packet. Finally, students had to buy a novel selected to complement the course materials, *Flowers for Algernon* (Keyes, 1966), a book that was on the reading list for

Psychology 101 and explored themes from the chapters we had selected from the course text.

In addition to exam questions, another display task is the book review, which requires students to analyze the novel from the perspective of psychological themes covered in the course. In short, this is a course that requires extensive reading: the course text, the novel, and the test questions (multiple-choice questions in particular constitute a difficult reading task, since the difference between selecting a correct answer and choosing an incorrect one often is a matter of understanding subtle vocabulary differences). And it is a course that requires extensive writing as well: reading and listening notes, study notes, short-answer questions, and the book review. The subtasks (vocabulary building, study skills—primarily reading strategies and notetaking strategies—and test-taking skills) constitute the basis for the pedagogical tasks.

Vocabulary Building

Vocabulary building is an extremely important aspect of EAP courses. Vocabulary is not something students just "pick up" through reading; we need to focus on it explicitly in the classroom. In this course, we emphasize two types of vocabulary: vocabulary students need to learn for production purposes and vocabulary they need to learn for recognition purposes.

Vocabulary for production refers to vocabulary that students need to be able to use. In other words, they must *know* what these words mean (have them in their internal lexicons) and be able to produce them when generating their own text (e.g., in short-answer questions and notetaking). In teaching vocabulary for production, we focus on three types of vocabulary.

1. *Discipline-specific vocabulary* constitutes the content of the course itself (psychology, sociology, etc.); it is the vocabulary that is often highlighted in the textbook, listed in the glossary, defined at the end of the chapter, and included on short-answer test questions (e.g., "What do psychologists mean by *personality?*"). These vocabulary items can be thought of as the concepts that students are learning in the process of studying a particular subject area. They constitute the fundamental building blocks of the course and, once introduced and learned, tend to be the concepts that are related to other concepts in the course and that recur throughout the text. In other words, it's not enough to know the dictionary definition of the word; students need to continue to widen their understanding of the term or concept as the course progresses. In some cases, students need to be able to distinguish these discipline-specific word meanings from the words' additional, nondisciplinary meanings (e.g., *stage* when referring to a stage of development as opposed to a theatrical stage) and to understand that some words have specific meanings in the context of the subject matter.

2. The second type of vocabulary that students need to learn is *general academic vocabulary* that they may have identified as problematic in a particular reading. These vocabulary items usually come from the vocabulary notebooks we ask students to keep—items that a majority of learners have

listed as both unknown and necessary to reading comprehension. These are words that students will see again and again in most of the courses they take, because they tend to be characteristic of all academic texts (e.g., *arbitrary, norm, analogy, versus*).

3. The third type of vocabulary for production is the study of *stems and affixes,* common morphemes that appear regularly in academic texts, including word roots, prefixes, and suffixes. Since these morphemes occur frequently in academic writing, once these few word "parts" are learned, students will have the key to understanding a significant amount of academic vocabulary. The stems and affixes we teach are ones that occur in material students are currently studying, and the examples given come directly from the text. For example, from the introductory chapter we selected stems such as *nat* (to be born)—example: *innate; psych* (mind)—examples: *psychology, psychohistory, psychosocial;* and *spec/spic* (to look at)—examples: *introspection, perspective.* Prefixes included *in/im/il/ir* (no, not)—examples: *irrational, imperceptible; intro* (within)—example: *introspection;* and *pre* (before)—examples: *prediction, preschoolers, preconception.*

Vocabulary for recognition refers to vocabulary students need to be able to recognize either by (1) having a "passive" understanding of the word itself or (2) using a variety of context clues. Understanding *vocabulary in context* is a particularly important skill to be practiced in the reading class, since we want students to be able to move away from word-by-word processing and focus on increasing both reading comprehension and reading speed. The importance of understanding vocabulary in context involves language-processing limits: the amount of information that a reader can hold in short-term memory. If students are looking up many (or most) of the words in a passage, comprehension suffers since they cannot retain the gist of a sentence while they stop to look up and grasp a particular word. We focus on a variety of strategies for understanding vocabulary in context, including recognizing (1) direct or explicit definitions, (2) indirect definitions (dashes and *such as* to introduce examples), (3) combined definitions (elaborations, criteria), (4) participation in a class, and (5) inference from the student's own experience.

To teach recognition vocabulary, we developed exercises in which we selected sentences from the text, highlighted a word in the sentence, and then asked students to write a definition based on that text/sentence and to identify the strategy they used to recognize the meaning. These sentences include a focus on strategies such as the following:

1. *Explicit definition:* "Piaget theorized that adolescents develop the capacity for **formal operations,** which enables them to reason abstractly." (p. 127)

2. *Direct definition:* "Young children wrestle with issues of trust, then **autonomy** (independence), then initiative." (p. 122)

3. *Indirect definition:* "The bad news: the body's disease-fighting immune system weakens, making the elderly more susceptible to life-threatening **ailments** such as cancer and pneumonia." (p. 133)

4. *Participation in a class:* "Note that Binet and Simon made no assumptions concerning why a particular child was slow, average or **precocious**." (p. 361)

These exercises do not always (or ever) prevent students from using dictionaries to figure out a word's meaning, but the strategy identification alerts them to the strategy they *could* have used to understand the word in context.

Study Skills

In addition to teaching productive and recognition vocabulary strategies, we directly teach reading strategies to help students access content and notetaking strategies to help them acquire content.

Reading Strategies. Reading strategies, like vocabulary strategies, are taught in the context of tasks students will need to perform in their academic coursework, and we practice these strategies by using study guides developed for each chapter. The reading strategies help students focus their reading to answer the study guide questions, and the study guide helps students focus on the important points in each chapter (i.e., those likely to be tested). A typical study guide would be something like the following:

Study Guide

Myers, Ch. 11, "The Dynamics of Intelligence," pp. 378–383

1. What evidence is there that a person's intelligence remains stable throughout the lifespan? What evidence is there that a person's intelligence changes over time?

2. What does it mean to be "gifted"? "Challenged"?

3. Identify the factors associated with creativity and describe the relationships between creativity and intelligence.

Terms and Vocabulary

mental retardation

Down syndrome

creativity

gifted

We introduce reading strategies (the usual ones: scanning, skimming, and reading for thorough comprehension) through a series of exercises geared to the text. For example, a scanning exercise would include the following questions:

1. Where would you look (what would you scan) to find information about the stages of adulthood?

2. Scan to find the name of a researcher who has studied stages of adulthood.

3. How would you go about answering this question: Do adults' physical capacities decline with age?

Skimming is used to help students learn to get a quick summary of the text—the main point. Skimming exercises would include these questions:

1. Skim the section on "Health," page 133. In general, what are the effects of aging on health?

2. Skim the section on "Death and Dying," pages 143–144. In general, how do adults react to death?

3. When is skimming a text a good way to read?

We also focus on reading for thorough comprehension. An example of this type of exercise follows:

Read the section on "Life Expectancy," pages 131–132.

1. Why does the author say that "Countries that depend on children to care for the aged are destined for major social changes"?

2. How does the ratio of males to females change with age?

3. Why do we age?

By differentiating the types of reading strategies needed to answer these study guide questions, students can learn to read differently to gather different types of information.

Notetaking. Notetaking of both readings and lectures is the second important study skill included in the course. Students begin with reading notes, since the static nature of written text makes the task of learning notetaking from reading somewhat easier than learning notetaking from spoken language. When listening notes are introduced, the teacher builds on what students have learned from taking reading notes, as well as pointing out differences that result from the dynamic, on-line nature of spoken discourse.

We have found that it is important to point out to students *why* notetaking is so important to academic success, and we begin with a class discussion that focuses on the function of notes as (1) information volume management and (2) memory storage. Information volume management is more important for reading notes, particularly in courses that require considerable reading (e.g., in History 113, students will need to read more than 835 pages over the term). Because students simply will not be able to reread the entire text to study for tests, reading notes provide a way for them to condense and manage the essential information to put it in a form that will facilitate acquiring that information. Memory storage is more important for lecture notetaking, since information given in class can be quickly forgotten.

Though notetaking clearly is an essential skill, it is also a very idiosyncratic activity. In its memory storage function, notes are crafted differently depending on how much information the notetaker already has in his or her head. In other words, a person who has significant background information about a topic will take more skeletonized notes than would a person who has little or no knowledge of the topic. The point needs to be made to students that there is no one "right" way to take notes and that the effectiveness of a student's notetaking can be measured only by how well those notes serve that student's study needs.

We have found that for the student, the rank importance of the reading and lecture material varies, as do the student's strategies for accessing that content.

Students are nothing if not efficient, and depending on the emphasis the professor puts on each of the sources and the cognitive complexity of the material, students often make a decision early on to attend to either the lecture, the reading, or both. For example, in our research (Carson, Chase, & Gibson, 1993) we found that in the entry-level political science course, where the material was accessible and repeated in both lectures and the course texts, students often chose to either take notes or read the text, depending on whether they perceived themselves to be better oral or visual learners. In biology, where the material was repeated in the lecture but was cognitively complex, students most often found that they needed both sources of information to render the content comprehensible. And in history, where the lecture material supplemented the course readings, students most often found the need to both read and take lecture notes to synthesize the material from the two sources.

When lecture material repeats textbook information, students develop different access strategies based on their own perceived reading or listening strengths and learning styles. A student who reads well is likely to read the material *before* the lecture, thereby making the lecture more comprehensible. Students who have better-developed listening skills will listen to the lecture first as a prereading activity, thereby setting up the necessary schema for understanding the reading. Students can use their reading notes in the lecture to help them fill in and clarify points in the professor's presentation that they do not understand well. By the same token, they can use lecture notes in reading to help clarify points in the text. These are choices that students can learn to make, thus exploiting their learning styles and strengths.

We directly teach notetaking skills, including recognizing the signaling of main points and organizational patterns, and the importance of developing abbreviation systems. When we introduce lecture notetaking, we vary the order of content presentation (reading then lecture, or lecture then reading). We also vary the type of content (first information that overlaps in lectures and readings, then information in one that supplements the other). In this way, students can both develop strategies appropriate for them as well as acquire an understanding of the relationships between lectures and readings (either to repeat information or to supplement it). We have found that live lectures given by the instructor work better for students than do audiotaped or videotaped lectures. A live presentation simulates classroom interaction, allowing the instructor to monitor student comprehension and also giving students the opportunity to ask clarifying questions as necessary. Visuals, such as chalkboard notes and overheads, also are more effective in a live presentation. Although there is some controversy about the necessity of ESL instructors becoming "experts" in a content field, we have not experienced this as a problem. When giving lectures that overlap with reading materials, instructors simply summarize and highlight important information from the text. For supplemental information, ESL instructors rely on the extensive supplemental materials provided by publishers of course texts.

Notetaking, of course, is not an end in itself, but is part of the process of acquiring information for the display task that follows: the exam. Students must also learn to integrate their reading and lecture notes into their own study notes, which will help them prepare to display the knowledge that they learn.

To emphasize the connection between study notes (the acquisition phase) and exams (the display task), we sometimes allow students to use their study notes on the first exam given in the course. (Students are then required to hand in both the exam and their study notes at the end of the exam period.) Students have been known to include on the exam virtually *everything* in their study notes, but they most often find that when their study notes are too detailed, they simply cannot access the appropriate information to answer the exam questions in the time allotted. In this way, they learn (1) that study notes need to contain *all and only* the information *likely* to be related to the exam (whether or not it is actually included on the exam) and (2) that study notes are indeed the text that allows them to both manage and acquire the information they will need to display.

Test-Taking Skills

The third component of the course focuses on skills needed to answer objective exam questions, in particular three common types: literal, application, and inference questions.

Literal Questions. Literal questions are those questions for which answers can be found *directly in the text,* and they represent the most common type of question that entry-level undergraduates will encounter on exams. It is helpful for teachers to correlate these literal questions with the cognitive operations that students will need to perform in order to answer the questions: (1) recognizing information (i.e., information is given in the exam and students must pick it out) and (2) retrieving information (i.e., information is not given in the exam and students must supply it from memory). We distinguish three types of literal questions, although there may be overlap among them, that may require recognition (true/false, matching, or multiple-choice) or retrieval (fill-in-the-blank):

1. Definition questions. ("The dependent variable is the factor _____.")

2. Questions that require general knowledge/information from the text. ("Carl Rogers emphasized the importance of _____.")

3. Questions that require related knowledge/information that results from synthesis of information in the text. ("Freud's theory of personality has been criticized because it _____.")

Application Questions. Application questions ask the student to apply information from the text to a new situation that was not mentioned in the text. This is the second most common type of exam question in entry-level courses. (Example: "John was riding his bike. He fell off and hit his head. He most likely has difficulty with _____.")

Inference Questions. Inference questions ask the student to draw from the text conclusions or inferences that the author intended. This question type, which occurs much less frequently in entry-level courses than the first two types, is like the application question in that the inference itself is not directly stated. However, with inference questions the author expected the inference to be drawn, whereas with application questions the novel situation is neither there nor intended to be understood in the text. (Example: [True/False] "The behaviorism that predominated in psychology through the 1960s had a wider focus than the current scope of studies in psychology.")

When we teach test-taking strategies, we emphasize these distinctions among types of exam questions and the cognitive operations associated with them, relating the question types to the study guide questions that students will be answering both in this class and in their future entry-level classes where study guides are commonly used to help them focus their studying for exams. We also help students identify reading and study strategies for answering the study guide questions. For example:

1. How could you answer definition questions?

   ANSWER: Use the glossary; use the index to find the term in the text.

2. What about inferences? Would the glossary help?

   ANSWER: Probably not, but the index would point you to the place where you would find sufficient context to help you draw the appropriate conclusions.

3. What about application questions?

   ANSWER: You would need to look at possible relevant concepts, which you could then look up in the index to find where to read more about them. You probably could not find the answer if you did not know where to start.

I have focused here on the three main components of this EAP course—vocabulary, study skills, and test-taking strategies—and have not described the other relevant components because they are not the heart of the course. Nevertheless, other components include charts and graphs from the text, extensive reading for the purpose of having students produce a book review, journal writing that helps students explore more personally concepts and strategies that they are learning, and computer skills that students are required to learn outside of class (for word processing, e-mail journal exchanges, and Internet resources).

Conclusion

The core of the EAP course is the display task that focus both the content and the pedagogical activities of the course in ways that help students make direct connections to the academic courses for which we are preparing them. In particular, we have developed this EAP course with the firm belief that EAP makes sense when reading and writing are taught together as they occur naturally in academic contexts. Because we have only recently implemented our task based curriculum, we have not yet conducted longitudinal studies to measure the effectiveness of this approach. Nevertheless, anecdotal evidence from students has been positive. Many students who have exited our program to begin their academic studies have returned to tell their ESL instructors how valuable their EAP courses have been. In particular, they have mentioned the importance of learning how to manage content for various assignments and of acquiring content knowledge in their ESL courses that they have been able to use in their academic courses. More subtle—and therefore less remarked on, it seems to me—is the fact that students have also learned the language of the academy: the discourse patterns common in reading and writing that they are able to understand and produce because these patterns have been the context of the students' language learning.

The value of sustained content for a task-based EAP curriculum is clear. The types of display tasks typical of entry-level undergraduate courses simply cannot be taught or learned without a sustained content framework to support them.

References

Carson, J. G., Chase, N. D., & Gibson, S. U. (1993). *Academic demands of the undergraduate curriculum: What students need.* Final Report to the Fund for the Improvement of Post-Secondary Education. Atlanta: Center for the Study of Adult Literacy, Georgia State University.

Carson, J. G., Chase, N. D., Gibson, S. U., & Hargrove, M. (1992). Literacy demands of the undergraduate curriculum. *Reading Research and Instruction, 31*(4), 25–50.

Keyes, D. (1966). *Flowers for Algernon.* New York: Bantam Books.

Leki, I., & Carson, J. G. (1997). "Completely different worlds": EAP and the writing experiences of ESL students in university courses. *TESOL Quarterly, 31,* 39–69.

Myers, G. (1996). *Psychology.* New York: Worth Publishers.

Chapter 3

The Old Man and the Sea
A Data-Driven, Corpus-Based Grammar-Reading Course

Charles S. Haynes
New York University

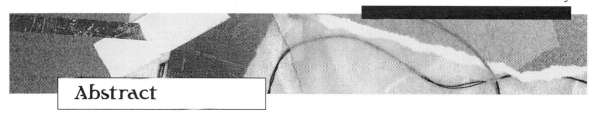

Abstract

This chapter describes a course to teach students to read an extended text, in this case Ernest Hemingway's novel *The Old Man and the Sea*. The students are taught a grammar of written English to understand the phrase structure, the clause structure, and the co-hering devices of sustained written texts. They are given a series of "discovery" exercises in the form of "analysis charts." By identifying and analyzing phrases and clauses in the Hemingway text and tracing the referents of "substitute" words, they practice the skills of reading and acquire the tools necessary to process written texts. This chapter provides samples of analysis charts, the ways they are used with the Hemingway text, class activities, and home assignments, and discusses excerpts of student work. ■

The Purpose of the Course

This data-driven, corpus-based course aims to help students to read English prose accurately by teaching them a method of grammar/analysis. The terms *corpus-based* and *data-driven* refer to learning a language by analyzing real language use and discovering the forms, functions, and organization of the language from this analysis.

The corpus of language used in this course is Ernest Hemingway's 1952 novel *The Old Man and the Sea,* for which, along with his other writing, Hemingway received the Nobel Prize in 1954. The data that drives the student's processing in this course is the words, the phrases, the clauses, the sentences, the paragraphs, and finally the entire corpus in the prose of the Hemingway novel, hereafter referred to as *TOM.* This course has been taught to lower-proficiency adult students of English as a Second Language (ESL), but it can also benefit all students, junior high age and up, who require the ability to read English prose easily and write it accurately. The corpus may be any corpus of English, and the analytical techniques can be applied by students with any degree of proficiency in English, whether English is a foreign language, a second language, or their mother tongue.

Modern linguistic research using the "data-crunching" power of computers has allowed researchers to examine vast numbers of sentences in English and write descriptions or grammars of this data that far exceed the accuracy and predictive power of traditional, Latin-based, parts-of-speech grammars that are still frequently used in ESL and EFL texts and the handful of texts written for native speakers in the few grammar classes remaining in American schools. (For a clear discussion of the linguistic research and its effect on language teaching pedagogy see *Corpus, Concordance, Collocation* by John Sinclair [Oxford University Press, 1991].) This research has established one central fact about "doing grammar": all language depends on surrounding context. Sentences written for display in traditional grammar texts lack context and thus are useless for learning a language. Another way of saying this is, unless you have a corpus, you don't have language. John Sinclair, professor of Modern English Language at the University of Birmingham (England) and a leading researcher in discourse and computational linguistics, writes:

> Any instance of language depends on its surrounding context . . . if we accept that the requirements of coherence and communicative effectiveness shape a text in many subtle ways. . . . The position of those who like to invent examples would be more plausible if, in practice, it was felt that they did a good job of simulation. However, it seems that sensitivity to context is very difficult to achieve, and even experts at simulating natural language are prone to offer examples which are extremely unlikely ever to occur in speech or writing. . . . Currently, there are signs of a growing recognition that the comprehensive study of language must be based on textual evidence. One does not study all of botany by making artificial flowers. (Sinclair, 1991, pp. 5–6)

This course aims to help students analyze large written texts. In a sense, this is the purpose of all liberal education: reading and understanding both spoken and written texts and then speaking and writing language that is related to this understanding. By reading a sustained text and performing the analytical tasks outlined in this chapter, students gain considerable linguistic knowledge about language in general and the English language in particular. Though this is certainly a bonus of this course, it is not the main goal. Primarily, reading and analyzing a corpus such as a complete novel alerts students to potential trouble spots in understanding texts, such as the boundaries of noun, verb, and participial phrases; problems of substitute reference and cohesion; and structures of modification. This kind of reading helps students to recognize and solve these and other difficulties. After they complete the course, this experience helps them to read other texts accurately and pleasurably.

Moreover, the total experience of reading *TOM* and applying the analytical tasks to solving problems of meaning gives students confidence that they can analyze and understand what they read and make judgments about it—skills that are necessary for successful work in any university and professional setting. They not only gain mastery of content but also control and become self-sufficient in the processes of learning.

In the course for "advanced beginners" in which *TOM* is the corpus, students spend the entire semester (approximately 90 hours) reading the text; more advanced students may complete *TOM* more quickly and move on to other books. One goal of the course is to read an entire book written for the entertainment of adults. This is often the first time students will have read a "whole book" in English that is not a grammar or a reader for students of English with short essays, articles, and stories with different subjects and often with controlled and simplified vocabulary and syntax.

Working with a sustained text such as *TOM* offers three important advantages. First and foremost, such reading is what educated people do when they read for pleasure. Second, a sustained text draws readers into a linguistic environment that engages all facets of their intelligence, which should be the goal of any teaching situation. Finally, a sustained text is easier to read than disconnected texts, such as collections of essays on different subjects or short stories; a single work teaches itself by reinforcement as vocabulary and stylistic choices are repeated.

Reading a Text

Successful reading of a text can be broken down into four discrete steps:

1. knowing the meanings of words or groups of words
2. recognizing groups of words and their functions, including the forms and functions of clauses as fundamental written structures and how they are joined
3. tracing the cohering devices in a text
4. deconstructing complex clause structures into constituent clauses to understand their derivations

This is at least part of what accurate reading involves, and reading well requires the reader to do all of these things simultaneously.

Knowing the Meanings of Words or Groups of Words

Students should be encouraged to infer word meanings from the text. For example, in *TOM*, the first sentence goes, "He was an old man who fished alone in a skiff in the Gulf Stream and he had gone eighty-four days now without taking a fish." In this context, the meaning of *skiff* as a "boat" might be inferred from the context. Allowing the context to define words is an elementary step in data processing. Also, the context above should suggest to the student that the verb *take* means "catch." Sinclair (1991) notes,

> By far the majority of text is made of the occurrence of common words in common patterns, or in slight variants of those common patterns. Most everyday words do not have an independent meaning, or meanings, but are components of a rich repertoire of multi-word patterns that make up text. This is totally obscured by the procedures of conventional grammar. (p. 108)

Analyzing the "rich repertoire of multi-word patterns that make up text" is one of the principal reasons for doing data-driven, corpus-based grammar in a sustained text.

Recognizing Groups of Words and Their Functions

Words do not stand alone but co-occur with other words in a text. These co-occurrences are more important than the words themselves. For example, in the first sentence of *TOM* we read, "He was an old man . . ." *Man* co-occurs with *an* and *old*. This noun phrase (NP) occurs only once in the data. Every other collocation of this kind will appear as *the old man*. With every repetition, this collocation is read as *theoldman* as if it were a single semantic unit, which it is *in this text*. Initially the words *an, the,* and *old* in the noun phrase modify or qualify the noun *man* in particular ways, but with repetition the collocation becomes fixed and the NP "coalesces" to one idea.

As we have seen with *the old man,* a sustained text provides reinforcement for learning by repeating vocabulary and structure. In another example of word function, the third page of *TOM* has the NP *a smell,* in which *smell* is clearly the last word of a noun phrase, a noun. On the following page, there is the NP *the sweet blood smell*. Those students trained in traditional grammar will likely read *the sweet blood,* knowing from earlier grammar lessons that *smell* must be a verb. Sixteen pages later in the text, students will read *the smell of the land,* where *smell* is clearly the last word of the NP, a noun. In the same sentence just five words later, they will read *the clean early morning smell,* where again *smell* could be read as a verb.

Functional shifts (*smell* as a verb and as a noun) account for much variety in English texts. The good reader knows this without understanding it, if we take *know* to mean "process for meaning" and *understand* to mean "acknowledging the process." Groups of words that are important in reading an English text are the noun phrase (NP), the verb phrase (VP), the participial phrase (PP), the substitute (SUB), the joint (J), and the adverb (ADV). Students identify and analyze these elements as they process the data and read the corpus. The clause (C) that joins NPs, VPs, and PPs is the fundamental unit of written discourse in English. Sentences are punctuated clauses in written English. Identifying and analyzing the forms and functions of the clause is essential in learning to read easily and accurately. It is also the fundamental task of the writer to write well-formed clauses, which also means using punctuation to help the reader over potential misunderstandings arising from ambiguity. We will examine this further when we look at the various analytical tasks that are assigned to readers.

Tracing or Mapping the Cohering Devices in a Text

The corpus is "glued together" using words that have only referential meaning. These words are called *substitutes (SUBs)*. For example, in the now familiar first sentence of *TOM*, "He was an old man who fished alone in the Gulf Stream and he had gone eighty-four days now without taking a fish," the words *He, who,* and *he* have the referential meaning "the old man." Functioning as the subjects of the three clauses in the sentence, these SUBs glue the separate clauses into a single unit, which is here punctuated as a sentence (S). Referencing of SUBs while reading a text is not necessarily automatic with native readers, and for non-native readers it constitutes a continuing challenge in data processing. Who is *who* is an important question from a teacher. If students can't answer questions about reference, they are not understanding the text.

Deconstructing Complex Clause Structures

After the forms and functions of the clause have been identified and analyzed, the reverse process of deconstructing complex clause structures is helpful in tracing the derivations, and therefore the meanings, of these structures. Again using the first sentence of *TOM* as an example, "He was an old man who fished alone in a skiff in the Gulf Stream and he had gone eighty-four days now without taking a fish," note clause identification and then deconstruction into *constituent clauses*. The sentence contains three clauses:

he was an old man

who fished alone in a skiff in the Gulf Stream

he had gone eighty-four days now without taking a fish

Deconstructing this sentence into constituent clauses results in:

an old man was an old man

an old man fished alone in a skiff in the Gulf Stream

the old man had gone eighty-four days now

the old man had not taken a fish

The purpose of identifying the constituent clauses is to see how these "simple" structures are transformed into more complex structures using referencing (the SUBs *he, who* and *he*), joining (Js—*who, and*), and clause reduction using PPs (*without taking*). By replacing the subject NPs in the constituent clauses with appropriate SUBs, inserting the J *and,* and reducing the final clause to a PP, we can reconstruct the Hemingway sentence. Doing the operations of clause and constituent clause analysis, of deconstruction and reconstruction, helps the student to understand the grammar of the written language in deeper and more subtle ways than traditional word-based grammars. Furthermore, learning to do these operations is fun because it engages the minds of the learners.

Classroom Procedures

The course is designed so that the analysis of the grammar of the text and the reading of the novel go together and complement each other. The students learn the basic phrases (NP, VP, PP); clauses (C); and parts (J and ADV) of the grammar by doing such activities as identifying them in the text and entering them on charts, taking them as dictation, and reading them aloud to sense the unity within phrases and clauses and the pauses between them. Here the teacher provides the model and the students repeat the phrases in the initial learning phase. Classes with advanced ESL/EFL students or native speakers use this "reading aloud" approach where passages present difficulties of length, ambiguity, and other syntactic and lexical problems.

Each homework assignment during the course starts with the reading of an assigned portion of *TOM*. It is the responsibility of the students to do this first reading of the text, finding in the dictionary the basic meanings of the words. Students can be encouraged to annotate their texts, keep personal dictionaries or glossaries, or do whatever is necessary to "translate" the text to their satisfaction to ready themselves for the classwork. The amount of text assigned for homework reading depends on the proficiency level of the students. Sustained content, with its repetition of key vocabulary and phraseology resulting from the sustained topic and the individual author's style, will acclimate students to the text and allow them to read greater amounts of text as the processing simplifies itself.

Each day the reading of the text in class proceeds in three steps: dictation, reading aloud, and discussion of the text.

Dictation

There are different dictation tasks, but the basic format holds for all tasks: listen, repeat, write. A paragraph or more of text is selected for dictation, with the teacher reading each phrase at conversational speed. As students' proficiency levels increase, the teacher can dictate larger chunks of text, but the unit of the clause should be respected. After students have had sufficient opportunity to hear the text, they are asked to repeat it orally, mimicking the teacher's pronunciation and phrasing. When they have repeated the text aloud after the teacher, they are asked to pick up their pencils and write down what they hear. The teacher continues to dictate the phrases of the text aloud, again repeating as necessary for maximum comprehension. Punctuation should also be dictated. When the entire text has been dictated, students are asked to open their texts and correct their dictation.

Later in the course, after students have learned the tasks (described in the next main section), the dictation may be used for another exercise, clause joining. Instead of dictating sentences from *TOM,* the teacher deconstructs sentences, dictates constituent clauses in numbered, unpunctuated lists, and then asks students to join the constituent clauses using Js or PPs. For example:

He was an old man who fished alone in a skiff in the Gulf Stream and he had gone eighty-four days now without taking a fish.

The teacher dictates the following constituent clauses:

1. the old man was an old man
2. the old man fished alone in a skiff in the Gulf Stream
3. the old man had gone eighty-four days now
4. the old man had not taken a fish

After these clauses have been dictated, the students try to join them into a single sentence. The goal is not necessarily to reproduce the Hemingway original but to produce a grammatical sentence that is well formed.

Reading Aloud

After completing the dictation exercise, students and teacher get down to reading the portion of the text that the students have studied as homework. There are different ways to do this. In the initial stages, the students read from their open texts. The teacher calls on students to read a sentence, a group of sentences, or a paragraph. After a student has read, the teacher reads and then the student rereads, imitating the breakup of the sentence into NP and VP phrases, joints, and adverbs. The goal is to produce "reading pronunciation" that correctly follows the phrase breakup of the text. Later in the course, students may close their texts and listen to student-teacher repetition as a practice exercise in aural comprehension, or they may read by scanning the text and looking up, attempting to repeat the text from short-term memory. Again, with more advanced classes, the method described here may be saved for passages of particularly difficult syntax or obscure meaning, but the teacher should be careful not to assume that students are too advanced or too sophisticated to benefit from this kind of "close" reading.

Discussion of the Text

Each homework reading assignment in the text is accompanied by separate worksheets in a workbook titled *The Old Man and the Sea. Study Materials*. After reading the assigned pages in the text, students are asked to answer, in writing, the questions on the worksheet. (See Figure 3.1 for a sample worksheet.) In class, augmenting the dictation and reading-aloud exercises, the teacher may direct students to respond orally to textual problems by referring to the questions on the worksheet or responding to students' questions about the text. When a tricky problem in text comprehension arises, one or more of the analytical tasks described next may be applied to solve the problem.

Analytical Tasks

Students can learn the steps needed to read a text easily and accurately by undertaking a number of analytical tasks that the teacher organizes and supervises. The teacher's job is not to lecture or to set rules. Rather, it is to assign tasks, answer procedural questions about doing the tasks, lead discussions about the results of

Figure 3.1 Sample Worksheet for *The Old Man and the Sea*

Questions for Comprehension (pp. 91–95)

1. "The fish was coming in on his circle now calm and beautiful looking and only his great tail moving" (p. 91). Can you write the constituent clauses of this sentence? There are at least three and maybe more.

2. "That way nothing is accomplished" (p. 92). Can you paraphrase this sentence? What is the referent of *that way*?

3. "I do not know. He had been on the point of feeling himself go each time. I do not know" (p. 93). What doesn't the old man know?

4. What words does Hemingway use in the paragraph on p. 94 beginning, "The old man felt faint . . ." that tell you that the fish is dead? Notice that Hemingway doesn't use the words *dead* or *died* or *was killed*.

5. "Even if we were two and swamped her to load him and bailed her out, this skiff would never hold him" (p. 95). There are three things that you need to know to understand this sentence: (1) you must know the referents of *we, her,* and *him;* (2) you must know the meaning of the words *swamped* and *bailed;* and (3) you need to know whether the VPs are fact or not-a-fact. Can you paraphrase this sentence to show the meaning?

6. Join these constituent clauses into a single sentence using joints and/or PPs:

    (1) the fish was silvery

    (2) the fish was still

    (3) the fish floated with the waves

    Hemingway's sentence is on p. 94, but don't look at it until you make your attempt. And don't change your sentence. It may be well formed.

the analyses, and suggest appropriate answers to questions of analysis. This chapter allows only brief descriptions of possible tasks and ways in which students approach them. Following are samples of analytical tasks.

Task: Noun Phrase (NP) Identification and Analysis

The NP is one of the fundamental units of written discourse. In English, the structure of the NP is distinguished by having the noun as the last word. In fact, the analysis of the NP reveals that one definition of *noun* in English is "the last word in a noun phrase." Using the chart illustrated in Figure 3.2, students are asked to identify the NPs in a selected paragraph of text. This exercise can be repeated until the students become thoroughly familiar with the form of the English NP. For students of ESL/EFL, this conditioning helps to alleviate the so-called article problem in learning English, that is, habitually failing to use articles or using them incorrectly. Over time students will note these other characteristics of the NP:

- Nouns rarely occur in isolation from other members of the NP.
- Some components of the NP occur with greater frequency (*the* heads this list).

Figure 3.2 NP Analysis Chart

PREP	ART	POSS Closed Mutually Exclusive SUB	DEMO	ADJECTIVE(S)	MODIFYING NOUNS(S)	NOUN	PL	FUNCTION
1								
2								
3								
4								
5								
6								
7								
8								
9								
10								
11								
12								
13								
14								
15								
16								
17								
18								
19								
20								
21								
22								
23								
24								

Source: From *Discovery Grammar* by Charles S. Haynes © 1993

- Some classes within the NP are mutually exclusive; that is, if *the* occurs, *my* and *this* are automatically excluded.

- There is a rough order of modifiers that places some kinds of modifiers before others in the phrase (e.g., "sweet blood smell" and not "blood sweet smell," at least in this context).

Students with different native languages will see that the requirements of well-formed NPs in English rule out some NP structures that they may wish to import from their languages, and native speakers of English will gain an intellectual understanding of what their competence in their native language entails—a goal of liberal education.

The selection of words in the NP and the position of the NP in a clause are functions of the larger context. Again, this is why students are asked to read a sustained corpus of text: so that they can work out and learn these external or contextual relationships. NPs may function as subjects, objects, modifiers, or adverbs in a clause. After analyzing many NPs, students will realize that NPs containing prepositions will function as adverbs or modifiers (the modifying clauses are normally marked by *of*) and NPs lacking prepositions will function as subjects or objects depending on their position relative to the verb in the clause.

Figure 3.3 is an NP identification and analysis task using a concordance for the word *bait* in *TOM* that clearly shows the form and function of NPs containing this noun.

Task: Verb Phrase (VP) Identification and Analysis

Following the NP, the verb phrase (VP) is the next most common part of speech of this written grammar. It is identified in the data and entered on a chart in the same procedure outlined for the NP (see Figure 3.4). When the NP was studied, the lead-in question was "What is a noun?" The analysis established that the noun is the *last* word in a noun phrase. A similar lead-in question may be asked in beginning the study of the verb phrase: "What is a verb?" After analysis, it is established that the verb is the *first* word of a verb phrase. Forms signaling time and tense of verbs are identified in context. As an additional task, students can make a "conjugation" chart for the various tense forms. The meanings of tenses can be learned only in context through the reading and examination of all the co-occurrences or collocations of tense forms with other words in different contexts.

The difficult part of verb phrase analysis is identifying the "type" or the "argument" of the VP. Is it complement, transitive, or intransitive? Here it is important that students have learned the functions of the NP, because knowing whether an NP functions as an object or an adverbial phrase determines the argument or type of verb. For example, consider this clause in *TOM:* ". . . they waited for the ice truck to carry them to the market in Havana." Is the base (citation) form *wait* or *wait for?* Is the verb transitive or intransitive? The answer is both. But the question is more interesting than the answer because it leads students to develop analytical abilities or an analytical stance toward language learning and confidence in their ability to "figure language out." This is one of the purposes of doing this kind of "grammar."

Task: Clause (C) Identification and Analysis

The basic structure of written English is the clause (C). Sentences are punctuated clauses. If beginning students are introduced to the form of the clause, clause functions, and ways of joining clauses at the earliest stages of their study, the common problem of writing fragments and run-ons can be avoided. Again, the text is used to identify the form and functions of the clause in English, and the data drives the analysis. Using the clause analysis sheet shown in Figure 3.5, students are guided toward identifying the clauses and entering them on their charts.

The following formula is used for clause identification: $NP_n + VP_n = C$, where NP stands for the subject noun phrase and VP stands for the verb phrase. The subscript n stands for number. This means that any number of subject noun phrases followed immediately by any number of verb phrases add up to only one clause. Students will understand this after they have analyzed several sentences from the text. Here is an example of a clause with multiple subject NPs and VPs:

Figure 3.3 "Bait" Collocation for NP Analysis

```
 1  so that any pull or touch on the bait would make the stick dip and each
 2 were concentrations of shrimp and bait fish and sometimes schools of squ
 3 ill work back to the forty-fathom bait and cut it away too and link up t
 4  the shank of the hook inside the bait fish, tied and sewed solid and al
 5 s drifting with the current.  One bait was down forty fathoms. The secon
 6 ce and there was no scattering of bait fish.  But as the old man watched
 7  had severed and the two from the bait the fish had taken and they were
 8 ed and twenty-five fathoms.  Each bait hung head down with the shank of
 9 ss of the stream there would be a bait waiting exactly there he wished i
10  what that fish was that took the bait just now.  It could have been a m
11 now dropping and dipping into the bait fish that were forced to the surf
12 of line.  There were two from each bait he had severed and the two from t
13 f the flesh is good.  He took the bait like a male and he pulls like a m
14 d taken the sack that covered the bait box and spread it in the sun to d
15 d leaping in long jumps after the bait. They were circling it and drivin
16  aloud.  "He'll make a beautiful bait.  He'll weigh ten pounds."      H
17 rising gently.       "I had better re-bait that little line out over the
```

	PREP	ART	POSS SUB	DEMO	ADJECTIVE(S)	MODIFYING NOUNS(S)	NOUN	PL	FUNCTION
1	on	the					bait		adverb
2	(of)					bait	fish		modifier
3	to	the				forty-fathom	bait		adverb
4	inside	the				bait	fish		adverb
5						one	bait		subject
6	of					bait	fish		modifier
7	from	the					bait		adverb
8					each		bait		subject
9		a					bait		complement
10		the					bait		object
11	into	the				bait	fish		adverb
12	from				each		bait		adverb
13		the					bait		object
14		the				bait	box		object
15	after	the					bait		adverb
16		a			beautiful		bait		complement
17									
18									
19									
20									
21									
22									
23									
24									

Figure 3.4 VP Analysis Chart

	BASE	Simple Completed Progressive Modal TENSE	Past Not Past TIME	VERB	Complement	Types Transitive NP OBJECT	(Intransitive) Ø OR ADVERB
1							
2							
3							
4							
5							
6							
7							
8							
9							
10							
11							
12							
13							
14							
15							
16							
17							
18							
19							
20							
21							
22							
23							
24							
25							
26							
27							
28							
29							
30							

The old man and the boy walked up the road together to the old man's shack and went in through its open door.

The formula for this sentence is $NP_1 + NP_2 + VP_1 + VP_2 = C$.

Other Analytical Tasks

Other analytical tasks of the course include the identification and analyses of the joint (J), the participial phrase (PP), and the substitute (SUB), with referent tracing (drawing lines in the text from SUBs to their referents (see Figure 3.6).

Figure 3.5 Clause Analysis Chart

JOINT J	SUBJECT (NP)	joint j	VP	FUNCTION
	he (the old man)		was an old man	IND
WHO	who (the old man)		fished alone in a skiff in the Gulf Stream	MOD
AND	he (the old man)		had gone eighty-four days now without taking a fish	IND
	CONSTITUENT		**CLAUSES**	
1	an old man		was an old man	
2	an old man		fished alone in a skiff in the Gulf Stream	
3	an old man		had gone eighty-four days now	
4	an old man		had not taken a fish	

Source: From *Discovery Grammar* by Charles S. Haynes © 1993

Also, the functions of the high-frequency substitute/joint *that* are studied (see Figure 3.7). Sentences with multiple clauses are broken down into their constituent clauses using a system of constituent clause analysis, as described briefly in the section on dictation.

Student Writing: *The Autobiography Project*

Students need to write well-formed NPs and VPs, join them into clauses, join the clauses into multiclause sentences using appropriate joints and reducing some clauses to participial phrases, and do all this with appropriate punctuation. In the course, students practice writing when they write answers to the worksheets (see Figure 3.1). In addition, they use a writing workbook titled *The Autobiography Project*.

This workbook contains a series of autobiographical sketches from the life of the teacher of the course. This original collection of sketches forms a sustained text and is read using the same procedures and tasks outlined for TOM. The students read the text of a sketch, answer comprehension questions as homework, read the sketch aloud in class, apply analytical tasks relevant to understanding the text, and, finally, write their own sketch following instructions for the "writing assignment." The three parts of Figure 3.8

Figure 3.6 Referent Tracing Exercise

He was an old man who fished alone in a skiff in the Gulf Stream and he had gone eighty-four days now without taking a fish. In the first forty days a boy had been with him. But after forty days without a fish the boy's parents had told him that the old man was now definitely and finally *salao*, which is the worst form of unlucky, and the boy had gone at their orders in another boat which caught three good fish the first week. It made the boy sad to see the old man come in each day with his skiff empty and he always went down to help him carry either the coiled lines or the gaff and harpoon and the sail that was furled around the mast. The sail was patched with flour sacks and, furled, it looked like the flag of permanent defeat.

The old man was thin and gaunt with deep wrinkles in the back of his neck. The brown blotches of the benevolent skin cancer the sun brings from its

---

give a sketch, questions for comprehension, and the writing assignment related to the sketch.

The teacher corrects the students' sketches by underlining those structures—NPs, VPs, Js, and so on—that are not well formed, and the students write a second draft of the sketches after analyzing the errors in their structures. The teacher looks at the second drafts and may suggest further analysis, correction, and other content revisions in a third draft. In other words, the students apply the same procedures they used in reading *TOM* to their own composing process.

Following is an example of a first draft of a composition by an advanced beginning student. The student, a Japanese woman, is following the writing assignment given in Figure 3.8. This is the first week of the program, and she has been learning to identify and analyze noun phrases in *TOM*. Only the noun phrase errors are underlined in the first draft of the student's composition.

Figure 3.7 THAT Function Analysis

```
 1   d steal from him, the old man thought that a gaff and harpoon were needle
 2   out after dolphin."      Are his eyes that bad?"      "He is almost blin
 3    could see him clearly with the light that came in from the dying moon.
 4   reat brown mountains.  He lived along that coast now every night and in
 5   and slept on the other old newspapers that covered the springs of the b
 6   ad seen.  The successful fisherman of that day were already in and had bute
 7   would you like to see me bring one in that dressed out over a thousand poun
 8      Who can we borrow that from?"      "That's easy.  I can always borrow two
 9   ave gone with us.  Then we would have that for all of our lives.  "I wo
10   ollars and a half.  Who can we borrow that from?"      "That's easy.  I can
11    boy said.  "But I will see something that he cannot see such as a bird wo
12   all he would have all day and he knew that he should take it. For a long t
13   hope no fish will come along so great that he will prove us wrong."      "Th
14   n said.  "He never went turtle-ing.  That is what kills the eyes."  "But
15    shirt had been patched so many times that it was like the sail and the pat
16    lost today,"  the boy told him.      "That means nothing.  The great DiMagg
17   er me."      "Can you really remember that or did I just tell it to you?
18   fore the mast on a square rigged ship that ran to Africa and I have seen li
19   d milk cans at an early morning place that served fisherman.      "How did
20   knew he would shiver himself warm and that soon he would be rowing.  The d
21   he eighty-fifth day."      "We can do that," the boy said. "But what about
22   s he rowed over the part of the ocean that the fisherman called the great w
23   pt and he smelled the smell of Africa that the land breeze brought at morni
24    "I can order one."      "One sheet.  That's two dollars and a half.  Who c
25   , and I take back the bottles."      "That's very kind of you," the old man
26    of water in the bow of the skiff and that was all he needed for the day. T
27    or the gaff and harpoon and the sail that was furled around the mast. The
28   tern of the skiff along with the club that was used to subdue the big fish
29         "You ought to go to bed now so that you will be fresh in the mornin
30    know," the boy said.  "All I know is that young boys sleep late and hard."
```

Substitute

DEMO	NP SUBJECT	NP OBJECT	JOINT		
			PHANTOM	NP SUBJECT	NP OBJECT (PHANTOM)

Source: From *Discovery Grammar* by Charles S. Haynes © 1993

Figure 3.8   The Autobiography Project

Assignment One

My Mother

My mom was a tightwad. There was no doubt about it. She hated to spend a buck, not that we ever had many bucks to spend. But if we had been much better off than we were, it is doubtful that my mother would have parted with a dime without a struggle.

For example, we never ate out. My father's idea of a big time was to go to a restaurant. Not that my mother's cooking was bad. It wasn't. In fact, it was magnificent, and that was the trouble. Whenever we went to a restaurant, once every two or three years it seemed, my mother would take the first forkful of whatever it was she had reluctantly ordered, always the cheapest dish on the menu, and declare, "I can do better than this at home, and for a lot less than this is costing." She was right, of course, and my father and my brother and I would know that it would be at least another two or three years before we could expect to eat out again.

Assignment Two

Questions: Copy the questions on another sheet of paper and write the answers below them:

1. What is a "tightwad"? (Read the rest of the first paragraph for the answer in context.)

2. How much is a "buck"?

3. Name something that costs a buck.

4. Why didn't the author's family ever eat out?

5. Was the author's mother's cooking bad?

6. How often did the author's family go out to eat?

7. What dish did the author's mother always order?

8. What did his mother say about the restaurant's food?

Assignment Three

Writing Assignment: Write a 200-word sketch describing one trait of your mother.

Rhetoric: In "My Mother" the author introduces one of her traits: She was a tightwad. She hated to spend money. This is the first paragraph. In the second paragraph, the author gives an example that illustrates this trait: She hated to eat out because the food was expensive, and she could make the same dishes at home for less expense.

Outline:

Paragraph 1: General: My mother was a tightwad.

Paragraph 2: Specific: For example, we never ate out because my mother hated to spend money at restaurants for food she could prepare just as well at home.

Following this model, write a short introductory paragraph introducing a trait of your mother's and a slightly longer second paragraph that illustrates this trait. Introduce the second paragraph with the phrase "For example . . ."

My mother

My mother is <u>a very cleanly woman.</u> She likes to clean. She cleans our home every morning. Everything in the house is neat and tidy. She does not like <u>a dust</u> and a dirty room. Of course, I like <u>clean room</u>. However, sometimes we are having difficulty in her conduct.

For example, after my mother got up, as soon as she found dust, she started to clean the house. She always finished it before breakfast. When she is cleaning, we can not move <u>to other room</u>. Because she thinks we will be raising <u>a dust</u>. So when she is doing that, we are staying <u>own room</u> or another room. And when we take a meal, we have to watch whether we made <u>floor</u> dirty. Sometimes, my brother and I make a mess of our rooms. Then my mother always gets angry and nervous. Probably <u>messy room</u> is a <u>nauseating</u> by her. And she always says, "Always keep your room clean." I think she takes things seriously. To keep <u>clean room</u> is <u>very good thing</u> but some day we will be tired. And of course I do not like <u>messy room</u> and she is <u>good mother</u> but she had better relax.

In doing her correction, the student is asked to analyze the underlined noun phrases, put them on the NP analysis chart if necessary, and make the required corrections. Here is the second draft with corrected noun phrase errors:

My mother

My mother is <u>a very clean woman</u>. She likes to clean. She cleans our home every morning. Everything in the house is neat and tidy. She does not like <u>dust</u> or a dirty room. Of course, I like <u>a clean room</u>. However, sometimes we are having difficulty in her conduct.

For example, after my mother got up, as soon as she found dust, she started to clean the house. She always finished it before breakfast. When she is cleaning, we can not move <u>to another room</u>. Because she thinks we will be raising <u>dust</u>. So when she is doing that, we are staying <u>our own room</u>* or another room. And when we take a meal, we have to watch whether we made <u>the floor</u> dirty. Sometimes, my brother and I make a mess of our rooms. Then my mother always gets angry and nervous. Probably <u>a messy room</u> is <u>nauseating</u> by her. And she always says, "Always keep your room clean." I think she takes things seriously. To keep <u>a clean room</u> is <u>a very good thing</u> but some day we will be tired. And of course I do not like <u>a messy room</u> and she is <u>a good mother</u> but she had better relax.

Note that the starred phrase, "our own room," has not been successfully corrected, but errors such as this are an inevitable part of the correcting process. Other correcting strategies are to (1) leave the incorrect phrase out of the second draft entirely or (2) substitute a phrase with another phrase with different words, sometimes correctly and sometimes not. For example, in another student essay, "to cafe" became "to a coffee shop." Sometimes this change of lexis will pull up whole phrases learned correctly as "chunks." Another example of this strategy is "is italian," with a lowercase spelling error. In the correction it becomes "comes from Milan, Italy," improving the composition with more specificity. Some students use still other strategies, showing that the correcting process may be as "creative" as the composing process.

Returning to our first example, the second draft with the corrected noun phrases was read by the teacher and additional corrections or revisions were suggested. It was decided that the composition would read better if the verb phrases in the second paragraph were revised with a consistent present tense. The final draft reads like this:

My Mother

My mother is a very clean woman. She likes to clean. She cleans our home every morning. Everything in the house is neat and tidy. She does not like dust or a dirty room. Of course, I like a clean room. However, sometimes we have difficulty with her conduct.

For example, after my mother gets up, as soon as she finds dust, she starts to clean the house. She always finishes it before breakfast. When she is cleaning, we can not move to another room because she thinks we will be raising dust. So when she is doing that, we stay in our own rooms or another room. And when we take a meal, we have to watch whether we make the floor dirty. Sometimes, my brother and I make a mess of our rooms. Then my mother always gets angry and nervous. Probably a messy room is nauseating to her. And she always says, "Always keep your room clean." I think she takes things too seriously. To keep a clean room is a very good thing but some days we are tired. And of course I do not like a messy room and she is a good mother, but she must relax.

Conclusion

The human brain is designed to solve problems. Adult students in a language class need to have their brains engaged in problem solving from day one, and problem-solving activities that engage the mind capture student interest. For example, the first task on the first day of the *TOM* class is for students to read the first sentence—"He was an old man who fished alone in a skiff in the Gulf Stream and he had gone eighty-four days now without taking a fish"—and determine the number of words in the sentence. Answers always vary. Some students will say 25, some will say 26, some will say 27, and a few creative types will decide that only the nouns are legitimate words and say 7 or 8. Each answer is correct, given an appropriate theory of *word*. Those who say 25 will have joined *Gulf* and *Stream*. Those who say 27 will have separated *eighty* and *four*. Those who say 26 will have counted the letters or groups of letters in between spaces. All are correct, but 26 is the "best" answer because it requires no appeal to meaning. It is simply a definition or theory based on physical evidence. We can easily agree to use this definition when we talk about a "word" as a letter or a group of letters in space.

This exercise is used to alert students to the kind of class *TOM* will be. They will be searching for meaning: What is a noun? What is the form of the NP in

English? The teacher will not give them the answers to these questions. They will be asked to "identify" and "analyze" as the zoologist and the botanist do, and in so doing they will learn not only English grammar but also analytical skills that are key to learning in any field. In the final test for this course, students are given a long sentence and asked to "parse" it into its NPs, VPs, PPs, clauses, and constituent clauses, using the appropriate charts. Student progress in "free writing" is assessed by reading students' autobiographical sketches throughout the term and noting how students use the analytical tasks to revise their writing.

The types of activities—dictations, reading aloud, analytical tasks—have proven to engage students in *TOM* classes because they challenge them to analyze texts for themselves rather than be passive receptors of teacher instruction. Students' growing mastery of the analytical tasks is evaluated by giving them an analytical chart such as the NP chart (Figure 3.2) and a sentence from *TOM* and asking them to identify the NPs in the sentence and enter them on the chart. Success at this activity shows that students are beginning to read the text accurately—in other words, to read English in a way that structures it correctly.

Chapter 4

Sustained Content Study and the Internet

Developing Functional and Academic Literacies

Loretta F. Kasper
Kingsborough Community College/CUNY

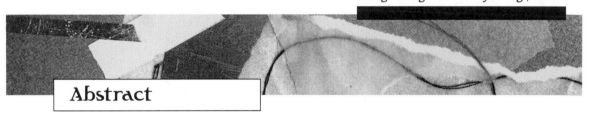

Abstract

This chapter describes a content-based ESL course that develops students' functional and academic literacies using the Internet as a resource for sustained and focused content-area study. The course provides a microcosm of the mainstream college experience and prepares students for this experience by offering them an introduction to the discourse patterns, rhetorical conventions, and conceptual content of several academic disciplines. Students build reading, writing, and research skills through their interactions with electronic texts representing these disciplines. Each student chooses one of these content areas as a focus discipline and engages in sustained, in-depth study of that focus discipline throughout the semester, articulating knowledge through a series of three progressive written reports and a research project. Through close reading and in-depth discussion of salient interdisciplinary issues, students acquire the linguistic and cognitive tools they need to succeed in an English-speaking academic environment. ■

Introduction

Academic literacy, which "encompasses ways of knowing particular content . . . [and] refers to strategies for understanding, discussing, organizing and producing texts" (Johns, 1997, p. 2), is key to success in college. Johns maintains that *literacy* is a multifaceted term, involving more than just reading and writing. Rather, the development of literacy is "a dynamic and ongoing process of perpetual transformation" (Neilson, 1989, p. 5) whose evolution is influenced by a person's interests, culture, and experiences, as well as by the responses of others to the texts he or she produces (Johns, 1997).

To be literate in an academic sense requires that one be able to access information from print, oral, and electronic sources; comprehend, analyze, and interpret it; evaluate its credibility and validity; and articulate conceptual relationships within and among disciplines (Farah, 1995; Mather, 1996). In a practical sense, a student who is academically literate should be able to read and understand interdisciplinary texts, analyze and respond to those texts through written and oral discussion, and expand knowledge through sustained and focused research.

Developing academic literacy is not an easy task for any college student, but it is especially difficult for ESL students who at the same time are attempting to become functionally literate in a second language. *Functional literacy* may be defined as a person's ability to function effectively as a member of the community—in this case, the academic community—and to be able to use language skills for his or her own and the community's development (Greaney, 1994). Thus, to sucessfully join the English-speaking academic and professional community, ESL students must meet a twofold goal: to function in English—to speak, understand, read, and write English in their everyday lives—and to use English to acquire, articulate, and expand academic knowledge.

The needs of college-level ESL students can best be met through a functional language-learning environment, one that engages them in meaningful and authentic language processing through planned, purposeful, and academically based activities (Adler-Kassner & Reynolds, 1996; Shea, 1996) that teach them "how to extract, question, and evaluate the central points and methodology of a range of material, and construct responses using the conventions of academic/ expository writing" (Pally, 1997, p. 299). A functional language-learning environment includes activities that teach students appropriate patterns of discourse and sociolinguistic conventions relating to audience and purpose (Soter, 1990). Sustained CBI provides a functional language-learning environment that enables students to acquire linguistic and cognitive tools through close reading and in-depth discussion of salient issues in science, psychology, business, and other academic disciplines.

When, as part of sustained CBI, students complete assignments of progressive complexity in which they define problems, examine evidence collected from a variety of sources, and make objective judgments on the basis of extended research (Wade, 1995), they learn to synthesize knowledge and practice the critical thinking skills necessary for a successful academic experience. In fact, research documents many positive results of sustained CBI, including high retention and pass rates, rapid progress through the ESL sequence, higher grade point averages in the mainstream, and, ultimately, higher graduation rates (Babbitt & Mlynarczyk, 1999; Kasper, 1995, 1997).

The extended research that is such an integral part of sustained CBI is more effectively carried out when an extensive body of instructional and informational resources is available to faculty and students. It is here that the value of computer technology as a tool for ESL education becomes most evident. With its vast stores of information, the Internet has given us the largest body of interdisciplinary resources in history. The Internet contains a wealth of information from archives, libraries, and databases all over the world, including texts, graphics, sound files, software, and full-motion video (Warschauer, 1996). Because it provides an extensive collection of reading materials and promotes numerous contexts for meaningful written communication, the Internet creates a highly motivating learning environment that encourages ESL students to interact with language in new and varied ways (Pennington, 1996). Used as a resource for sustained content study, the Internet is a highly effective international medium that may be used to help ESL/EFL students develop and refine the literacies functional in a successful college experience.

This chapter describes a high-intermediate to advanced-level ESL course that develops reading, writing, and research skills using the Internet as a resource for sustained and focused content-area study. Students are introduced to academic discourse as they read and write texts within and across a variety of mainstream college disciplines. Knowledge is expanded as students choose one of these content areas as a focus discipline and pursue in-depth study over the semester through a series of three progressive written reports and a research project.

The introduction to several academic areas and in-depth research in this course provide ESL students with a microcosm of the mainstream college experience. During their college years, ESL students will be required to enroll in a wide variety of courses spanning a number of different disciplines. This ESL course prepares students for this experience by offering them an introduction to the discourse patterns, rhetorical conventions, and conceptual content of several of the academic disciplines in which they may enroll.

In addition to taking courses to meet requirements in various subject areas, students choose a major area of study based on personal interest and/or career plans; their studies are then sustained and focused within that major discipline, becoming progressively more complex over time. The focus discipline component of this course not only allows ESL students to learn academic course material but also gives them the opportunity to develop and refine reading, writing, and critical literacy skills as they build a strong knowledge base through sustained research in a discipline they have *chosen* to study over time. Because they have elected to do extensive research in that discipline, they are invested in a learning experience that is personally meaningful and important. Thus, focus discipline research immediately promotes active involvement in learning.

Focus discipline study also provides a valuable opportunity for cooperative and collaborative learning through "focus discipline groups," in which students work both individually and collectively to gather information and construct knowledge. Peers become resources for furthering knowledge and understanding content-area and linguistic information (Strommen & Lincoln, 1992) as students elaborate and reflect on both their own ideas and those of their peers.

Research shows that this kind of student collaboration benefits instruction by promoting active engagement in learning, creating common group goals, and encouraging mutual help among students to achieve these goals (Bracey, 1994).

Developing Reading Skills

Sustained CBI presents ESL students with sophisticated academic reading that contains cognitively demanding language and linguistic forms. The Internet provides an even greater range of vocabulary forms through its inclusion of academic, journalistic, and personal texts. Moreover, the Internet encourages students to read widely across these texts through hypertext links that allow easy access to cross-referenced documents and screens (Tierney et al., 1997). As students engage in this type of reading, vocabulary and language structures become increasingly familiar, intertextual associations become clearer, and students build a wider range of schemata and a broader base of knowledge, which are then available to help them grasp future texts.

Internet texts further promote reading skills because they visually reinforce academic subject matter in the form of pictures and/or slideshows usually included on web pages. The collaborative effects of visual and verbal cues aid comprehension of the often abstract concepts presented in academic readings (Chun & Plass, 1997; Kasper, 1998a).

Developing Writing Skills

Thus, the combined effects of reading related print and electronic texts, reinforced by the multimedia and hypertext format of the Internet, help to facilitate comprehension, clarify concepts, and consolidate learning. By familiarizing students with this range of texts, formats, and conventions, the combination of print and electronic reading also helps them to write in various rhetorical modes. In this way, the Internet also becomes an ideal instructional resource for teaching writing skills.

The readings encountered in sustained content study serve as models for various academic rhetorical modes that require in-depth analysis of key intra- and interdisciplinary concepts. These texts suggest many topics through which students may practice and develop academic writing skills. Students work individually and with peers, producing analytical responses to the course materials and to one another's writing. The course activities require that students formulate questions, analyze evidence, and consider diverse interpretations of issues, thereby providing practice in and refinement of critical thinking skills. In addition, through sustained study of one chosen content area, students are given the opportunity to practice vocabulary and discourse patterns as they pertain to the particular discipline under study.

It is important to make ESL students aware that some discourse traditions are discipline-specific (Kaufer & Young, 1993; Prior, 1992), while many are formed across disciplines with minor stylistic changes. Far too often, however, the rhetorical modes commonly practiced in ESL courses (for example, personal exposition and narration) neither accurately represent nor are appropriate for written discourse in many mainstream disciplines. Thus, ESL courses that focus on these modes do not allow students to develop academic writing skills. Leki and Carson (1994) maintain that because strong academic discourse skills are so critical to ESL students' success in college, ESL programs must do more to prepare students adequately for the demands of other academic settings. These researchers contend that "ESL programs need to move away from writing tasks that require students only to tap their own opinions and experiences and toward work that encourages them to integrate those opinions and experiences with external sources of information and argument" (p. 95).

According to statistics published by *Open Doors* (1996/1997), many ESL students choose to study business or the sciences, so let us consider the discourse modes appropriate to these disciplines. Writing effectively in both of these fields entails the ability to collect and interpret data, to compare/contrast and explain the causes and effects of various events, and to argue a point of view (Arani et al., 1998). Therefore, a number of rhetorical modes, including description, definition, cause/effect, comparison/contrast, and argumentation, are appropriate for the articulation and analysis of relationships among the various issues and principles in both business and the sciences. However, neither personal exposition nor narration is considered an appropriate discourse mode in either of these fields. Note too that modes of discourse in business and the sciences involve analysis and persuasion, both of which take more cognitive effort than narration and require critical thinking and argumentation skills effectively developed through sustained CBI (Bensley & Haynes, 1995).

Developing Research Skills

Research papers require students to gather information from a variety of sources, to present that information in a form appropriate to the discipline, and finally to cite the sources used to prepare that report. Students may also be asked to examine how an issue in one discipline affects other areas of life. Academic research skills are often underdeveloped in ESL courses, which makes research reports especially challenging for students with limited English-language skills (Horowitz, 1986).

The research skills students need to complete focus discipline projects in this course are the same skills they will need to succeed in mainstream college courses. Students must be able to find appropriate resource materials, and they must be able to deal with the sophisticated language often found in these materials. The sequenced assignments involve students in genuine inquiry and encourage them to view research as "an integral part of the writing process" (Profozich, 1997, p. 304).

The Internet as an Informational Resource

Used as a tool for sustained content study, the Internet is a powerful resource that offers easier and more rapid access to interdisciplinary information than do traditional libraries. Using the Internet allows ESL students to control the direction of their reading and research, teaches them to think creatively, and increases motivation for learning. The Internet makes integrated, focused research easier and more feasible by providing information not only on the web page accessed but also through the hyperlinks that lead to other, related sources (Liu, 1998). By hitting the "back" and "forward" keys, students are able to navigate hypertext links and can easily return to reread or review any site visited during the computer session.

Although the Internet may be compared to a library containing almost every book in the world, it is one that often lacks organization (Harvey, 1998) and also contains a good deal of inaccurate and unreliable information. To reap the benefits of the multitude of resources on the Internet, ESL students must develop strong critical literacy skills; they must learn how to navigate through, and then evaluate, the information presented there. This requires learning to use search engines, web browsers, and meta-sites to locate, retrieve, and evaluate information. Web browsers such as Netscape and Microsoft Explorer facilitate the location and retrieval of documents from the Internet by assigning a specific URL (Uniform Resource Locator) to each web page. Meta-sites help to bring order out of Internet chaos by providing well-organized hyperlinks divided into clearly labeled categories (Harvey, 1998).

Lepeintre and Stephan (1995) maintain that a successful Internet search is useful in developing both literacy and critical thinking skills because it involves more than simply finding information. A successful Internet search also requires the use of critical reading skills such as predicting content, categorizing, guessing meaning from context, skimming, and scanning. These researchers believe that as students navigate through the vast amounts of information on the Internet, they unconsciously practice these critical reading skills. To guide their Internet search and to help make them aware of the critical reading skills they are using, Lepeintre and Stephan recommend giving students a set of questions that direct them to specific URLs and ask them to provide information on their search procedures and on the content of the Internet sites accessed (Appendix A provides examples of questions used).

After locating information, students must evaluate it in terms of its validity and reliability, as well as its relevance to the topic under study. According to Carlson (1995), "sources have credibility to the extent that they derive their conclusions from the most relevant, objective, and explicit methods available . . ." (p. 40). To guide them in determining whether an Internet source is reliable and credible, students may be given a list of questions that ask them to consider factors such as the source and time frame of the information (see Appendix B).

After completing their research, students must learn how to organize a research paper and cite the research sources they have used. Exercises contained in Online Writing Labs (OWLs), which are linked to many university web pages, contain worksheets and instructions for the citation of research sources, both within the body of the paper and in a bibliography. For example, the Purdue OWL provides a hyperlinked web page, *Research Papers,* located at http://owl.english.purdue.edu/Research-Papers.html. As students follow the hyperlinks on this page, they are taken step by step through the process of writing a research paper. The page links contain a variety of exercises that offer practice in outlining, paraphrasing, quoting, and citing resources in several formats.

Instruction that targets the development of research skills teaches ESL students the rhetorical conventions of term papers, which subsequently leads to better writing and hence improved performance in courses outside the ESL program (Mustafa, 1995). In addition, learning how to conduct and write up research helps students develop critical reading and writing skills through the acquisition of a general knowledge structure for argumentation (Bensley & Haynes, 1995) and enables them to manage information more effectively. These are skills that will serve them long after they have left the ESL course, throughout their college years and into the work force.

Illustrating the Approach: Sample Lessons

Teaching reading, writing, and research skills through Internet technology requires a bit of planning and the use of appropriate content-based materials. After teaching content-based ESL courses for over a decade, I developed materials spanning ten disciplines—linguistics, environmental science, computer science, mathematics, business and marketing, psychology, sociology, physical anthropology, biology, and diet and nutrition—and combined them in the text *Interdisciplinary English* (Kasper, 1998b). Reading, writing, and critical literacy skills are developed through sustained CBI that engages students in activities consisting of several stages of progressive difficulty. Each text is accompanied by vocabulary and comprehension questions, as well as essay prompts that require students to explore the topic in written pieces of an academic nature. Finally, each unit is followed by a list of related print and electronic resources to guide students' research efforts.

The overall course spans content areas from the humanities to the social and physical sciences, and students may complete focus discipline research projects in any of these areas. This pedagogical approach is illustrated through detailed descriptions of the units on business and environmental science, described next.

Business

Business is a major field of study for many ESL students. According to statistics published by *Open Doors* (1996/1997), 21 percent of ESL students enrolled in United States colleges are business majors. As part of their study, students are required to take courses in the areas of marketing and advertising. Because the principles of marketing and advertising play a large role in the American culture, it is important that all ESL students, whether business majors or not, become familiar with them. The lesson on marketing involves multiple stages that introduce a number of business concepts, among them product development, consumer behavior, marketing utilities, and market targeting.

Prereading Activity In preparation for the lecture on marketing, students are asked to cut out an advertisement from a magazine or newspaper. They are told to choose the ad because it stands out in a way that would either lead them to buy the product or cause them not to buy the product. The class discussion focuses on the prominent elements, such as color or design, that make the ad effective or ineffective, and we consider whether or not we would be likely to buy the product on the basis of the advertisement. This classroom discussion introduces business vocabulary and concepts, and prompts comparisons between advertising strategies used in the United States and those used in students' native countries.

Reading the Texts Next, students read two texts, one on product development and merchandising and the other on consumer behavior. The first reading covers several key concepts in product development and merchandising, such as marketing utilities and the law of supply and demand. The second reading enumerates the steps in the consumer decision process and discusses the basic determinants of consumer behavior. This text also describes three market coverage strategies, with examples, as it discusses how and why a business might follow a specific market coverage strategy. After reading each text, students write responses to open-ended comprehension questions, and we discuss their answers, clarifying any confusion that may remain.

Synthesis of Concepts Through Writing The first essay prompt for the unit on business requires synthesis of knowledge as well as both critical and creative thinking, targeting the rhetorical modes of description and cause/effect:

> Describe a new product that you have developed, identify the target market for the new product, and then explain how you would market this new product. Be sure to provide detailed information on how considerations such as merchandising and consumer needs would affect your marketing strategies. (Kasper, 1998b, p. 88)

Students have produced many interesting responses to this essay prompt. For example, one young woman described her new product, a computerized car that would help drivers avoid accidents. She believed that many accidents result from drivers' failure to pay attention to or unawareness of changing road conditions. She explained that sometimes fatigue, dim light, or inclement weather makes it difficult for drivers to judge road conditions. She proposed that computer technology could be used to help make driving safer under these conditions. Her computerized car would automatically detect when road conditions had changed or when another car was coming too close, and would automatically compensate to avoid an accident. In her essay, this student explored the question through several rhetorical modes: she described the problem, explained the causes and effects of the problem, and proposed a solution to it. The resulting piece not only was very creative but demonstrated the use of higher-order critical thinking skills and an understanding of the discourse patterns necessary for effective business writing.

Furthering Knowledge Through an Internet Search In the next phase of the lesson, students are asked to search the Internet to find information on advertising, another major topic in business. To conduct research on advertising, they need to become familiar with Internet search engines such as Yahoo!, Infoseek, or AltaVista. They must learn how to enter keywords to identify the information they want. Then, once the Internet search engine has returned a list of "hits" for the keywords, students must go through the list to identify the most appropriate and/or useful information.

To guide students in their research, they are given a copy of the Internet search activity provided in Appendix A, which directs them to a web site called *Advertising Strategies* (http://www.executive-printing.com/20steps/20ad.htm). After students have accessed this web site and answered the corresponding questions, they are required to continue on their own, finding additional web sites related to advertising. As they carry out this search activity, they become actively engaged in the *linguistic* tasks of reading English, developing vocabulary, and interpreting language structures used in the Internet texts, as well as in the *research* tasks of searching for, accessing, and evaluating information.

Whatever students' personal viewpoints, the topic always sparks lively discussion. Because advertisements are everywhere, students become very involved in researching this topic, and almost all of them—even those who are typically shy and quiet—express an opinion. Because it encourages students to take control of their own learning, Internet research is a highly motivating vehicle to developing language and content knowledge as students actively practice the skills necessary for college-level work.

Building the Knowledge Network The final writing assignment for the unit targets two rhetorical modes important in business—comparison/contrast and argumentation—and requires students to bring together everything they have learned as it asks them to discuss effective advertising, considering its place in a variety of media:

> Choose one print, one television, and one Internet advertisement for (a) a wristwatch and (b) an automobile. Compare and contrast the effectiveness of the print, the television, and the Internet ad for the wristwatch versus the automobile. Was each advertising medium equally effective for both products? Why/why not? Support your statements with concrete examples drawn from your reading and your research.

This writing task encourages students to link new knowledge to what they have learned from previous reading, other classes, and personal experience, and to build a more sophisticated body of knowledge that they will be able to use to facilitate performance on future linguistic and academic tasks.

Focus Discipline Research While the entire class studies marketing and uses the Internet for additional research, students who have chosen business as a focus discipline continue to research this subject area throughout the semester, reporting on their research in three progressive papers. The information in these papers is then put together into a research project that culls all of the information acquired. Students must cite each of the sources they have used.

Students who choose business as a focus discipline are asked to use both print and electronic texts as sources for information on the following three topics:

1. Psychological factors involved in advertising

2. Television infomercials

3. Internet commerce

In their first paper, students discuss how advertisers use the basic determinants of consumer behavior in designing product advertisements. They describe the types of ads that are most likely to appeal to or change consumer behavior. In their second paper, students explain how and why infomercials are effective in inducing consumers to buy advertised products. They also explain how and why products sold through infomercials cost more or less than those sold in retail stores, and they describe the psychological and/or sociological needs to which infomercials appeal. In their third paper, students explain how the Internet has changed the face of sales and marketing, and describe the advantages and disadvantages of selling and/or buying products over the Internet.

As students do the research necessary for the three progressive essays, they actively practice searching for, sorting through, and organizing related pieces of information. They also practice a number of rhetorical conventions commonly used in the field of business and thus build their linguistic and discipline-specific knowledge in preparation for a longer research report.

In a final research project of five to seven pages, students bring together all of the information they have gathered to discuss how advertising strategies have changed as a result of developing technology. They do a historical analysis of advertising, beginning with the pre-television days of the early to mid-1900s, and answer the following questions: What advertising strategies were used at that time? How effective were these strategies? How did television change advertising? What were businesses able to do with television that they could not do before? What additional changes occurred in advertising with the development of computer technology? How has developing technology expanded the marketplace for both businesses and consumers? Students are asked to include a bibliography in which they cite each source used to prepare the research project.

As they prepare this research project, students read additional print and electronic material and rethink the information from previous papers. Thus, the overall experience of focus discipline research exposes these ESL students to texts taken from a variety of sources, including electronic and paper versions of newspapers and magazines such as the *New York Times* or *Business Week*, Internet articles, and print books. In addition, focus discipline research gives students the opportunity to practice the analytic and synthetic reading and academic writing needed in college.

Environmental Science

Along with business, the sciences represent a popular area of study for ESL students. In fact, statistics published by *Open Doors* (1996/1997) indicate that approximately 40 percent of ESL students attend American colleges to study one of the sciences. Issues in environmental science often appear in the news, and their effects influence other disciplines and students' lives, which motivates student interest. One topic covered in the environmental science unit is the greenhouse effect, its immediate and possible future impact on our weather, and the resulting effects on issues ranging from business to nutrition.

Prereading Activity The greenhouse effect is an abstract topic that requires some understanding of complex chemical principles. I direct students to a web site that illustrates the greenhouse effect through a diagram depicting the earth, the sun, and the ozone layer:

http://www.epa.gov/globalwarming/reports/slides/cc&i/b-ghouse.html

As they view this visual, students go step by step through an analysis of what happens when the sun's ultraviolet radiation mixes with man-made pollutants. The web page facilitates comprehension in two ways: it serves as a visual pre-reading exercise, and it provides students with an imagery link that they can later access to clarify the complex scientific concepts that will be presented in the textbook reading.

Interaction with Text The textbook chapter on environmental science details the environmental, chemical, and political implications of ozone depletion and global warming, discussing their effects on everyday life and possible consequences if not addressed in the near future. As students read the chapter, they engage in vocabulary building and express their understanding of the text through written answers to open-ended comprehension questions. We then discuss the contents of the chapter in class to check comprehension and clarify any questions students have.

Furthering Knowledge Through an Internet Search Now students are asked to search the Internet to find additional information on the greenhouse effect. Once again, to direct their Internet search and help make them aware of the critical reading skills they are using, students are given a set of questions.

An article published on the web page of the *Washington Post* (http://www.washingtonpost.com) describes some of the potential consequences of global warming (Warrick, 1997), and an article on the web page of the *New Scientist* (http://global.newscientist.com/970719/features.html) dismisses the greenhouse effect as a hoax (*New Scientist*, 1997). These essays expose students to contrasting opinions on this issue, providing a wonderful opportunity to teach the discourses of comparison/contrast and argumentation in which differing viewpoints are described and evaluated. To prepare students for this writing, we list the arguments for treating the greenhouse effect as a genuine problem versus those for viewing it as simply a hoax, and we analyze the strengths and weaknesses of each argument.

Synthesis of Concepts Through Writing A final Internet search activity directs students to narrow the focus of their search to the impact of global warming on the world's economy and food supplies. This search prepares them for the final writing activity, an interdisciplinary analysis. In this writing assignment, students must put together all of the information they have gathered through the textbook reading and the Internet research:

> Considering all the information you have gained from this unit, what are the potential effects of global warming on world nutrition? How may what we eat be affected by our changing global climate? What other areas of our lives will be affected by nutritional changes caused by the greenhouse effect?

Both linguistic and content knowledge are developed as students acquire information for this project, thereby offering students skills that they can use in future linguistic and academic tasks.

Focus Discipline Research Students who choose environmental science as a focus discipline are asked to use both print and electronic media as sources for information on the following three topics:

1. Recent changes in global climate
2. Recent changes in geographical patterns due to climate
3. The effects of a weather phenomenon known as El Niño

In their first paper, students describe recent changes in global climate, addressing the predictions of scientists and trends in global temperature and weather patterns. In their second paper, students describe recent changes in geographical patterns as a result of the changing global climate. In their third paper, students describe the weather phenomenon known as El Niño, addressing the environmental changes resulting from it, the frequency with which it occurs, and its overall effect on global climate.

In a final research project of five to seven pages, students draw interdisciplinary connections between environmental science and another content area by synthesizing the information they have gathered to discuss the effects of a changing climate on either business or government. Focusing on one of these areas, students describe the specific effects and problems brought about by climate changes and make predictions for the future in light of a continually changing climate. They are asked to include a bibliography in which they cite each source used to prepare the research project.

In one particularly interesting paper, "The Earth Is in Danger," a Russian student wrote a powerful analysis of the effects of a changing climate on the behavior of the world's governments. Her research led her to print sources, books and magazines, and Internet sources—electronic newspapers and articles. The following is an excerpt, reprinted with permission, from the student's paper:

> About 150 years ago, the earth's atmosphere had remained unchanged for several thousand years. Since the mid-1900's, people's actions have been changing the heat ability of the atmosphere. Scientists who study the earth's atmosphere and climate have been talking about the greenhouse effect and finally about "global warming". Changes in climate have an effect on the Earth's landforms. The soils of regions also depend on climate. Sea level rise presents a serious threat to some coastal regions in the different parts of the world.
>
> Politicians, who for years have ignored the warnings of scientists and environmental protection movements, are becoming alarmed. They are announcing and making decisions on an international scale. A conference on the environment took place in Stockholm in 1972. The first world conference on climate gathered the scientists almost from all of the world in Geneva in 1979. During these meetings, the scientific world

began to talk seriously to the political world. In 1988, in order to protect the stratospheric ozone layer, 120 countries agreed to limit their use of CFCs and signed the Montreal Convention. In 1989, several heads of state and heads of government of the industrialized nations signed the Hague Appeal to turn public opinion to threats to the environment. Government authorities realized that climatic change is one of the questions on which the planet's future depends. The United States and Sweden had already prohibited the use of CFCs in aerosol cans towards the end of the 1980s; Germany has announced that it will have reduced its use by 95%.

The Clinton administration believes that scientists stand against devastating effects. Three years ago U.S. joined the international community in signing the historic Framework Convention on Climate Change. It was the beginning of a process to design a kind of insurance policy. It was a treaty that called on all nations to work together in an effort to protect the global environment. The industrialized countries were urged to take the lead by stabilizing greenhouse gas emissions to 1990 levels by the year 2000.

The International community has a serious problem, which has direct relation to global climate change. This is the problem of ozone depletion. Ten years ago the nations of the world came together in Montreal to take wise steps toward protecting the Earth's stratospheric ozone layer. These efforts were expanded in the scientific discovery—a hole in the ozone layer above Antarctica, which was the size of the North American continent.

After that discovery was confirmed the world's political system began to sign any agreement much easier than before. Copenhagen Agreement was signed in 1990. Nations have agreed on the nature of the climate change threat, and we have taken the first initial steps to destroy that threat. All the nations of the world will need to work together to develop our steps after the year 2000. So we must achieve a new aim for the future.

The great poet William Butter Yeats wrote, "I have spread my dreams under your feet. Tread softly because you tread on my dreams". Unless we tread softly, our dreams for the future will be nothing but dreams. Let us make sure that our next steps are the right ones.

This paper shows the development of the student's linguistic, rhetorical, and content knowledge. In her paper, she combines factual information drawn from science and government and analysis of cause and effect, and concludes with a persuasive argument that clearly advocates world governments working together to solve the problem of global warming. She begins by describing some of the dangerous effects of global warming and scientists' warnings about them. She then presents a chronological listing of the steps the world's governments have taken to address the problem, weaving scientific evidence into her description of these events. The student concludes by quoting the poet Yeats as she offers the reader her own caveat for the future. Her paper is well organized and cogent. She has presented the facts—both scientific and political—analyzed them, related scientific knowledge to governmental action, formed a clear opinion of the issues and their relevance across disciplines, and argued for further action on the part of world governments.

This student's paper is a strong indication of the type of work students can produce when they are engaged in cognitively demanding tasks that foster the development of language skills through the exploration and analysis of academic content material. The student herself expressed both pride and amazement at her accomplishment in an e-mail message (reprinted with permission):

> My DEAR TEACHER:
> As you noticed, I tried to put as much efforts on my project as I could. If you remember from our first lessons, this topic attracted me. To be honest, I was scared by your first lessons, when you were telling us about our future assignments. I could never imagine before that I, ESL student, would read, understand, and discuss by writing of global warming, greenhouse effect, and El Nino. I am very proud of myself that I could reach it. (June 19, 1998)

Student Accomplishments

The accomplishments of each student in this course were very impressive in terms of students' overall performance in the course as well as the quality of the projects produced. In fact, in addition to improved language and cognitive skills evinced by the thoughtful, coherent, academic essays these students produced, the pass rates in this course were significantly higher than those in the overall ESL program at my college.

These students were enrolled in ESL 91, a high–intermediate to advanced-level course, which is the final course in the ESL sequence. On the basis of their scores on departmental reading and writing examinations, 73.3 percent of the students in this course were able to skip a level and move from ESL 91 to ENG 93, a course for both native and non-native speakers. This is significantly better (chi-squared = 28.47; $p < .001$) than performance in the ESL program overall, where only 21.4 percent of students were able to skip a level and move from ESL 91 to ENG 93. In addition, the percentage of students who needed to repeat the ESL 91 course was significantly lower (chi-squared = 5.64; $p < .02$), at only 8.3 percent, compared with 21.2 percent of students in the overall program who needed to repeat ESL 91.

Student Feedback on Sustained CBI

Students' performance and research in SLA, cognitive psychology, and transformative pedagogy support the value of sustained CBI (see Chapter 1 of this volume). But how do ESL students view this experience? When asked to complete questionnaires requesting their feedback on sustained CBI, students' response is overwhelmingly positive and supports the theories underlying this pedagogical approach. Students say that they enjoy reading and writing about one subject area because, along with learning English, they learn a lot of new and interesting information about another subject. They say that studying a subject area in depth teaches them to think more logically and helps them to organize their thinking process. Students believe that focus discipline projects help them learn how to get information from reading and how to analyze and present that information in writing, and that this type of learning experience will be helpful in other college courses. Finally, as they work individually and collectively, interacting with Internet texts written in English, 95 percent of students express increased confidence in both interpersonal and academic language skills (see Cummins, 1981).

Using the Internet as a resource for sustained content study produces additional positive outcomes. As evinced through student feedback and classroom behavior, motivation increases. Students are eager to begin class and often arrive early to computer lab, logging on to the Internet and beginning research on their own. They also often stay after class to continue working on the Internet, alone or with other members of their focus discipline group. Stronger students help weaker ones, and both benefit. Students form multicultural friendships, fostered by their collaborative efforts to achieve common goals in a learning environment that is both social and academic.

Conclusion

Although Internet technology can be a powerful resource for ESL education, to maximize its potential, instructors must be careful that it is used to enhance the language-learning experience. To do so, instructors themselves must become proficient users of, or at least comfortable with, Internet technology and should learn ways to use it to improve language instruction. Oxford, Rivera-Castillo, Feyten, and Nutta (1998) advise that "teachers need to develop competence in teaching students how to use technology, so that it becomes a vehicle for meaningful learning, not just an exercise in operating software or hardware or a trivial encounter with noise and images" (p. 12). Technology is most beneficial when it offers students something they cannot obtain from an in-class communicative activity.

Finally, while it represents a valuable educational tool, technology must never become a replacement for personal interaction, whether student-teacher or student-student. Rather, technology should be used to increase opportunities for such interaction. For example, students who are unable to visit an instructor during office hours or who experience a problem while completing an assignment at home over a weekend may use Internet e-mail to conference with that instructor. Students can also communicate with one another via e-mail, exchanging ideas or collaborating on group assignments. When students work together to produce focused research projects and use Internet technology to increase social interaction, the computer becomes a tool that both builds interpersonal bonds and strengthens instruction.

According to Ira Shor (1992), "meaningful learning involves examining subjects in depth and from several perspectives" (p. 171). As students engage in sustained content study and focus discipline research, they examine the "deep meanings, personal implications, and social consequences [of issues and become] active researchers who make meaning" (Shor, 1992, p. 169). In so doing, students take charge of their own learning as they develop and refine literacy.

By offering new paths and ways to think about interdisciplinary concepts, sustained content study fosters the development of both functional and academic literacies. Using the Internet and focused research further reinforces the development of these literacies. By providing information that must be classified, sorted, compared, contrasted, and evaluated for relevance, the Internet promotes critical thinking skills and engages students in sustained study and practice of skills needed in future class and work settings. In their attempts to understand and consolidate the information in diverse textual media, students call on the cognitive and linguistic resources developed through their experiences with other, related texts and events. Working through the "complex intermingling of meanings, embedded within [these] different texts" (Tierney, 1994, p. 1177), ESL students learn how to define equivalencies among experiences and how to perceive differences involving similar phenomena (Dyson, 1994).

Extended research involving the collection and analysis of varied informational sources helps students acquire expertise in their chosen focus discipline and strengthen their academic and critical literacies. Students learn not only "content information, but also how to gather, synthesize, and evaluate it" (Pally, Chapter 1, this volume), articulating their expanded content expertise and academic/critical literacies through a variety of rhetorical formats. As they engage over time in Internet research, discussions with peers, and written examination of various content-area issues, ESL students hone the skills they need to succeed in college and in the workplace.

References

Adler-Kassner, L., & Reynolds, T. (1996). Computers, reading, and basic writers: Online strategies for helping students with academic texts. *Teaching English in the Two-Year College, 23*(3), 170–178.

Arani, M., Bauer-Ramazani, C., Deutsch, L., Doto, L., Russikoff, K., Smith, B., & Velasco-Martin, C. (1998). *Preparing ESL students for academic content courses.* Colloquium presented at the 32nd annual meeting of TESOL, Seattle, WA.

Babbitt, M., & Mlynarczyk, R. W. (1999). Keys to successful content-based programs: Administrative perspectives. In L. F. Kasper, *Content-based college ESL instruction* (pp. 26–47). Mahwah, NJ: Erlbaum.

Bensley, D. A., & Haynes, C. (1995). The acquisition of general purpose strategic knowledge for argumentation. *Teaching of Psychology, 22*(1), 41–45.

Bracey, B. (1994). Emergent learning technologies/ Common themes. *Institute for Alternative Futures Report.* [Online]. Available: gopher://unix5. nysed.gov/ [1998, March 10].

Caprio, M. W. (1994). Easing into constructivism, connecting meaningful learning with student experience. *Journal of College Science Teaching, 23*(4), 210–212.

Carlson, E. R. (1995). Evaluating the credibility of sources: A missing link in the teaching of critical thinking. *Teaching of Psychology, 22*(1), 39–41.

Chun, D. M., & Plass, J. L. (1997). Research on text comprehension in multimedia environments. *Language Learning and Technology, 1*(1), 60–81.

Cummins, J. (1981). The role of primary language development in promoting educational success for language minority students. In J. Cummins (Ed.), *Schooling and language minority students: A theoretical framework* (pp. 1–50). Los Angeles: Evaluation, Dissemination, and Assessment Center.

Dyson, A. H. (1994). Viewpoints: The word and the world—Reconceptualizing written language development or, "Do rainbows mean a lot to little girls?" In R. B. Ruddell, M. R. Ruddell, & H. Singer (Eds.), *Theoretical models and processes of reading.* (4th ed., pp. 297–322). Newark, DE: International Reading Association.

Farah, B. D. (1995). Information literacy: Retooling evaluation skills in the electronic information environment. *Journal of Educational Technology Systems, 24*(2), 127–133.

Greaney, V. (1994). World illiteracy. In F. Lehr & J. Osborn (Eds.), *Reading, language, and literacy: Instruction for the twenty-first century.* Hillsdale, NJ: Erlbaum.

Harvey, J. (1998). TESL meta-sites on the Internet: A review. *TESL-EJ, 3*(2). [Online]. Available: http://www-writing.berkeley.edu/TESL-EJ/ej10/m1.html [1999, June 22].

Horowitz, D. (1986). What professors actually require: Academic tasks for the ESL classroom. *TESOL Quarterly, 20*(3), 445–462.

Johns, A. M. (1997). *Text, role, and context: Developing academic literacies.* Cambridge: Cambridge UP.

Kasper, L. F. (1995). Theory and practice in content-based ESL reading instruction. *English for Specific Purposes, 14*(3), 223–230.

Kasper, L. F. (1997). The impact of content-based instructional programs on the academic progress of ESL students. *English for Specific Purposes, 16*(4), 309–320.

Kasper, L. F. (1998a). Interdisciplinary English and the Internet: Technology meets content in the ESL course. Paper presented at the TCC '98 Online Conference, April 7–9, 1998. Available: http://leahi.kcc.hawaii.edu/org/tcon98/paper/kasper.html [1999, June 22].

Kasper, L. F. (1998b). *Interdisciplinary English* (2nd ed.). New York: McGraw-Hill.

Kaufer, D., & Young, R. (1993). Writing in the content areas: Some theoretical complexities. In L. Odell (Ed.), *Theory and practice in the teaching of writing: Rethinking the discipline.* (pp. 71–104). Carbondale and Edwardsville, IL: Southern Illinois UP.

Lankes, R. D. (1997). The bread and butter of the Internet. *ERIC Digest (EDO-IR-97-02).* [Online]. Available: http://ericir.syr.edu/ithome/digests/David.html [1999, June 22].

Leki, I., & Carson, J. G. (1994). Students' perceptions of EAP writing instruction and writing needs across the disciplines. *TESOL Quaterly, 28*(1), 81–101.

Lepeintre, S., & Stephan, L. (1995). Telnet treasure hunts: Learning to read (on) the Internet. In M. Warschauer (Ed.), *Virtual connections* (pp. 331–335). Honolulu: University of Hawaii Press.

Liu, K. (1998). Electronic communication, new technology, and the ESL student. In T. Smoke (Ed.), *Adult ESL: Politics, pedagogy, and participation in school and community programs* (pp. 289–311). Mahwah, NJ: Erlbaum.

Mather, P. (1996). *World Wide Web: Beyond the basics* (Chapter 6). [Online] Available: http://ei.cs.vt.edu/~wwwbtb/book/chap6/critical.html [1999, June 22].

Mustafa, Z. (1995). The effect of genre awareness on linguistic transfer. *English for Specific Purposes, 14*(3), 247–256.

Neilsen, L. (1989). *Literacy and living: The literate lives of three adults.* Portsmouth, NH: Heinemann/Boynton-Cook.

New Scientist (1997, 19 July). Features. [Online]. Available: http://global.newscientist.com/ns/970719/features.html [1999, June 22].

Open Doors 1996/97. (1996/1997). New York: Institute of International Education. [Online]. Available: http://www.ne.org/opendoors/forstud6htm [1998, April 17].

Oxford, R., Rivera-Castillo, Y., Feyten, C., & Nutta, J. (1998). Computers and more: Creative uses of technology for learning a second or foreign language. *INSA de LYON.* [Online]. Available: http://www.insa-lyon.fr/Departements/CDRL/computers.html [1999, June 22].

Pally, M. (1997). Critical thinking in ESL: An argument for sustained content. *Journal of Second Language Writing, 6*(3), 293–311.

Pennington, M. C. (1996). The power of the computer in language education. In M. C. Pennington (Ed.), *The power of CALL* (pp. 1–14). Houston: Athelstan.

Prior, P. (1992). Redefining task: Academic writing in six graduate courses. Paper presented at the 23rd Annual TESOL Conference, Vancouver, Canada.

Profozich, R. (1997). Coping with the research paper. *Teaching English in the Two-Year College, 24*(4), 304–307.

Reilly, B. (1996). New technologies, new literacies, new problems. In C. Fisher, D. C. Dwyer, & K. Yocam (Eds.), *Education and technology: Reflections on computing in classrooms* (pp. 203–220). San Francisco: Jossey-Bass.

Shea, P. (1996). Media, multimedia, and meaningful language learning: A review of the literature. Web-Net 96, October 15–19, San Francisco, CA. [Online]. Available: http://aace.virginia.edu/aace/conf/webnet/html/159.htm [1999, June 22].

Shor, I. (1992). *Empowering education: Critical teaching for social change.* Chicago: University of Chicago Press.

Smoke, T. (1997). The challenges of technology in ESL. *Selected papers from ESL for the 21st century.* A New Jersey Statewide Higher Education Conference, October 18, 1997, Union County College, Elizabeth, NJ

Soter, A. O. (1990). The non-English-speaking student. In G. E. Hawisher & A. O. Soter (Eds.), *On literacy and its teaching* (pp. 224–242). Albany, NY: State University of New York Press.

Strommen, E. F., & Lincoln, B. (1992). Constructivism, technology, and the future of classroom learning. *ILTweb.* [Online]. Available: http://www.ilt.columbia.edu/k12/livetext/docs/construct.html [1999, June 22].

Tierney, R. J. (1994). Dissension, tension, and the models of literacy. In R. B. Ruddell, M. R. Ruddell, & H. Singer. (Eds.), *Theoretical models and processes of reading* (4th ed., pp. 1162–1183). Newark, DE: International Reading Association.

Tierney, R. J., Kieffer, R., Whalin, K., Desai, L., Moss, A. G., Harris, J. E., & Hopper, J. (1997, May). Assessing the impact of hypertext on learners' architecture of literacy learning spaces in different disciplines: Follow-up studies. *Reading Online.* [Online]. Available: http://www.readingonline.org/research/impact/index.html [1999, June 22].

Wade, C. (1995). Using writing to develop and assess critical thinking. *Teaching of Psychology, 22*(1), 24–28.

Warrick, J. (1997, November 12). Consensus emerges earth is warming—Now what? *Washington Post,* p. A01. [Online]. Available: http://www.washingtonpost.com [1999, June 22].

Warschauer, M. (1996). Computer-assisted language learning: An introduction. In S. Fotos (Ed.), *Multimedia language teaching* (pp. 3–20). Tokyo: Logos International.

Appendix A

Internet Search Activity

Business and Marketing Unit

Directions: Answer the following questions as you search for information on advertising on the Internet. Try to make your answers as specific and as descriptive as possible.

- Step One: Get into Netscape, and enter the following URL in the line marked *Location:*

  http://www.executive-printing.com/20steps/20ad.htm.

This URL will take you to a web site called *Advertising Strategies*. Be sure that you type it EXACTLY as written on this sheet.

- Step Two: Now follow the hypertext links to access each of the web pages contained on this site on advertising by clicking on the underlined words.

- Step Three: Now you will practice accessing sites on your own. Answer the following questions to help guide you in your search:

  1. Which keyword should you enter into the search engine to find information on *advertising?*

  2. What do you have to do to access a web file on *advertising?*

  3. Once you have accessed this file, how do you get information on *advertising?*

  4. After reading the article that you accessed on the Web, write *two new things* you have learned about advertising using this web site.

- Step Four: Now narrow the focus of your search to information on *the effect of the advertising medium on marketing success.*

Do a new search and answer the above four questions to guide you in this new search.

Questions to Guide You in Evaluating Internet Resources

1. Does the information add anything to what you already know about the topic?
2. Who is providing the information contained on the Internet page?
3. Where did the information come from?
4. Do they provide evidence to support the points they are making?
5. How old is the information?
6. When was the Internet page last updated?
7. How broad is the topic?
8. Is the information provided in a WWW or gopher document, a text file, a newsgroup posting, or an e-mail message?
9. Is the information clear and well organized?
10. Who recommended this site as a good source of information?

Chapter 5

Frames for Reference
Content-Based Instruction in the Context of Speech

Neil R. Williams
New York University

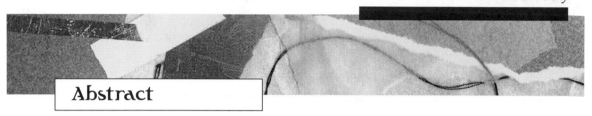

Abstract

For many students, "academic discourse" is synonymous with academic writing. This belief stems chiefly from certain misconceptions they hold about the primacy of writing in an academic context. This chapter describes five aspects of speech ("frames") that students need to access: the emotional frame, the lexical frame, the referential frame, the discourse frame, and the attitudinal frame. While it is impossible to teach all language used within these frames, students are led to discover aspects of it through analysis of sustained "spoken like" text: a comic book. Using worksheets to isolate these aspects of speech, students categorize spoken English while comparing it with their own spoken L1. Students refine their categorizations in class discussion and in continued encounters with the authentic language in the comic book. As an added benefit, they gain practice in inductive reasoning, a skill they can use in any academic context. ■

To learn something new one must first notice it. This noticing is an awareness of its existence, obtained and enhanced by paying attention to it. Paying attention is focusing one's consciousness, or pointing one's perceptual powers in the right direction and making mental "energy" available for processing. Processing involves linking something that is perceived in the outside world to structures (patterns of connection) that exist in the mind (van Lier, 1996, p. 11).

The Role of Speech in Academic Discourse

The inclusion of a chapter on speaking in a book that focuses on academic discourse may at first blush seem somewhat anomalous—but, truth to tell, it *ain't!* To many students, "academic discourse" is a synonym for academic writing, with speech relegated to the linguistic sidelines. As many of the books cited in Chapter 1 remind us (e.g., Johns, 1997; Spack, 1988), this is a dangerous simplification. Many students seem unaware of the range of linguistic options open to a native speaker to "do speaking" effectively. For example, even in a relatively formal context, such as making a presentation, a speaker may vary his or her language to create an effect (as I did in the opening sentence) while in the relatively unstructured context of the classroom. In this setting, teachers and students interact in a wide variety of ways, and the language constantly evolves to accommodate shifts in the informational and interpersonal dynamic. ESL students may recognize the need to understand and eventually use such variation, but they often come to the academic context painfully ill equipped to deal with the vagaries of English speech or seriously limited in their understanding of what academic spoken discourse involves. Consider the following extract from the opening of an academic presentation by a teaching assistant in a science department at a university in the northeastern United States:

> [Writes name on blackboard]. This is my first name and you can call me this. I come from [city name] in [state], and my major is biology. I pursue my Ph.D., and my specialization is molecular biology. That deals with something about DNA. That is their structure and today I'm teaching about human reproduction.

The presenter is a non-native speaker of English, and though at a grammatical level her language is for the most part correct (she gets her information across), it hardly succeeds at a discourse level. American English-speaking undergraduates would find her presentation rather stiff and awkward, which might compromise how much effort they would expend to follow what she was trying to say. Her speech somewhat resembles the way academic prose reads: it is information dense and seems to be aimed *at* an audience rather than *to* an audience. There is no greeting, very little repetition to aid comprehension, and none of the confirmation-checking devices commonly used by native speakers of English. The speaker appears to be unaware of the fact that spoken English, even academic spoken English, is vastly different from the written academic English she may have encountered so far in her academic career.

Why should this be? The fault, I suggest, lies with her understanding of what constitutes English in an academic context. This understanding may be a result of the academic discourse she has been exposed to, where the only English she encountered was in the textbooks she studied. It may also, regrettably, stem from her pre-university ESL speaking classes, where she may have picked up certain myths and misconceptions about the nature of spoken English.

The first, and perhaps most disturbing, of these myths is that spoken English is merely a sloppier version of written English that one can somehow "acquire" through "communicative practice." We ESL teachers often do little to dispel this common misconception. How often do we put our ESL students in groups to "have a discussion" or accomplish a task through speech and then leave them to get on with it? On one level, of course, there is good reason for this. Group activities are very effective in developing a certain ease in communication. And we are happy when students come up with an outcome. This validates the activity: the students have negotiated an outcome, and they have done so in English. They must therefore have been acquiring "fluency." But have they really? A facility with speech, yes, but fluency? What do we teachers do while students are doing such activities? Often we monitor the syntax of what they are saying and give feedback on structures that they could have used. We rarely comment on the language they did use to structure the discussion itself, or on the interpersonal nature of the discussion (how members of the group reacted to what others said).

Following are some other misconceptions that permeate ESL learners' schemata of what constitutes spoken English.

Speech is made up of words. This is simply not true. Speech consists of much more than words. Beyond the whole overlay of stress, rhythm, intonation, and body movements that goes into a speech message (paralanguage), many groups of words (chunks) function as single meaning units. While students may recognize the importance of paralanguage and chunking, in their ESL classes they may not have had the opportunity to focus on them as extensively as they have on grammar, and so may accord them little importance.

Speech is essentially unidirectional. This too is untrue. Speech can occur only in the presence of a listener or listeners. Solidarity must be negotiated and listener reactions constantly monitored for signs of incomprehension. In the absence of such signs, we routinely ask explicitly for them through confirmation-checking language. Students may be unaware of how to ask for listeners' reactions in English, given the nature of the speaking they have been asked to do in class. "Communicative practice" often relies on information transfer, in which the listener's role is relegated to that of "information recipient." While in theory such "information gap" activities require interpersonal negotiation, often students will be able to transmit the information with a minimal amount of spoken language, relying instead on paralinguistic signals, such as pointing. As a result, there is little need for negotiation; one student speaks, the other responds, and so on—hardly realistic communication.

In any context, the register will remain the same, either formal or informal. This is only partially true. Speakers constantly shift their stance toward the listener in light of the feedback they receive. In the following exchange between a husband and wife, the register shifts from "informal" to "uneducated" to "mock-regal" in the space of four turns as the wife capitalizes on her husband's praise to negotiate a neck rub:

A: I found it! I actually found that hibachi you were looking for! Took me most of the afternoon, but they finally had one in [store name].

B: C'mere, woman. You done good. [Kisses her]

A: Well, good then. Now come do your duty, varlet. [She places his hand on her neck]

B: Indeed I shall, milady. [Rubs her neck]

Such playful uses of register shifting for humorous, sarcastic, or insulting effect are not only very common between friends and intimates but are also remarkably common in academic and business contexts, whether a lab or an office. They rarely appear in language presented in ESL textbooks.

Spoken language is inferior to written language, and is used only by lazy speakers. This is the biggest misconception of all. It may stem from the belief that because written language is more permanent and has to be learned, it should be accorded much more importance than spoken language. As a corollary, ideally "good" spoken language should approximate written language. In fact, spoken language is far more subtle than the corresponding written language, since the listener's presence and reaction to what is being said requires the speaker to alter the tone of what he or she is saying "on the fly" to ensure good ongoing relations and continued communication.

Native speakers, especially native speakers in the ESL profession, can be held at least partly to blame for such beliefs, though, admittedly more through sins of omission than of commission. Simply put, in speaking we may be unaware of the discourse styles we use or the discourse choices we make. Unlike writing, speech has never been taught to us; we have never had to consciously learn or monitor the forms we use because we have unconsciously acquired them through repeated use in multiple contexts. Speech is second nature to us; even if we recognize that it differs from writing, we tend to think of it as the easy part of language, to be picked up simply through use. For the non-native learner of English, however, once he or she has become aware of it, speech proves by far the most difficult aspect of English to use successfully.

Thus, before ESL students can become aware of how spoken English works, native speakers (instructors) must first step back and look at what really constitutes English when it is spoken. Unfortunately, in the applied linguistics literature, where systematic descriptions of spoken English grammar systems are beginning to appear, there is still considerable divergence in how or what to describe. Students (and teachers) confront a bewildering array of descriptions of spoken English. At the utterance level, one can read about the "telling increment" (Brazil, 1993, 1995) or about the Left-Dislocation, proposition, Right-Dislocation model of Geluykens (1992, 1994), with its various permutations of REF (a topic referred to, usually in phrase initial position), GAP (a word inside the phrase—generally a pronoun—referring to the REF), and PROP (the information being given about REF), modified by Carter and McCarthy (1995) into the (THEME) CORE (TAIL) unit. At the discourse level come the adjacency pairs of the conversation analysts (e.g., Sacks, Schegloff, & Jefferson, 1974), where language is considered in terms of two-turn units (e.g., greeting-greeting or question-answer), and the hierarchical models (outgrowths of Halliday's systemic/functional grammar), where language consists of transactions made up of exchanges made up of acts (Sinclair & Coulthard, 1975; Tsui, 1994), not to mention the macro levels of discourse exemplified in Grice's (1975) maxims and Sperber and Wilson's (1986) relevance theory.

Is it necessary for teachers to be aware of and teach all the competing theories complete with their individual jargons, or should they choose just one theory and teach that? Neither approach seems satisfactory. On the one hand, students stand to become confused as they encounter competing and/or contradictory terms and frameworks. On the other, they may be limited by the framework of the single descriptive apparatus presented to them. Yet people clearly have learned a target-language spoken grammar well, without ever having to memorize the different labels used in the various descriptive frameworks. I would suggest that because they had noticed certain aspects of speech in their own language, these people taught themselves to "notice" the same aspects of speech in the target language.

The remainder of this chapter presents a sustained content-based instructional methodology that emphasizes the tools and strategies students need to acquire an understanding of speech. This methodology has been used successfully with low to intermediate pre-academic students, though it certainly would be appropriate for higher-level students who have had no formal training in the pragmatics of speech. By training them to look and compare, the methodology alerts students to many of the pragmatic, interactional, "here and now" aspects of spoken English while at the same time giving them practice in many of the skills required for both university and professional work. For instance, starting from raw data, students are asked to classify and differentiate aspects of the data; from these primary classifications, they then derive patterns. These patterns, in turn, lead them to predict other possible patterns, which they can then check and modify or reinforce in light of new data. In-class discussions focus on having students justify their categorizations. Such reasoning and support of hypotheses is a necessary concomitant to any academic or professional work. The benefits of the methodology are thus twofold: an alternate, complementary understanding of the nature of speech and, at another level, practice in skills students will need in many academic and professional settings.

Course Content: English in Context

Speech by its very nature is difficult to examine and analyze. It exists in real time, in a context, and, in its usual form, is evanescent: the message has already disappeared even as the sounds that make it up are being decoded. There is no way a student can go back to check what was said, other than by asking the speaker for repetition. Even if infinite repetition by a speaker were feasible (and few native speakers would have that kind of patience!), the utterance would likely be different at some level, either in stress or in intonation. Speech changes as the speaker's emotional state changes. Given the speed required to process any utterance, it is quite likely that the student would have no time to attend to its form, being preoccupied with matching the jumble of sounds just heard to words he or she could recognize. Somehow students need to be exposed to authentic speech, but in a form that allows them sufficient time to process it. One such form, which I have used successfully in class, is a comic book written for English-speaking Americans rather than adapted for ESL students. Students are thus exposed to raw data: a body of English that will not always break down into neat grammatical sentences and as such often needs to be interpreted rather than analyzed.

The pedagogical reasons for using such a text are many:

- Comic strips are both *permanent* and *visual.* They are therefore much easier to study than other potential sources of spoken English. Videotapes, for example, are visual, but they are *timebound:* language can be caught only fleetingly as the action progresses. Even if they are stopped and replayed over and over, the sounds need to be decoded before the language can be studied. Movie scripts, on the other hand, are time*less:* though the language is available for study, there is no visual context to refer to as an aid to meaning.

- Comic strip characters interact in a real (for them), self-contained, predictable context. As most people do when they actually speak, characters talk about *here* and *now* and *you* and *me* rather than the *there* and *then* or *him* or *her* of narrative or newspaper reports.

- Unlike one-panel cartoons, which have a local context that changes from one cartoon to the next, comic strips often have sustained context: a continuous storyline over three or four strips, which in turn boosts comprehension and ease of decoding. Comic strips are full of paralinguistic clues; feelings can often be inferred from facial expressions or posture, and the language understood accordingly.

- Comic strip language lies between real spoken English and "grammatical" English. Although it doesn't capture the pauses, false starts, and overlapping of casual speech, it reflects real people speaking real English, contains frequent examples of "interactional language," and is rich in formulaic expressions uttered in response to many different situations.

- Characters in each strip exist in the same social context, so it is easy to see when they are making use of register shifting and to discuss why they are doing it.

- Given its limited size (roughly 16,000 words in 1,400 panels in 285 strips), the comic book provides more than enough data for use over one term in a low-to-intermediate ESL classroom, while advanced students may be able to study more than one book without having to come to the characters and contexts "fresh."

- Finally, the comic book serves as a jumping-off point for further analysis/interpretation of the language students encounter around them outside the classroom. As students become increasingly competent and confident in decoding the sounds of spoken English, they attend to speech patterns in movies, in television programs, and on the street, and apply and extend their initial rules of use based on patterns they have already observed and discussed.

The cartoon book I have been using is *Yukon Ho!: A Calvin and Hobbes Collection* (Watterson, 1989). It was chosen because of the limited number of characters, which would give students a chance to get to know each character in depth. Most of the dialogue takes place between two characters: Calvin, a six-year-old with a hyperactive imagination, and Hobbes, his stuffed tiger and imaginary friend. Their relationship veers from the cordial to the acrimonious. Minor players are long-suffering Mom and Dad, who spend their days wondering what they have done to deserve such a child; Rosalyn, the mean baby-sitter; Miss Wormwood, the teacher nearing retirement whose lot it is to attempt to get Calvin to pay attention in class; and Susie, the smart "girl next door" with whom Calvin has an intense love-hate relationship.

The Content: Descriptive Frameworks

> It is difficult to see how we can draw attention to everything that learners need to know. We can, however, encourage learners to make important generalisations for themselves. (Willis, 1993, p. 90)

The following sections briefly describe "important generalisations" in the form of provisional frameworks or heuristics that have emerged from intensive study of the language in *Yukon Ho!* There are five such heuristics: the emotional frame, the lexical frame, the referential frame, the discourse frame, and the attitudinal frame. These frameworks refer to "noninformational" aspects of speech and have been useful in training students to know where to look and what to look for as they encounter native-speaker speech. Their provisional nature must be stressed, however. The frameworks correspond (more or less) to aspects that are unique to speech and serve as points of repair against which students can measure their emergent knowledge of speech and register. These frameworks undergo modification and refinement as students derive their own patterns from the context and recycle them in the light of new data.

Framework 1: The Emotional Frame

Speech is more than words. A speaker is invested emotionally in what he or she says, and this is realized either lexically or suprasegmentally. The lexical realizations can be termed *reactions.* Figure 5.1 provides examples.

Reactions fall into two categories: *nonlexical sounds* or *sound clusters* (e.g., *uh-oh, blecch!, mhm,* and *augh!*) and *lexical expletives,* which Stenström (1991) describes as "taboo words related to religion, sex and the human body, which are used figuratively: and express the speaker's (genuine or pretended) emotions and attitudes" (p. 240). Examples of these would be words used to express surprise (*Oh my God! Fuck ME!*) or frustration (*Jesus! For Chrissake! Shit! Fuck!*).

The emotional frame is a useful place to begin an analysis of the speech in *Yukon Ho!* because it can be used to raise the question of register and appropriateness. In the book, visual clues betray what the character is feeling/thinking, and often a linguistic clue accompanies the nonverbal clue. In most cases, the character uses language that is mild in tone (newspapers will not publish characters using taboo language) but apposite. Such terms as *phooey, sheesh, geez,* and *heck* are typically used in place of an obscene or blasphemous variant beginning (usually) with a similar phoneme that students may have heard from the mouths of many Americans (even if only in movies). Students presented with

Figure 5.1 The Emotional Frame

Reaction	Sounds/Words
Surprise/awe	Wow!; Gosh!; Gee, . . .
Surprise/shock (good/bad)	Uh-oh; Oh NO!; Well, I'll be! . . . ; Why, . . .
Disbelief of context	Can you believe it?; I don't BELIEVE this!; This isn't happening; OH boy . . .
Frustration/anger (no success)	Man!; Phooey.; Rats!; Sheesh!; Geez, . . .
Satisfaction/joy/success	YES! (+ paraling.); GREAT!; Oh BOY!
Disgust	BLECCH!; YUK!; GROSS!
Irritation/exasperation	(God) Damn (it); For . . . sake!; For crying out loud!

these examples of emotional language gain in two significant ways. First, they come to recognize that not all reactions and taboo words they hear around them or in the media can be used freely in all contexts. They also have the option to use reactions that will not offend. Second, students encounter reactions that are both acceptable and commonly heard (e.g., marked surprise: *Wow!* [= wonder], *Uh-oh* [= unfortunate outcome], *Oh NO!* [= unhappy outcome], *Well, I'll be . . .* [= totally unexpected/shocking]). Once they have become aware of such reactions, students invariably have been surprised at how frequently they occur in speech, and have started listening for them in earnest.

A second emotional framework lies at the level of suprasegmentals. Stress and intonation often betray a speaker's feelings toward the listener. In the following utterances, the informational load is the same, but the emotional load is very different:

Where have you BEEN?!?

Where have YOU been???

The first example conveys an air of irritation at the listener's nonarrival, while the second suggests genuine surprise at the listener's appearance. Stress and intonation are also frequently manipulated for pragmatic effect: for contrast (*This is MY room, not YOUR room*), for intensification (*Get down here NOW!!*), or for ironic or humorous effect (when words do not match the expected pitch contours).

As another example, consider the following sentences:

- *Charlie arrived in a car* (unmarked form). Charlie the person arrives in a real car (pictured in my mind's eye). Chances are that I will go on to tell my interlocutor something about the car that Charlie arrived in.

- *Charlie arrived in some car* (marked lexically but not suprasegmentally). The vehicle itself is of no interest, other than the fact that it was not a bus or a bicycle. Chances are that without further prompting from the interlocutor, the car will not be mentioned again in the conversation.

The Content: Descriptive Frameworks

- *Charlie arrived in SOME CAR* (marked with a high rise-fall on *car*). Charlie arrived in *very much* an example of a car—be it good, bad, or strange—which the context would help define.

Exploring such utterances helps students interpret the meanings of capital letters and the tones, emphases, and intentions they represent.

Framework 2: The Lexical Frame

Much of speech, like much of writing, is remarkably formulaic. In a given context, we are likely to access certain "chunks" of language that we use as single-meaning units. Where applied linguists (Lewis, 1993; Nattinger & DeCarrico, 1992) have found it necessary to classify and subclassify such groups of words, students have found it useful to classify such groupings in one of three ways: as idioms, as frames, and as chunks.

Idioms are relatively rare (*a dime a dozen, dead as a doornail*), whereas frames and chunks are very common in speech. Frames are phrases in which there is a fixed form containing slots that can be filled (e.g., *[noun] isn't (exactly) the [superlative + noun] I've ever [verb]*. Chunks are groups of words with a meaning different from the words that constitute them, and occur everywhere in spoken language (e.g., *at first blush, chances are, by and large, pretty much of a [noun phrase]*). Interestingly, many chunks have written counterparts, and discussion of the differences between oral and written forms furthers understanding of register. Here the concept of *markedness* (an attitudinal overlay to a base meaning) is crucial. For example, students ponder why a character uses *rarely* in a given context and how the effect would be attenuated if the character used *every so often, once in a blue moon,* or *from time to time* in the same context. To answer this query, they are directed back to the strip where they first met the form to identify what sets that context apart from the context where they are meeting the alleged "synonym."

Figure 5.2 presents additional examples of idioms, frames, and chunks.

Framework 3: The Referential Frame

Spoken language makes use of words that can be interpreted only through reference to the context (see Figure 5.3). They fall into three categories: general verbs, prepositions with metaphoric extensions, and minimal reference words.

1. *General verbs.* These are verbs with a "basic" meaning that the listener can adapt to derive a meaning that is sufficient for the context. A good example is the verb *get,* which can be reduced to a simple, abstract base meaning: *someone did something and as a result someone [be]/[have]/[can do] something.* When a speaker says *Bill got John drunk,* what is important is that John is or was drunk as a result of something Bill did. If *Chris got the dog,* what is important is that someone did something and as a result Chris now has the dog, whether it was captured, killed, bought, stolen, taken, or given to him.

2. *Prepositions with metaphoric (or literal) extension* (Lakoff & Johnson, 1980). If a book is *out* of the library, it is not the same as being *out* in the bookstores, though the bookstore manager could conceivably be *out* collecting copies of the book that he ran *out* of. Similarly, I may have been *in and out* all day, but

Chapter 5   Frames for Reference

Figure 5.2 The Lexical Frame

Marked forms	How come SVO? [= why? + surprise]; great [= good + I like it]
Idioms	Sticks and stones may break my bones Kick the bucket
Frames	[X] beats [Verb]-ing (e.g., *Renting videos beats going out to the movies*) S [be (present)] such a [negative NP] (e.g., *You're such a dweeb!*) S [be] not THAT [adj] (to [Verb]) (e.g., *It isn't THAT difficult [to do]*) All S [have] to do [is/was] (e.g., *All he had to do was tell me*)
Chunks	It takes one to know one; I'll tell you what . . . ; . . . and then, to cap it all, . . . ;

I have to be *in* in half an hour to meet someone. The immediate context is the only place a listener can look to make sense of how to interpret these words.

3. *Minimal reference words.* These words are used when a speaker cannot find the exact word or decides it is unnecessary to make the referent explicit. Common examples are *that, it, so,* and *then.* A speaker facing the impossibility of seeing a project through to completion might say *That's that, then,* expecting the listener to infer something along the lines of *That* (what I can see happening or not happening) *is that* (the end of my/your/our hopes) *then* (which I or you had already mentioned before). An important subcategory of such reference words is chunks or frames using the word *stuff* or *thing(s)*. These words are used either to refer to a contextually recoverable object, material, or argument (*Throw your stuff/things over here*) or to qualify a noun close enough in meaning for the speaker's communicative purpose (e.g., *I had my shots and stuff*). Another, similar qualifying frame is *the (whole) [modifying phrase] bit* (e.g., *I didn't really enjoy the "I'm-your-father-so-don't-argue-with-me" bit*).

Framework 4: The Discourse Frame

A spoken message is often prefaced or followed by words or phrases used to "do conversation," to signal how the listener should understand what will be or has just been said, or to indicate how the speaker is feeling in or about the context. These words have little or no meaning beyond interactional signaling, and most speakers accord them little importance because their use is second nature to them. If ESL students give them so little status in their own language, it is hardly surprising that they consider them unnecessary for learning "good" English. It often comes as quite a shock for them to realize that fluent speakers of English use the same kinds of "sloppy" words that they do when speaking in their own language. Figure 5.4 summarizes these "doing words."

Figure 5.3 The Referential Frame

	Example	Meaning to Be Inferred
General words [*get*] [*let*] [*keep (on)*]	I got the dog	I bought/took/stole/was given/found the dog
	I got her in	I persuaded the dean/bribed the guard/pushed hard/brought her home/forced the zipper up
Extension [*get/be/have*]+	1. *up*	I was up late; you're up to bat; are you up for . . . ?
	2. *in*	I'll be in by nine; they [had]/[got]/[called] the doctor in
	3. *on*	the TV's on; I have nothing on; he has nothing on tomorrow; you're on; you're having me on!
	4. *off*	the meat's off; he's off work; I'm off; we got off early; it went off [people *get*, things *go*]
	5. *out*	my book's [come] out; he's [run] out of time; he's out; we had it out [fought]; we got out alive
	6. *over*	it's over; I got over her; I'm over it; I was over at John's; I had John over last night
Reference	1. *it/this/that*	it's going to rain; isn't it nice how he does that?; that's that, then; that's it!; this is it; that's nice
	2. [*make*] [+ *it/NP*]	Just made it!; we made the train; he made me (do it)!
	3. [*do*][+*so/that/it/* Ø]	you can't do that; just do it, OK?; that'll do; we had to make do with what we had; she'll do
	4. *so*	just so; I think so; I hope so; he did so; I will SO!!
	5. *stuff/thing*, etc.	. . . , and stuff; . . . , or something; . . . , and all; the (opinion adj) thing IS; your stuff

Framework 5: The Attitudinal Frame

Possibly the most difficult aspect of spoken English for ESL learners to grasp is the way speakers commonly take a stance toward an utterance, making explicit their opinion of what they are saying. For example, when given the opinion *That dress is pretty,* a speaker can assert a degree of prettiness (intensification):

That dress is SO pretty,

That dress is the prettiest dress I ever saw, or even

That is QUITE a dress.

Figure 5.4 The Discourse Frame

"Doing Words":

		Examples
Signals	1. For topic management	offer – new: SO; So Dad, . . .
		offer – parallel: By the way, ... That reminds me, . . .
		takeover: Well, . . .
		invitation: How about . . . ?
		continue: And, . . .
		return: . . . , then.
		discount preceding: Anyway, . . .
		topic recall: You know . . . ? Well, . . .
	2. Qualification	. . . , though; . . . , not to mention . . . ; Mind you, . . . ; In all fairness, . . . ; I mean, . . .
	3. Comment [how to understand]	Of course, . . . ; actually, . . . ; naturally, . . . ; as far as I'm concerned, . . . ; needless to say, . . . ; frankly, . . . ; we might as well . . .
Requests	1. Attention [self/words]	Listen, . . . ; Look, . . . ; You know, . . . ; Say, Dad, . . . ; Hey, Dad, . . . ; See, . . . (= explanation coming)
	2. Action	Quiet! Sit down! Come quick! C'mon!
Other	1. Acknowledgment [new info]	Oh.; Hey!
	2. Alignment/ nonalignment	Yeah! Right! I'LL say! Sure. You bet! || Sorry, No way! Forget it! Heck no!
	3. Consideration/ thought	Hmmm . . . ; Let's see (now), . . . ; Ummm . . .
Confirmation Checks	1. Align! (agree!) [initiate]	Isn't she nice? ↘; It's good ↘, isn't it ↗?; You're Jane, right?; Don't you think . . . ?; . . . , don't you think?; Pretty smart, huh↗?
	2. Align? [understand?]	I made a mistake, OK?; Let's not fight, all right?
	3. Clarify! [response] [echo (context/ message)]	**A:** Jane came. **B:** Jane. ↘ (= So?) or Jane? ↗ (= I didn't hear correctly); **A:** How about Guam? **B:** GUAM? ↗↗ (= Why Guam? I'm surprised. Expand); **A:** We're eating salad tonight. **B:** You mean, there's no meat? ↘ It's good, is it? ↗; Yeah? ↗ (or ↗↗); Really? ↗ or ↘; No ↘↘!!; (rhetorical) You don't like it? ↗ FINE ↘↘!! I won't give you any!
	4. Clarify? [neg. question (ITB) (I thought, but)]	Aren't you HAPPY? ↗ (= I thought you were); Didn't YOU have a best friend? ↗ (= I thought we all did; I know I did)

Alternatively, the speaker can mitigate the nature of what she or he is saying:

I guess it's a pretty dress.

I think it's a pretty dress.

Intensifiers and mitigators function (often together) to mark just how far the speaker is prepared to assert or commit to the truth of what he or she is saying. Figure 5.5 gives examples of mitigation and intensification.

Intensification is most often realized through word stress (graphically realized through the use of capital letters: *you IDIOT:* through underlining: *you idiot;* through exclamation points: *you idiot!!!;* or through any combination of the three). It can also be seen in lexical phrases (*What a . . . ; How . . . !; [be] such a . . .*), intensifying lexis (*so, real, really, sure*), or through intensifying disjuncts (*Boy, [+ stress]; Geez, [+ stress]*). In a few cases, it appears in the speaker's use of intensifying particles (e.g., *eat up* rather than *eat)* or through lexical intensification (e.g., the opinion *good* can be marked: *great* [= *good + I like it*] or *amazing* [= *great + I like it + It was surprising*]).

A final group of intensifiers (e.g., *just, even*) serve to isolate, focusing the listener's attention on the word or phrase following them. Consider how the placement of *just* in the following example changes the meaning of the message:

Just say what you want.

Say just what you want.

Say what just YOU want.

Say what you just wanted to.

Mitigators are used to signal to what degree the speaker's words express a personal opinion. The generic mitigators *kind of (kinda)* and *sort of (sorta)* mark an utterance with the message: *I'm NOT sure; I could be wrong; this is only MY opinion.* Like the focus particles, *kind of* and *sort of* can be used to modify whole utterances or specific parts of them: *I sort of ate the ice cream quickly; I ate the ice cream sort of quickly.* Interestingly, they usually do not modify nouns unless "quoted off" (*I ate the "sort of" ice cream quickly.*)

While *sort of* and *kind of* offer a generic way to mitigate, mitigation is also achieved lexically. Lexical options open to speakers include overt marking (*I think* [strong opinion], *I THINK* [but I could be wrong], *I guess* [don't quote me on this], *I imagine* [though I'm probably wrong]) and marked words (using *I wish* instead of *I want* to mean [*"I want" + "but I know I cannot"*]).

Methodology: Applying the Frames for Reference

Many teachers . . . try to hold a mirror up to (linguistic) nature—to let students see something of the organized chaos which is out there. This is as it should be. Trying to protect students from it, by pretending it isn't there, does no-one any service. We need to find ways of reflecting it, but at the same time filtering it, so that students are not dazzled by

Figure 5.5 The Attitudinal Frame

Intensifiers (a degree of certainty, affirmation of absolutes: "I **can't** be wrong")

Generic	**word stress** (CAPS/<u>Underline</u>/!!!); **lexis** (what (a) . . . !/How . . . !) S *sure/really* VO; S [Be] *really/real/so* Adj/Adv; S [Be] *such a* [N]. *Boy,* SVO [+stressed element]
Lexical intensity (ironic)	*great* (<*good*<*nice*); *dumb/lousy (rotten) (stinking)* (<*bad/stupid*) *SOME* (Cf. *That's SOME car!* and *SOME CAR <u>THAT</u> is!*) *pretty* [Adj/Adv] (e.g., *pretty average* vs. *pretty good*)
"++"	[Consumption verb] *up* (e.g., *eat up/burn up/use up*) [Motion verb] *on* (e.g., *walk on/go on out/talk on and on*)
"Complete"	*the whole* [N], *every* [N]; *all* [N/NP]; *not one/not a single* [N]; *not even* [NP]; *ever/never/always* (in VP); *You* [epithet (+N)]!
Isolating particles	*just/only/even/too*

Mitigators (a degree of uncertainty, denial of absolutes: "I **could** be wrong")

Generic	*sort of/ kind of (like)* [Verb] [Adj/Adv] [NP]
I want	*I wish* [+ 2F subjunctive] *I hope* [+ will/can (+) 1F/1F-ing]
I think	*I think* *I guess* } [(that) SVO] *I suppose* *I take it* [it + epistemic modal] (e.g., *it must be the wind.*)
Someone or Something [BE]	*seems* [*to be*] [*as if* SVO] [*like* NP/SVO] *it/he looks/smells/tastes/feels/sounds* [*like*] [*as if*] *would appear to be*
Someone [*state*]	**epistemic modals**: will/must/should/may/might [e.g., *She [will/must/may] have a gun*] +/- **intensifying lexis**: certainly/probably/maybe/possibly [e.g., *He [may possibly]/[will probably] have a gun.*]
Someone [*action*]	**mitigating lexis**: certainly/probably/maybe/possibly [e.g., *She probably ate dinner at 6 o'clock;* *He's certainly coming to school tomorrow.*]

the spectrum of alternatives which are part of sociolinguistic reality. (Crystal, 1996, p. 16)

The methodology described in this section is very much in keeping with that posited by Pally in Chapter 1 in that it relies on training students to look for patterns that are refined and differentiated as they become more familiar with the

---

Figure 5.6 Figuring Out the Sequence

Write the following sentences in the correct order:

How come they float?

There's no qualifying exam to be a dad.

It's evaporated water.

Why are they white when the rest of the sky is blue?

There are some other gases, too.

What are clouds made of?

We ought to look this up.

They're mostly water.

---

content and the text. The sustained text exposes students to the language in its entirety while students use a series of "filters" to initially throw into relief, and later to increasingly refine, their understanding of the underlying regularities they find there. The more students see of the text, the more familiar those regularities become. The teacher's role in this process has been to raise and maintain awareness of pragmatic forms, first by presentation of frameworks (if you don't know to look for something, how can you hope to see it?) and later by intensive questioning, to keep students refining and redefining what they are looking at.

Raising Awareness

Once students have been introduced to the main characters in the textbook, they are given the dialogue from a Calvin and Hobbes strip in random order with all the speech grammar apparatus removed, and asked to order it (see Figure 5.6). Since the text is information dense and full of logical reference (e.g., *they* = *clouds*), it is fairly easy for students to complete this task. They are then given the actual strip (Figure 5.7) to check their results in the dialogue-ordering exercise.

Below the strip are listed all the other words from the original, and students are now asked to consider why these words are there and what they might mean. Naturally, this task is much more difficult (none of the words adds anything to the information being transmitted) and leads to a discussion of how there are two kinds of language: informational and attitudinal. Homework during the first week involves students reading two or three strips a night and identifying which is which. At a certain point, students begin to realize that most of the attitudinal vocabulary occurs either before or after the main grammatical message, and the stage is set to introduce the frameworks described earlier.

Probably the most extensive way to help students analyze the spoken language is to provide frames-for-reference worksheets to filter the language in comic books. The first worksheet, shown in Figure 5.8 (abandoned as soon as practicable), serves to establish the idea of context as intrinsic to language. It requires students to look first and decide on such basics as "Where are these people and what are they doing?", as well as "What is being said beyond the

Figure 5.7   Calvin and Hobbes Cartoon #1

Here is the original text. What do these other words mean?

I'm not sure. / Hey dad, / sort of / I think / Well, / I take it / Maybe / So / I guess / Hmm . . . / So / Heck, beats me. / stuff / I used to know that.

Could any of the words go anywhere else?

Figure 5.8   Comic Book Frame I—Categories

Page #   Strip #

Context (Where? Doing What?)	Body Expressions		Reactions		Vague Words + Meaning (*it/that/so/up/get/do/stuff/thing*)
	Drawing	Meaning	Word/Sound	Emotion	

Confirmation Checks (SVO? *or* [Repetition]?)	Mitigators and Intensifiers	CAPS + Pronunciation *ff* [loud]; # [stress]; ↓, ⇓ [contrast]	"Doing Words" (. . . , SVO. or SVO, . . .)

message?" The answers to the latter question are found through observation of facial expressions and posture that requires students to focus on the nonverbal as well as the verbal. At the same time, students are asked to look for the "noninformational" language: "doing words" (words "comma-ed off" from the sentence), confirmation checks (normal sentences with a question mark), mitigators and intensifiers (words to give an opinion), and capital letters (words said differently). Once looking for noninformational language has become second nature (usually over a couple of weeks), the other frames (Figures 5.9 through 5.11) are introduced as a way to refine the analytic tools. Frames are introduced sequentially: first, Figure 5.9; then, after two weeks, Figure 5.10; and two weeks later, Figure 5.11. Each frame essentially refers to all the noninformational aspects of speech, but in each, one or two elements have been expanded to help students extend the patterns they have initially recognized.

Classroom discussions now center around word choice—around the *why* of utterance rather than the *what* of meaning. Students search the context to find the *reasons* for the words. These discussions may be in the mother tongue at lower levels (if the class has more than one representative of the same language) and may continue to make reference to L1 even at higher levels, though the discussion will be in English. At the same time discussions are going on, the teacher stimulates the process by asking questions to help students actively search for coordinates for a *pragmatic mapping* of L2 on L1, and vice versa. Once the words have been tied in to the context, the next logical step is to ask, "How would this be said in *your* language?" Sometimes students shoot back, "*We* don't say that," which may indeed be the case (though this may betray an unconscious refusal on students' behalf to admit to the "sloppy" aspects of their own language, stemming perhaps from the "received truth" in their culture of "good" language (careful, educated, and error-free) in contrast to "bad" language (lazy, uneducated, and ungrammatical). If indeed there is no pragmatic equivalent for

---

Figure 5.9   Comic Book Frame—II

Marking Language	Quote: (Strip, Frame #)	Meaning

Doing Words:
  Requests: (R)
  Signals:
   Topic Managers(TM)/Comment(C)/Other(O)

Reactions: (*Wow! Nuts. Boy!*)

Intensifiers/mitigators:
(*just/real/great/what a . . . !/kind of/pretty*)

Vb/PP? (*look up/look+up*): Preposition means?
(**ONLY:** *UP / IN / ON / DOWN / THROUGH*)

Confirmation checks (SVO? *or* [REPETITION]?)

It/this/that/them/th*se/[do]/some/so(+stuff/thing[s]) Get

CAPS = *ff*,↓, ⇓, #

Other vocabulary/questions

Figure 5.10 Comic Book Frame—III

Marking Language	Quote: (Strip, Frame #)	Meaning

Doing Words—Requests:
Quick!, Look!, Shut up!, Listen!

Doing Words—Signals: Topic Managers:
so, well, then, I mean, you know, mind you, anyhow/anyway

Doing Words–Signals: Comments:
actually, of course, to tell the truth, as far as I'm concerned

Confirmation Checks: Require(**R!**)/Expect(**E**)/Request(**R?**)

Intensifiers/Mitigators/Reactions

Vague Words: *up/in/on/down/through/get/it/do/some/stuff etc.*

CAPS = *ff*,↓, ⇓, #

Other vocabulary/questions

Figure 5.11 Comic Book Frame—IV

Marking Language	Quote: (Strip, Frame #)	Meaning

Signals (TM): *so, well, then, I mean, you know, sure, anyway*

Signals (C): *actually, of course, to tell the truth, as for me*

Confirmation Checks: Require *Isn't it warm!* ↓

Confirmation Checks: Expect *Isn't it warm?* ↑

Confirmation Checks: Request—Clarify *[REPETITION]?;*
you mean,?

Confirmation Checks: Request—Clarify [+I DON'T BELIEVE
YOU]. *Yeah?!;* ⇑ *Really?!;* ⇑ *I am,* ⇓ *am I?* ⇑

Confirmation Checks: Request—Clarify: [+I DON'T
UNDERSTAND WHY YOU SAID THAT].
[REPETITION] ↓ *So?* ↑ *And?* ↑

Intens./Mitigs./Reacs./Vague/Caps:

---

a lexeme, this still contributes to pragmatic mapping: at least students have become aware that there are contexts where L1 functions differently from the L2 they are learning.

Other questions address other aspects of language:

What is the character thinking (look at the paralinguistics), and how will this affect the way she or he says the words?"

"How would you say this if you were to mitigate it rather than intensify it?" (i.e., "What is a pragmatic opposite, an opposite of effect rather than a lexical opposite?")

Figure 5.12 Calvin and Hobbes Cartoon #2

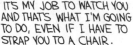

"*How* does this expression mean this in this context?"

"Is this vocabulary useful or not?"

Finally, as the semester progresses, the question of register shifting for ironic or sarcastic effect is raised. Confronted with the strip in Figure 5.12, students are asked to decide why Calvin would speak German in panel 3 and why Rosalyn would use a very polite register in panel 4.

Student Reactions

Students have found working with *Yukon Ho!* challenging but rewarding. In end-of-term evaluations, the words *at first I thought* are usually juxtaposed with *but then I found out.* One Korean student wrote:

> I was surprised when I found out that our textbook was a comic book. . . . At first I was dubious about whether I would really learn much from a comic book. However, I was soon surprised to see how much I was learning from this collection of comic strips.

An Italian student was equally shocked—and impressed:

> I thought it was a simple book for children, but I learned day by day many new words with the help of the figures. . . . I think that this is a good method to learn English with a smile!!!

As more objective evidence of how students individualize and refine their learning process, consider Figure 5.13. This shows one student's mapping of language in the context of the attitudinal frame.

Unlike the earlier frames, this one is much more abstract, with the four "cardinal" attitudinal characteristics in the four corners of the page. While you may not agree with the placement (or even the inclusion) of certain words, you can

Figure 5.13 One Student's Mapping of Mitigators and Intensifiers

	OPINIONS	CLOSE TO	
MITIGATORS	*I guess* we're all packed *I doubt it* we *should* save 'em why *should* I do all this if you're seceding? we *might as well* record our progress		**MITIGATORS**
MIXED	See? I . . . I . . . TRIED it (cough) it . . . *almost* (wheeze) killed . . . me for THIS amazing trick I need an *ordinary* American Express card we *probably* won't get to Northern Canada until this afternoon Why should I do *all* this if you're seceding? I guess we're *all* packed double rations for *all* officers I'm not going *at all* This won't take any time *at all* The *only* reason Mom and Dad are my parents is because I was BORN to them! We've *only* been walking twenty minutes You *only* packed two sandwiches?		**MIXED**
INTENSIFIERS	*Geez!* what kind of mom are you! If you were littler than me, *boy* I'd pound you! energy *to spare* a long way *away* This is *the last straw!* Look *how close it is!* it's been nice . . . but not *REAL* nice	you *just* stole my helmet we *just* have one apiece I wasn't *even* consulted We don't *even* have a car our *entire* trip your *own* family	**INTENSIFIERS**
	VERY MUCH	**EXACTLY/COMPLETELY**	

Source: Based on language in Watterson (1989), pp. 54–58.

see that the student included words according to a consistent set of rules: words go together and are contrasted with one another while placed in the "absolute matrix" of intensification and mitigation. Needless to say, this midterm classification was later modified in light of the student's exposure to further examples of language within the attitudinal frame. By retaining these records of how his classification system had developed, over the course of the semester the student was able to refer back to them constantly and thus monitor how and why his classification system evolved.

Conclusion

Such continuous comparison of language with language in given contexts lays the foundation for students to develop an awareness of spoken contrastive rhetoric. As the semester progresses, they open up to the idea that spoken language is subtle and multifaceted, and that with the right tools to help them observe and infer, they can become well equipped to analyze and extrapolate from language they will encounter in the multiple contexts of their student world. As they become aware of language in more and more sophisticated contexts, they learn to map spoken English rhetorical conventions onto those of their own L1, actively "noticing" the *variation* inherent in English and in spoken English in particular.

And along the way, they are taking an important first step toward acquiring the skills of inductive reasoning, skills that will serve them well in any academic situations they encounter in the future.

So does a chapter on speaking have a place in a book about using sustained content to teach academic discourse? You betcha! And how!

References

Brazil, D. (1993). Telling tales. In J. M. Sinclair, M. Hoey, & G. Fox (Eds.), *Techniques of description: Spoken and written discourse. A* festschrift *for Malcolm Coulthard* (pp. 154–169). New York: Routledge.

Brazil, D. (1995). *A grammar of speech*. Oxford, UK: Oxford University Press.

Carter, R., & McCarthy, M. J. (1995). Grammar and the spoken language. *Applied Linguistics, 16*(2), 141–158.

Crystal, D. (1996). Language matters: Reflecting linguistic change. *The Teacher Trainer, 10*(1), 15–16.

Geluykens, R. (1992). *From discourse process to grammatical construction: On left dislocation in English*. Philadelphia: John Benjamins.

Geluykens, R. (1994). *The pragmatics of discourse anaphora in English: Evidence from conversational repair*. New York: Mouton de Gruyter.

Grice, H. P. (1975). Logic and conversation. In P. Cole & J. Morgan (Eds.), *Syntax and semantics: Vol. 3. Speech acts*. New York: Academic Press.

Johns, A. (1997). *Text, role, and context: Developing academic literacies*. New York: Cambridge University Press.

Lakoff, G., & Johnson, M. (1980). *Metaphors we live by*. Chicago: University of Chicago Press.

Lewis, M. (1993). *The lexical approach: The state of ELT and a way forward*. Hove, UK: Language Teaching Publications.

McCarthy, M. J., & Carter, R. (1995). Spoken grammar: What is it and how can we teach it? *English Language Teaching Journal, 49*(3), 207–218.

Nattinger, J. R., & DeCarrico, J. S. (1992). *Lexical phrases in language teaching*. Oxford, UK: Oxford University Press.

Sacks, H., Schegloff, E., & Jefferson, G. (1974). A simplest systematics for the organization of turn-taking for conversation. *Language, 50*(4), 696–735.

Sinclair, J. M., & Coulthard, M. (1975). *Towards an analysis of discourse.* London: Oxford University Press.

Spack, R. (1988). Initiating ESL students into the academic discourse community; How far should we go? *TESOL Quarterly, 22*(1), 29–51.

Sperber, D., & Wilson, D. (1986). *Relevance.* Cambridge, MA: Harvard University Press.

Stenström, A.-B. (1991). Expletives in the London-Lund corpus. In K. Aijmer & B. Altenberg (Eds.), *English corpus linguistics—studies in honour of Jan Svartvik* (pp. 239–253). London: Longman.

Tsui, A. B. M. (1994). *English conversation.* Oxford, UK: Oxford University Press.

van Lier, L. (1996). *Interaction in the language curriculum: Awareness, autonomy & authenticity.* New York: Longman.

Watterson, B. (1989). *Yukon Ho!: A Calvin and Hobbes collection.* Kansas City, MO: Andrews & McMeel.

Willis, D. (1993). Grammar and lexis: Some pedagogical implications. In J. M. Sinclair, M. Hoey, & G. Fox (Eds.), *Techniques of description: Spoken and written discourse. A festschrift for Malcolm Coulthard* (pp. 83–93). New York: Routledge.

Chapter 6

Critical Thinking Development and Academic Writing for Engineering Students

Lynne Flowerdew

Hong Kong University of Science and Technology

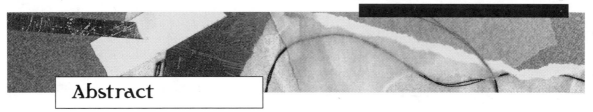

Abstract

This chapter describes how a technical communication skills course for engineering students has been designed with the main aim of developing the type of critical thinking skills necessary for academic study at the tertiary level.[1] These skills are developed initially through reading exercises based on the discipline-specific engineering content that students will be expected to produce in their content courses. Students then carry out a discipline-related ESP project that demands the application of these cognitive skills to an in-depth writing task. Because the linguistic dimension is also important, key language functions and structures are introduced within the contextualized framework of the report. The cognitive pedagogy outlined in this chapter, which is developed through sustained content-based teaching, can better equip students to cope with the interdependent cognitive and linguistic demands they encounter in their academic disciplines. ∎

---

[1]I wish to thank Marcia Pally for her valuable comments on an earlier version of this paper.

Introduction

Certain terms abound in the literature on needs analysis and syllabus design in the area of ESP (English for Specific Purposes): EAP (English for Academic Purposes), EST (English for Science and Technology), EOP (English for Occupational Purposes), and the more recently coined term EPC (English for Professional Communication). This chapter argues that in an academic or a workplace setting where English is used as the medium of instruction or communication, underlying these "academic," "occupational," or "professional" purposes is the notion of EIP (English for Intellectual Purposes) (Ballard, 1996; Ballard & Clanchy, 1991), which I take to mean cognitive ability—that is, critical thinking skills. What counts as "intellectual" obviously differs from one culture to another, but here the term refers to those critical thinking skills associated with the British and American traditions of rhetorical practices (but see Atkinson [1997] and Swales [1998], who argue that because these skills are a form of social practice, their imposition on other cultures can be regarded as a type of academic imperialism). The following glossary definition provided by Gardner (1996) is consonant with Ballard's concept of critical thinking skills:

> *Critical thinking:* Looking beneath the surface of words to understand a writer's meaning and intention. Critical thinking involves *analysis, synthesis,* and *evaluation.* (p. 271)

Gardner elaborates on this definition as follows:

> *Analysis:* A type of *critical thinking* involving the division of something into its parts and an explanation of their relationship to the whole. (p. 269)

> *Synthesis:* A type of *critical thinking* involving the combination of ideas in a way that shows the relationships among them. (p. 276)

> *Evaluation:* A type of critical thinking whereby one judges the significance or worth of something. (p. 272)

Many writing practitioners have emphasized the need to develop students' critical thinking skills in the EAP language classroom. Ballard (1996) highlights the importance of developing such analytical approaches to learning at the tertiary level, where students are expected to show in their academic courses that they can "systematically organize their ideas and the evidence they have selected into an argument that will produce an intellectually satisfying evaluation of some controversial topic" (p. 161). With this emphasis on critical thinking skills, language instruction at the tertiary level should not be relegated to the teaching of correct linguistic structures and manipulation of genre conventions, but in addition should focus on language as a tool for the kind of thinking required in academic classes. Ballard and Clanchy (1991) also maintain that such skills are essential for students to become socialized into a university learning culture. Other prominent writing researchers (see, for example, Belcher, 1995; Bunker, 1992; Cumming, 1995; Swales & Feak, 1995) have also emphasized the value of focusing on higher-order cognitive skills in EAP.

Developing these skills is of prime importance in the field of science and technology, where writing demands higher-order cognitive skills involving analysis and interpretation of experimental results, and relating these to underlying theory:

> Time after time, teachers in ESP for Science or Engineering feel that they need to perform a double function for their students. The first is to teach correct English, as defined by grammar, lexis, vocabulary, sentence structure, and, at advanced levels, elements of style. The second function teachers become aware of is the need for what is loosely labelled as teaching students "how to think." (Bunker, 1992, p. 229)

Ballard (1996) further remarks on the problems first-year undergraduates encounter in learning how to think critically and analytically since they are used to a more reproductive learning style in school, where the learning strategies focus on memorization and imitation. She points out that these problems are further compounded for students from Asian learning backgrounds, which emphasize rote learning and respect for the authority of the teacher and tend to discourage critical questioning of the teacher or the text.

It would seem that, as at the secondary school level, tertiary preparation programs are failing to equip students with "thinking skills." Leki and Carson (1997) comment on the cognitively unchallenging nature of most EAP writing classes: "Hearing ESL students repeatedly describe writing classes as friendly but not intellectually challenging . . . is alarming and disheartening and calls for, we believe, deeper reflection on how we as teachers ask our students to spend their time" (p. 64). Their interviews with EAP students reveal that students are writing without responsibility for the content of source texts, whereas they are held responsible for the content in their disciplinary courses. Braine (1989) makes the obvious but much neglected point that if academic writing is to be taught successfully, EFL/ESP teachers have to be aware of the type of writing students undertake in their major disciplines. EAP classes therefore should require students to engage intellectually with the type of subject matter they will have to grapple with in their content courses. As Johns (1997) remarks in her comments on the similarities between CBI and ESP:

> Practitioners in both movements recognize that language classroom activities should be designed to assist students in interacting with content and discourse in cognitively demanding ways, or at the very least in ways that are similar in use to those in the target language situation. (p. 364)

Another aspect of developing critical thinking skills using content-based material is the *sustained* nature of the instruction, meaning students acquire and refine these thinking skills through extensive practice over a period of time (see Chapter 1 of this volume). Building on Ballard's concept of EIP, this chapter describes how an ESP course for higher-intermediate, second-year, undergraduate engineering students at a tertiary institution in Hong Kong has been designed to develop students' critical thinking skills by drawing on aspects of the sustained CBI theoretical underpinning outlined above. The primary aim of this course is to help second-year engineering students write up their final-year engineering project reports (FYPs), which gives the course a very specific focus. To complete the FYP, students must be able to perform such academic subtasks as using secondary source material to write a literature review, summarizing, paraphrasing, and so forth. Therefore, this course has much in common with the linked adjunct model of CBI (see Brinton, Snow, & Wesche, 1989; Snow & Brinton, 1997) in that the primary purposes of both are to "introduce students to L2 academic discourse and develop transferable skills" (Brinton, Snow, & Wesche, 1989, p. 19). See Brinton and Master (1997) for examples of critical thinking activities that introduce students to the L2 academic discourse of CBI.

In this sustained CBI model, however, the content is dealt with in the ESP classroom and is not adjuncted; rather than running in parallel and closely interlocking with the content courses, the course exploits FYPs from content classes given in previous semesters as reading material to prepare students for those very same assignments they will be undertaking in six months' time.

The following sections of this chapter describe the rationale for the ESP course, followed by an overview of the research project students complete, which is designed in part to simulate an engineering project from the students' own subject discipline. The second part of the chapter provides examples of content-based reading and exercises in the course, followed by an illustration of the kind of written output students produce. Finally, the chapter considers the role of language instruction in a course in which this is not the primary aim.

Rationale for the ESP Course

A recently completed English-language needs analysis (Noakes & Wong, 1997) targeting the academic needs of engineering students and the engineering departmental guidelines for the final-year projects provide ample justification for focusing on the development of students' critical thinking skills. The needs analysis reports that both students and lecturers have identified students' lack of ability in organizing FYP content as a key area needing improvement. Interestingly, the subject lecturers comment that this is not solely a linguistic problem but is also a pedagogical one, as students lack adequate training in organizing and articulating ideas and information according to English-language conventions of logic and clarity. Students' inability to function in an academic environment where the medium of instruction is English is due not only to linguistic deficiencies but also to a lack of awareness of the discourse structure of academic texts. This suggests that students do not possess the critical thinking skills necessary to produce the "linear" kind of analytical writing required for academic study in English.

After examining this needs analysis, I also examined the Final Year Project departmental guidelines (1996) for the engineering projects in content classes to ascertain the types of strategies and skills students require. These guidelines call for a first chapter that describes the problem under investigation and provides general background material and an overview of the project, including the solutions explored. The section of the guidelines on project accomplishments asks, "How creative and motivated is the student (or team) in finding interesting solutions to problems?" (p. 4). The identification of this problem/solution structure for the report (see Hoey, 1983, for a detailed description of this discourse pattern in written text), coupled with the emphasis on creative/interesting solutions, shows that the report is analytical rather than purely descriptive, demanding the application of critical thinking skills and an ability to search for new possibilities and explanations. Interestingly, the report guidelines also warn against an overly descriptive (i.e., reproductive, using Ballard & Clanchy's term) approach as they caution the student not to include excess background material and redundant results, which suggests that this is an area of weakness in students' writing.

Having established that the main objective of the ESP course is to equip students with critical thinking skills to help them with the writing of their FYPs in their content courses, the next step was to identify suitable material to achieve this goal. Since the cognitive skills outlined earlier can be regarded not only as a general set of critical thinking skills necessary for English-language requirements but also as discipline specific, they can best be developed through using relevant subject matter. A decision therefore was made to utilize the content-based material from the discipline courses—that is, very good models of the FYPs—as reading material for cognitive skills development in the ESP classroom. This sustained content thus provides meaningful and useful subject matter for skills-based instruction in a context with which students can identify. As Pally points out in Chapter 1 of this volume, "A cyclical, synergistic relationship exists between content and critical thinking skills: in order to learn content, students must learn critical thinking skills, but in order to learn these skills, students must study content that is complex and enduring enough that argumentation and rhetorical conventions can be identified, practiced, and questioned."

Comparison and Contrast of ESP Project and FYP

This section gives an overview of the type of research project students produce in the ESP course and compares it with the FYP from the content courses. It also discusses similarities and differences between the two projects and the reasons for them. Both the ESP project and the final-year engineering project are similar in that they are groupwork (usually three to four students in each group) and rely on a problem/solution organizational macrostructure. Both types of projects also span several months. This *sustained* nature of the instructional process is, as reflected by the title of this volume, a prerequisite for the skills developed in this course, as students can hone their critical thinking skills and analytical writing ability only through continual reflection and revision of their work over a period of time. Both projects are design-based in that they either report on the construction of or evaluate a mechanism or system. However, they differ somewhat in the identification of an initial problem, need, or demand prompting the investigation and in the analysis of the design process (i.e., solution), which is explained in detail next.

In the FYPs, students are expected to identify a real-life problem, need, or demand. Indeed, some FYPs, most notably those in the mechanical engineering field, are sponsored financially by outside bodies with interests in specific, real-world engineering problems. So identifying an appropriate "real-world" problem would be a particularly important aspect for reports that fall into this category. In response to this identified problem, need, or demand, students construct a mechanism/system as a solution, test it, and determine if it meets the design specifications. For example, past projects have explored the development of a seawater treatment system for seafood restaurants. Hong Kong has a large number of seafood restaurants, and many of them keep the live seafood in tanks with water taken from the harbor, which is polluted. Thus, the need for a water treatment system for restaurants to keep their seafood in a contamination-free environment has been established, and the design of such a system provides a solution.

The ESP research project has also been designed to mirror the problem/solution organizational macrostructure of the FYPs. The main components of this project are as follows:

- Choosing an area for investigation
- Identifying a problem/need/demand within this area
- Collecting data from primary and secondary sources to provide evidence of the problem (e.g., interviews, observations, survey questionnaires)
- Analyzing and interpreting the data collected from secondary and primary sources
- Stating implications, making recommendations, and putting forth a design proposal

The ESP projects resemble the FYPs in that students are encouraged to choose an area for investigation from their own subject disciplines. For example, computer science/computer engineering students have chosen to investigate the need to computerize the university's manual booking system for the sports facilities or the provision of software and hardware in the university computer labs. However, whereas in the FYPs the problem statement is usually outlined in one or two paragraphs in the introduction section of the report, in the ESP project it constitutes a section on its own in which the need for the project is demonstrated by various primary source data. For example, to investigate deficiencies in the manual booking system for the sports facilities, students design and administer survey questionnaires, carry out observations of the booking system, and interview personnel from the sports section.

Although it may seem rather unusual to cover these data collection methods, which tend to be associated with humanities and social science courses, in an ESP course aimed at engineering students, I believe the following reasons provide fairly strong grounds for doing so. First, some FYPs (albeit only a few) do require students to collect evidence from primary sources. For example, in the project on the seawater treatment system for seafood restaurants, students had to contact various seafood restaurant owners to arrange interviews with them and administer surveys on the water quality in the restaurants' fish tanks. Second, engineering students' oral communicative abilities are weak. Employers of recent graduates have commented that although these students are very hardworking and have a responsible attitude toward work, they tend to lack interpersonal skills and are not proactive in establishing contacts in an outside workplace situation, such as when meeting potential clients at a software exhibition fair. By collecting these primary source data to justify their choice of project, students will thus have an opportunity to improve their oral communication skills. Third, many computer science/computer engineering students enter the software design field after graduation and could well be expected to design and administer questionnaires for improvement of the programs. Finally, I view the construction of a survey questionnaire as an additional means for honing students' critical thinking skills, as experience shows that students have considerable difficulty organizing their survey questions in a logical and coherent manner.

Let us now consider how the FYP and ESP project differ as to the solution aspect of the reports. As stated previously, FYPs concentrate on the conceptualization, construction, and testing of a design project or system. ESP projects design a solution to a problem, but, in contrast to FYPs, the design is a "notional" one; that is, it is a detailed proposal rather than the execution of an actual design. For example, with regard to the ESP project on computerizing the sports facilities booking system, the students put forth a detailed proposal on the necessary hardware and software configurations for computerizing the system, but do not actually implement the system; their proposal is addressed to the university's CCST (Centre of Computer Services and Telecommunications) in the form of a recommendation report or proposal.

Thus, this ESP project relies on content-based FYPs as reading input for the course and as models for the written reports. But the written output, while similar to the FYPs in terms of the overall problem/solution structure, deals with the problem and solution from a rather different perspective. In Widdowson's (1993) words, therefore, this task-based ESP project is "discipline referred rather than discipline specific" (p. 35), and students engage in activities "which are not directly *derived* from disciplines, but *contrived* from them in reference to their basic principles of design and more general generic features" (p. 35). However, in spite of these differences, I would like to maintain, and hope to illustrate in the following sections, that the ESP course develops the same kind of critical thinking skills—namely synthesis, analysis, and evaluation—that will be called on for the writing of FYPs.

I will now explain why my college has implemented this sustained CBI model rather than the linked adjunct one. As Brinton, Snow, and Wesche (1989) state, a full-fledged linked adjunct model is an ambitious undertaking that requires a large amount of coordination to ensure the smooth running of the parallel discipline-specific and CBI courses. Snow (1993) also refers to the extra administrative support for coordination time or release time necessary to run the course. Such CBI programs, while of proven benefit to students (Kasper, 1997), are time-consuming and impose an extra burden on teachers who have to respond daily to the material presented in the content courses (Brinton, 1997). Unfortunately, when language teachers have a heavy teaching load (which involves preparation, grading time, and consultation with students outside class), it often is not practical to implement such a course.

Another reason for not implementing a fully linked adjunct model is that many teachers shy away from teaching such a course because they feel uncomfortable with the technical aspect. This problem is partly avoided in our modified course because the content of the reading material (FYPs from earlier se-mesters) is accessible to ESP teachers. This is a different situation from that of teachers in the adjunct course, who have no choice in the technical material they are required to cover. Although understanding of technical content is necessary for the proposed solution in the ESP project, the teacher's task is to help students organize the technical information rather than supply it. Students are expected to check with a subject lecturer or technology administrator to ensure that their proposal is technically sound as well as operationally and economically feasible. For example, the students who are proposing computerization of the sports booking facilities would arrange an interview with a technology administrator from the university's CCST to double-check any technical details. This has the added advantage of providing extra oral practice for students, who, as stated previously, need to improve their oral communication abilities.

From the students' perspective, this course has been well received. Students have commented on their end-of-course evaluation forms that this course has been very useful in teaching them report writing, although further follow-up is necessary to ascertain to what extent they are capable of applying these skills to the writing of the FYP in their final year of study. Students have also said that they appreciate the interactive, "hands-on" nature of the project, which is practically based and involves them in a variety of both oral and written communication tasks. On the negative side, though, they have criticized the data collection (for evidence of a problem) as being very time consuming. Some also have misgivings about working with three other group members, claiming it is difficult to find a mutually convenient time to meet to discuss their ESP project. However, in spite of these logistical issues, the main motivating factor for these projects is that students perceive them as "real-life" projects. As with FYPs, students write in response to an actual, proven need and to a specified audience rather than an imaginary one. The best ESP projects are sent to the departments concerned, and in several cases a department has responded to students' concerns by implementing their proposals.

Developing Critical Thinking Skills in an ESP Writing Context

Stage 1: Reading Input

To select suitable material for the ESP course, the engineering faculty was asked to provide the Language Centre with what they considered to be very good models of FYPs. These reports were used as reading samples for students, but were edited to correct some mechanical and minor content and organizational errors, and compiled into an in-house Language Centre ESP textbook. Although all the examples of material in this chapter are from the field of computer science, discipline-specific material for each engineering field (e.g., electronic and electrical engineering, civil and structural engineering, chemical engineering, mechanical engineering) has been produced and includes the exercise template described below. Each unit in the in-house textbook takes students through all the main sections of the final-year project report—Abstract, Introduction, Literature Review,

Results, Results Analysis, and Conclusion—for one engineering field. The first unit in the textbook deals with introductions. After working through various reading/controlled writing exercises designed to familiarize students with the rhetorical conventions of introductions, students apply what they have learned to writing the introductions of their ESP projects.

For example, Appendix A is an extract from the introduction section of a computer science report. Some key words/phrases have been deleted, and here the blanks in the original exercise are indicated by underlining. The reading task requires students to do two things: fill in the blanks in the extract and complete the outline in Appendix B of the generic structure of the introduction. Since the needs analysis highlighted the difficulty students have in organizing their writing, I believed that using this "move structure" generic model (Swales, 1990), which focuses on the microfunctions of the various sections of the report, would aid them.

This genre-based framework is also an ideal vehicle through which to develop students' critical thinking skills. For example, in Appendix B, the *Need for Project* section requires students to analyze the reasons for the inadequacy of the traditional keyboard interface method. In the *Value of Study* section, students have to evaluate their proposed new interface method by putting forward its potential benefits. In the *Gap in Research* section, students are expected to synthesize information from different sources to show how their research project extends present research in the area. Appendix C provides an answer key for this exercise.

Students learn to develop the other main sections of the FYP (Literature Review, Results, Results Analysis, and Conclusion) in a similar manner, using reading samples of those sections from "real" FYPs and a variety of exercise types (e.g., jumbled paragraphs, information gap). As class time is limited, I have suggested to students that they also try to read a wider selection of FYPs from previous years, which are kept in either the university library or departmental libraries. I have explained to them that the greater their awareness of the genre conventions of each section of the FYP, the easier they should find it to produce such writing.

The following section explains how the critical thinking skills of analysis, evaluation, and synthesis are further developed in a typical project outline produced by students.

Stage 2: Project Outline

The approach taken to drafting, redrafting, and writing up the ESP research project is very much a process-based one. Before students embark on writing up their project, they are required to produce an outline and have several one-on-one consultation sessions with their language instructor to refine and edit its content and organizational structure. In this preliminary writing stage, students are expected to apply, and further develop, the critical thinking skills they acquired in the reading stage. When students have produced a reasonably detailed outline, and before they begin writing up their project, I have introduced a presentation stage where students defend their outlines as an additional means of honing their critical thinking skills. Each project group gives copies of their outline to the other project groups, who ask for clarification or elaboration on the outline content in a 15-minute question-and-answer session for each group. The following sections examine a typical student outline to demonstrate in greater detail the subskills within the critical thinking skills—analysis, evaluation, and synthesis—needed to produce an outline such as the one in Appendix D.

Analysis The skill of analysis, which involves dividing a topic into various parts and then considering their relationship to the whole, is developed through giving students practice in the following subskills (adapted from Bunker, 1992): distinguishing relevant from nonrelevant information, understanding conceptual divisions of a subject and its subdivisions, distinguishing more essential from less essential information and ordering this information appropriately, and looking below the surface of text to make inferences, offer explanations, and so on. This sorting of information into logical, discrete categories can be represented through sets of headings and subheadings similar to those in Appendix D (see Flowerdew, 1998/1999, for an overview of this cognitive skills pedagogy).

1. *Distinguishing relevant from nonrelevant information*. This feature mainly concerns the scope of the project and the background section. In the project in Appendix D, for example, students must ensure that any information following the "scope" is related to the student dial-up service and the use of this service during the semester; otherwise their writing will contain irrelevancies. The background section is also of concern here, as students tend to include too much descriptive information that is unrelated to the scope of the project, an observation also made in the departmental guidelines for the engineering projects.

2. *Understanding conceptual divisions of a subject and its subdivisions*. Students often have difficulty formulating appropriate topical subheadings, especially for the *Major areas of investigation* section, indicating a limited grasp of conceptual subdivisions. Conceptual divisions can be examined through their use of subheadings, and the content students supply for the subheadings acts as a check on whether they understand these conceptual divisions.

3. *Distinguishing more essential from less essential information and ordering it appropriately*. In the *Major areas of investigation* section, one would expect utilization of the service to be the most important consideration in order to ascertain the high demand, and therefore mentioned first.

4. *Looking below the surface of the text to make inferences, offer explanations, etc*. In a corpus-based study of 90 ESP project reports similar to the one analyzed here (Flowerdew, 1997), I found that the results and discussion sections focused mainly on reporting and describing the data and lacked adequate explanations and interpretation of the data collected. Likewise, the needs analysis (Noakes & Wong, 1997) also recommends that students need practice in writing skills that focus on the interpretation of results and conclusion sections to help them write up their lab reports. In this outline, students are required to provide explanations for their findings. For example, the higher usage rate of the dial-up service among engineering students

can be explained by the greater frequency of computer-related assignments in engineering compared with business.

Evaluation Evaluation, in which one judges the significance or worth of the project, is done by judging the evidence provided by the data in the *Major areas of investigation* section to arrive at a logical conclusion from which to propose suitable solutions. This evaluation task also hones students' critical thinking skills, since they must attend to the overall coherence of the outline and ensure that any proposed solutions are adequate ones for the problems identified in the previous section of the report. Within this section, students are also expected to evaluate the feasibility of their proposed solutions, by considering the drawbacks and advantages of each one, to arrive at a sound recommendation or to propose a combination of recommendations.

Synthesis Synthesis involves combining two types of content—primary and secondary sources—to show the relationships among ideas as well as content in different sections of the report. First, it involves the integration of primary sources—observations, interviews, and survey questionnaires (indicated in italics between brackets in Appendix D) with secondary sources (indicated in bold between brackets). This type of synthesis can be either at a macro level (different sources for different sections within one outline) or a micro level (different sources within one section). At the macro level, the Centre of Computing Services and Telecommunications (CCST) newsletter contains information relevant for the *Background* section, whereas a survey questionnaire is the main source for obtaining data for the *Major areas of investigation* section. At a more micro level (i.e., within the *Utilization* section, the peak versus nonpeak hours can be ascertained via the questionnaire responses, which can also be verified from CCST's graph printouts of utilization rates for the modem pool.

In addition to considering *synthesis* as the combining of both primary and secondary sources, I use the term to refer to synthesis of content across sections. Students should be encouraged to look for correlations in the data and patterns of similarities and differences (e.g., is there any correlation between the level of satisfaction with the service and the types of problems mentioned in the *Major areas of investigation* section?). In this particular project, students found that the greater the number of problems reported, the lower the level of satisfaction with the service, which they commented on as follows: "Not surprisingly, the more problems students reported, the less favorable they were toward the service."

Although I have considered analysis, evaluation, and synthesis as discrete categories for ease of discussion, in reality these features operate interdependently, as "the whole is more than the sum of its parts." For example, examining correlations among different sets of data involves both synthesis and analysis.

Stage 3: Written Output

This section demonstrates students' grasp of the critical thinking skills outlined earlier by comparing their writing on the ESP course with similar writing from an FYP. If we compare the introduction from an ESP report (Appendix E) with

Chapter 6   Critical Thinking Development and Academic Writing for Engineering Students the exemplar report in Appendix A, we can see that, apart from minor differences in organizational structure and the use of subheadings, the two reports are very similar in terms of their generic structure and, consequently, the critical thinking skills employed to produce this type of academic writing. Each report sets the scene with a short, introductory paragraph giving some general background information. Each then moves on to an analysis of some inadequacy in the present situation, which provides the need/justification for the project:

Appendix A

Traditionally, humans interface with the computer via the keyboard. However, training is required before one can become familiar with the keyboard. . . . Sometimes the keyboard is too bulky to use when portable applications are needed.

Appendix E

As the number of UST students has been increasing gradually in recent years, the demand for this service has become higher. However, it is inconvenient for those students who need to access the network frequently for academic purposes to do their work on the system since most of the time the modem pools are difficult to connect to.

Both introductions continue with an evaluation of the proposed or modified system, which will, of course, be expanded on in the body of the report:

Appendix A

Thus, there is a great demand for a natural and user-friendly communication system. The most natural and efficient way to communicate is via speech.

Appendix E

Hence a better, more reliable and secure network is needed.

As mentioned previously, the FYP and ESP projects differ in terms of their orientation toward an engineering design: the FYP projects describe the actual construction of a mechanism or system, whereas the ESP projects put forward a detailed proposal for possible implementation. However, in spite of these differences, the overall generic "move structure" is very similar in that both reports would consider various aspects of feasibility criteria (e.g., technical, economic, environmental) and thus hone discipline-specific critical thinking skills.

Linguistic Dimension

The main focus of this ESP research project is on developing the critical thinking skills students will need for their subject discipline projects, but what role does language have to play? In fact, many practitioners consider language to be distinct from writing competence, which involves the application of the cognitive processes discussed in this chapter.

Teachers as well as students need to recognize that writing competence and linguistic competence are different. Writing competence encompasses knowledge about writing and writing strategies, which is reflected in the overall coherence of the text. Linguistic competence is knowledge of language code and is reflected in the lexical and grammatical aspects of the text. (Mitchell Scott, 1996, p. 18)

In this critical thinking pedagogical approach, although the main aim is to improve students' writing competence, it is also necessary to focus on language work. To accomplish this, it is critical that students simulate a project, such as the one described in this chapter, that is complex enough to warrant practice in these different but complementary skills. When reviewing the content and organizational aspects of the students' outlines, the teacher can also introduce the grammatical choices available for key rhetorical functions. For example, with regard to the analytical skill, the language for offering explanations (e.g., "This can be accounted for by the fact that . . . "; "This may be due to . . . ") can be introduced in the discussion section of the report, where students discuss which particular modal choice would be the most appropriate one. In a corpus-based study of cause-and-effect markers (Flowerdew, 1998) I found that students failed to mitigate causal expressions, overusing the phrase "It is because . . . " when the context called for a more tentative phrase. To illustrate, in the case of the dial-up service, students can be asked to suggest possible reasons for the low/high level of satisfaction with the service. Such reasons, although valid, would still be expressed using modality phrases such as "This is probably due to the fact that . . . " or "This could be attributed to . . . ," since they are based on the students' own analysis and interpretation of the data. However, when positing reasons for the difficulty in connecting to the dial-up service (e.g., heavy demand during peak hours), such reasons would be worded more strongly—for example, "This is because . . . " or "This can be accounted for by the fact that . . . " —since they comprise part of the factual data collected from primary or secondary sources. This type of contextualized grammar work can be done with a wide range of grammatical and rhetorical structures throughout the development of the ESP project.

Conclusion

This chapter has emphasized the central role that the refining of students' critical thinking skills should play in the design of ESP courses. For engineering students, these critical thinking skills of analysis, evaluation, and synthesis can perhaps best be developed initially through reading exercises based on the discipline-specific engineering content that students will be expected to produce. In the writing stage, students carry out an ESP project that to some extent mirrors the engineering FYP, and thus tests whether they can apply these cognitive skills to an in-depth writing task. However, in addition to writing competence, linguistic competence is important, and key language functions or structures are introduced within the contextualized framework of the report. It is thus the author's contention that the cognitive pedagogy outlined in this chapter can serve as a means of developing students' intellectual and linguistic ability simultaneously, thereby better equipping them to cope with the interdependent cognitive and linguistic demands made of them in their academic disciplines.

References

Atkinson, D. (1997). A critical approach to critical thinking in TESOL. *TESOL Quarterly, 31*(1), 71–94.

Ballard, B. (1996). Through language to learning: Preparing overseas students for study in Western universities. In H. Coleman (Ed.), *Society and the Language Classroom* (pp. 148–168). Cambridge, UK: Cambridge University Press.

Ballard, B., & Clanchy, J. (1991). Assessment by misconception: Cultural influences and intellectual traditions. In L. Hamp-Lyons (Ed.), *Assessing second language writing in academic contexts* (pp. 19–35). Norwood, NJ: Ablex.

Belcher, D. (1995). Writing critically across the curriculum. In D. Belcher & G. Braine (Eds.), *Academic writing in a second language* (pp. 135–154). Norwood, NJ: Ablex.

Braine, G. (1989). Writing in science and technology: An analysis of assignments from ten undergraduate courses. *English for Specific Purposes, 8,* 3–15.

Brinton, M. (1997). The challenges of administering content-based programs. In M. Snow & D. Brinton (Eds.), *The content-based classroom* (pp. 340–346). White Plains, NY: Addison Wesley Longman.

Brinton, M., & Master, P. (Eds.) (1997). *New ways in content-based instruction.* Alexandria, VA: TESOL.

Brinton, M., Snow, M., & Wesche, M. (1989). *Content-based second language instruction.* Boston: Heinle & Heinle.

Bunker, V. (1992). Thinking skills in English for professional purposes: Parameters and implementation. In T. Boswood, R. Hoffman, & P. Tung (Eds.), *English for professional communication* (pp. 229–245). Hong Kong: Department of English, City University of Hong Kong.

Cumming, A. (1995). Fostering writing expertise in ESL composition instruction: Modeling and evaluation. In D. Belcher & G. Braine (Eds.), *Academic writing in a second language* (pp. 375–397). Norwood, NJ.: Ablex.

Final Year Project: Final Report Guidelines. (1996). Departments of Electrical and Electronic Engineering and Computer Engineering, Hong Kong University of Science and Technology.

Flowerdew, L. (1997). Interpersonal strategies: Investigating interlanguage corpora. *RELC Journal, 28*(1), 72–88.

Flowerdew, L. (1998). Integrating expert and interlanguage computer corpora findings on causality: Discoveries for teachers and students. *English for Specific Purposes, 17*(4), 329–345.

Flowerdew, L. (1998/1999). Developing critical thinking skills in ESP. *TESOL Matters:* TESOL Publications.

Gardner, P. S. (1996). *New directions: An integrated approach to reading, writing, and critical thinking.* New York: St. Martin's Press.

Hoey, M. (1983). *On the surface of discourse.* London: George Allen & Unwin.

Johns, A. (1997). *Text, role, and context.* Cambridge, UK: Cambridge University Press.

Kasper, L. (1997). The impact of content-based instructional programs on the academic progress of ESL students. *English for Specific Purposes, 16*(4), 309–320.

Leki, I., & Carson, J. (1997). "Completely different worlds": EAP and the writing experiences of ESL students in university courses. *TESOL Quarterly, 31*(1), 39–69.

Mitchell Scott, V. (1996). *Rethinking foreign language writing.* Boston: Heinle & Heinle.

Noakes, N., & Wong, K. (1997). *English language needs analysis.* Language Centre, Hong Kong University of Science and Technology.

Snow, M. (1993). Discipline-based foreign language teaching: Implications from ESL/EFL. In M. Kreuger & F. Ryan (Eds.), *Language and content* (pp. 37–56). Lexington, MA: D. C. Heath.

Snow, M., & Brinton, D. (Eds.) (1997). *The content-based classroom.* White Plains, NY: Addison Wesley Longman.

Snow, M., Met, M., & Genesee, F. (1989). A conceptual framework for the integration of language and content in second/foreign language instruction. *TESOL Quarterly, 23*(2), 201–217.

Swales, J. (1990). *Genre analysis: English in academic and research settings.* Cambridge, UK: Cambridge University Press.

Swales, J. (1998). Language, science and scholarship. *Asian Journal of English Language Teaching, 8,* 19–40.

Swales, J., & Feak, C. (1995). From information transfer to data commentary. *Functional approaches to written text: Classroom applications. TESOL France, 2*(2), 79–93.

Widdowson, H. (1993). The relevant conditions of language use and learning. In M. Kreuger & F. Ryan (Eds.), *Language and content* (pp. 27–36). Lexington, MA: D. C. Heath.

Continuous Cantonese Speech Recognition System

1. Introduction

1.1   Introduction

Traditionally, humans interface with the computer via the keyboard. However, training is required before one can become familiar with the keyboard. Moreover, there are occasions when <u>one's hands are occupied and are not free to use the keyboard</u>, for example, when driving. Sometimes the keyboard is too bulky to use when <u>portable applications are needed</u>. Thus, there is a great demand for a natural and <u>user-friendly</u> communication system. The most natural and <u>efficient</u> way to communicate is via speech. A machine that can "hear," "understand," and "speak" would be the solution.

However, to produce such a machine is not an easy task. First of all, we need to implement speech recognition. Up to the present, quite a lot of academic research has been carried out on isolated word recognition. What we should do is extend this research to design the <u>continuous speech recognition</u>. However, most of the research on speech recognition is of spoken English and Mandarin. As we live in Hong Kong, we realize that there is a need to have a recognition system for <u>spoken Cantonese</u>.

In speech recognition systems, one of the frequently used models is the Hidden Markov Model. One of the advantages of the Hidden Markov Model is that a continuous speech recognizer can be constructed based on the models built from isolated words. In this project, we plan to adopt the Hidden Markov Model to construct a Cantonese continuous speech recognizer.

1.2   Objective and Scope

The overall objective is to build a system to translate an acoustical speech sequence to a sequence of numbers which can then be dialed out automatically. There are two requirements:

1. Software:
   To construct a Cantonese continuous digit recognition system using the Hidden Markov Model (HMM).

2. Hardware:
   To build a telephone dialing box using the D6106 and the DTMF chips.

Appendix B

Student Exercise (Completing an Outline)

Need for Project

Traditional interface method: _____

Inadequacy:

(a) _____

(b) _____

(c) _____

Value of Study

Proposed new interface method: machine that can hear, understand, and speak
Benefits: natural, _____ and _____
communication system

Gap in Research

Previous research:

(a) _____

(b) _____

Proposed research:

(a) _____

(b) _____

Student Exercise (Answer Key)

Need for Project

Traditional interface method: <u>keyboard</u>

Inadequacy:

(a) <u>training required</u>

(b) <u>hands occupied</u>

(c) <u>keyboard bulky</u>

Value of Study

Proposed new interface method: machine that can hear, understand, and speak
Benefits: natural, <u>efficient,</u> and <u>user-friendly</u> communication system

Gap in Research

Previous research:

a) <u>isolated word recognition</u>

b) <u>mostly on spoken English and Mandarin</u>

Proposed research:

(a) <u>continuous speech recognition</u>

(b) <u>for spoken Cantonese</u>

Investigation of Student Dial-up Service: Outline

Purpose

to investigate dial-up service

Scope

dial-up service for students' use during semester (weekdays vs. weekends)

Justification

High demand for dial-up service, especially by engineering students

Complaints about logins, especially during peak hours

Background   **[CCST Newsletter]**

168 student regular pool lines (1 hr time limit)

60 express pool lines (15 min time limit)

Calculate   **[Questionnaire responses]**

% of students living off campus who have a modem and therefore use dial-up service

No. of lines to student ratio

Major areas of investigation

Utilization   **[Questionnaire responses verified from CCST's graph printouts of utilization]**

Which time period—to establish peak vs. nonpeak hours

Frequency of use

Duration of use

Differences between schools or departments

Purpose

Which applications used—for academic or nonacademic work?

Types of problems encountered

e.g., cut off; line busy; slow response

Level of satisfaction with service

Any correlation with types of problems encountered?

Conclusions reached on basis of above evidence

insufficient no. of phone lines for great demand

Possible solutions   *[interviews with CCST staff]*

1. Increase number of modem lines
   Technically feasible and economically viable

2. Set up modem pools for departments
   Departments may not want to bear the cost from their internal budget

3. Increase transmission speed
   Technically feasible

4. Implement time login quota for each student
   Not easy to estimate most suitable time quota for each student

Recommendations

Two of the above solutions are technically and economically feasible:

Increase no. of modem lines

Increase transmission speed

Investigation of Student Dial-up Service: Report

Introduction

Due to the rapid growth in the popularity of computer applications, UST students are now more dependent on using computers to complete their homework assignments. The student dial-up service is currently provided by the Centre of Computing Services and Telecommunications (CCST) for UST students to connect their computers at home with the university network by using their modems. CCST provides 168 regular pool lines with a one-hour time limit and 60 express pool lines with a 15-minute time limit.

As the number of UST students has been increasing gradually in recent years, the demand for this service has become higher. However, it is inconvenient for those students who need to access the network frequently for academic purposes to do their work on the system since most of the time the modem pools are difficult to connect to. Hence, a better, more reliable and secure network is needed. This report will analyze the problems in the system and suggest some potential solutions to them.

Description of the Project

As the dial-up service is provided for the convenience of UST students, we would focus on the present situation of this service. In order to see whether the service can accomplish its original purposes, this project has two goals. The first goal is to reveal the present problems concerning the dial-up service and the second goal is to provide possible solutions to these problems. The present study focuses specifically on three major criteria:

1. to consider only UST undergraduate students and not postgraduate students or staff

2. to consider off-campus students only

3. to investigate the student dial-up service only and not any of the other services that are provided by CCST

Chapter 7

Well-Formedness Principles on Syntactic Structures

Paul J. Camhi

Borough of Manhattan Community College

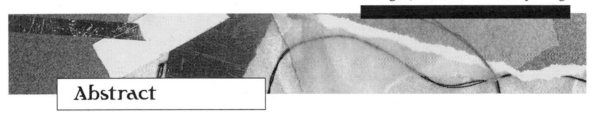

Abstract

Through a teacher-guided process of analysis and discovery, ESL/EFL students build a set of metalinguistic principles that govern the syntactic structure of English sentences. These principles comprise the sustained content of this course. As students learn the course content, they form metacognitive strategies for analyzing and successfully correcting the errors they make in their English writing. In addition, they develop the kinds of critical thinking skills needed to function successfully in academic and professional communities. This chapter provides a description of the course, including background information, pedagogic rationales, methodology, exemplars of classroom activities, critical thinking skills development, and evidence of student accomplishments. ■

Introduction

The sustained content of this course is of a conceptual nature. It offers a consistent set of metalinguistic principles of English grammar that predict syntactically well-formed English sentences and preclude syntactically ill-formed ones. Mastery of these metalinguistic concepts provides students with a formal mechanism to look at English sentence structure analytically, in a way not dissimilar from the way mastery of the basic principles of physics or chemistry facilitates deeper understanding of the content of those fields.

It is important that students at the college level have a command of the variety of critical thinking skills that they will be called on to use in their college/professional work (see Chapter 1 of this text). It is also important that they have command of the surface-level aspects of English grammar in their writing and speaking. Students taking this course can make significant strides toward achieving both these ends as they (1) build a theory about language (the course content) and (2) apply this theory to the language data (i.e., edit their writings for grammatical correctness). The analytical tools needed to successfully perform these two processes are essentially the same. These include classification, comparison and contrast, exemplification, inducing principles from data, checking hypotheses of principles by applying them to new data, synthesizing principles, questioning principles, and forming judgments about concepts and ideas.

Using these analytical tools, students move through incremental steps, each building on the previous ones, through which they derive linguistic principles from language data. They acquire these principles, use them to question previously learned ones, develop more complex and refined analyses, and apply these principles to their writing. Thus, as students learn to master sentence structure using this system, they learn critical thinking skills they will find useful elsewhere.

Grammar as a Set of Components

How the term *grammar* is defined is an essential consideration in teaching this course. Linguists (e.g., Chomsky, 1986) for the most part conceive of grammar as a multicomponent system, including syntactic, semantic, rhetorical, morphological, phonetic, and phonological components. Each component has its own system of organization, with distinct principles governing interrelationships among all the components. Most language teachers and writers of grammar materials (e.g., Azar, 1989; Celce-Murcia, Larsen-Freeman, 1983), on the other hand, present *grammar* as an umbrella term, combining the syntactic, semantic, and rhetorical components and making little formal distinction among the three. For example, the manner in which the active versus passive voice is taught in grammar texts usually includes the *syntactic* choice between active (*have* + past participle) and passive (*be* + past participle) triggered by varying *semantic/rhetorical* environments (see Exemplar 2 in this chapter for more details). Given the highly interrelated nature of these components, this is a logical and efficient way to *describe* how the active-versus-passive system is organized. However, whether this is always the optimal way to *teach* it is questionable.

In designing this course, I have found it productive to anchor it on the linguist's perspective of grammar—separating out the component grammar systems—since this perspective often provides a more comprehensive and systematic body of information from which to extrapolate pedagogically efficient principles. For example, from the work of transformational generative linguists (Chomsky, 1965, 1986), as well as of linguists designing computer systems that translate one language into another (Hovy, 1993; Scott, 1993), we learn that the syntactic component is the simplest one comprising the grammar of a language in that it requires the fewest rules to explain its structure in a principled way. Due to its simplicity, it serves most efficiently as the fulcrum through which the inter-relationships among the other, more complex components can be explicated.

Paralleling the observation of these linguists, I have found, through trial-and-error experiences in the classroom, that when students master the relatively simple aspects of syntactic organization in a pedagogic environment that is relatively free from the nonsyntactic aspects, they become more free to attend to the infinitely more complex semantic/rhetoric aspects of language. They thus gain greater conscious command over language structure in general, enabling them to more proficiently analyze their writings for grammatical correctness.

Metalinguistic Principles

This course provides an in-depth analysis of metalinguistic principles that define the syntactic component of English grammar. Metalinguistic principles govern the way language-related rules may be formulated and thus the way sentences may be constructed. These metalinguistic principles might be called *well-formedness principles,* taken from Chomsky's (1965) term. Although these principles are inspired by theoretical considerations, their form and manner of presentation are governed primarily by pedagogic considerations. It is pedagogically efficacious for ESL/EFL students to master these metalinguistic principles because the potential number of ad hoc rules that we can teach our students is vast, as is the number of unique combinations of rules that each student might need to master. This makes the teaching of ad hoc rules to an entire class highly inefficient. By providing students instead with a way to master metalinguistic principles that govern the form of rules, rather than learning the lower-level rules themselves, students can access a systematic means of focusing only on the specific areas of grammar they need to address. Also, gaining mastery of metacognitive principles gives students independence from the teacher in editing their work. They can work at their own rates and can sustain this process after they leave the classroom.

Metacognitive principles are grasped in two ways: through metacognitive ability and metacognitive awareness. Native users of a language are presumed to have largely unconscious knowledge (metacognitive *ability*) of the principles governing the grammar of their language, whereas non-native (especially post-pubescent) learners are presumed to lack or have limited access to this system. Some researchers (Ellis, 1994; Rutherford, 1988; Sharwood Smith, 1981; Sorace, 1985) suggest that these non-native users might benefit from at least some conscious knowledge of language form (metacognitive *awareness*).

Student Population

This course has been taught, either in full or in part, to intermediate and advanced ESL classes at community and senior colleges (public and private) in New York, New Jersey, and Connecticut, and at English-language institutes in private and public universities in New York. The student populations at these institutions are heterogeneous: ages range from 18 to 50-plus; native languages include Spanish, Mandarin, Korean, Japanese, Haitian Creole, Russian, Arabic, Polish, French, Hindi, and Farsi; students have varying grasps of what Cummins called *cognitive academic language proficiency* (CALP) (Cummins, 1981). Sections of the course have also been taught at a public high school in New York City to sophomore and senior ESL students, most of whom are native Spanish speakers with limited CALP.

Methodology

Through an inductive process of analysis and discovery, students arrive at a set of metalinguistic principles governing syntactic structure. At each step along the way, students are presented with a carefully controlled corpus of English utterances reflecting the particular principle being considered. Each step builds on previous ones. Through this scaffolding technique, students are able to produce and evaluate increasingly complex structures.

The Course Content

The topics covered in this course are listed in the table of contents (see the appendix to this chapter). The list seems daunting at first. However, the reader should bear in mind that these topics are not presented to the student in an ad hoc fashion. Rather, they are developed sequentially as students acquire the conceptual tools (i.e., metacognitive principles) needed to interpret the content in a coherent way. In fact, it is through the sequential presentation of the topics that the list becomes undaunting. This and the following sections present exemplars of how students derive some of these principles and how they apply them to language data.

Exemplar 1

The first exemplar is from Section One, early in the term. Prior to Exemplar 1, students are introduced to steps one and two of the three-step test for a complete sentence (adapted from Troyka & Nudelman, 1986). Those steps are (1) find the mutable verb (MV) and (2) find the subject of the MV. (The full meaning of the MV is developed inductively by students in Exemplar 2.) Knowledge of these two steps is necessary to activate this system of analysis and is a precursor to establishing the more complex principles later on. In addition, as a precursor to this course, students are expected to know what the seven parts of speech are, or at least to be able to identify them. They should also be able to identify subjects and objects in sentences.

In this exemplar, students follow a simple line of argumentation leading to the principles: (1) *a noun can be the subject of the MV or the object of the MV* and (2) *step one for a complete sentence must precede step two*. Students are presented with sentence 1 below and, in applying steps one and two, need to determine if it is a complete sentence or a fragment. In applying step one of the three-step test, students observe that

1. *The young man

lacks a verb of any sort. Because the principle of step one is not met, (1) is a fragment. (The asterisk before the string signifies that it is ungrammatical. The asterisk is added after students assess the string as ungrammatical.) Many students guess that "the young man" is the subject of the sentence, such as in (1a):

1a. The young man saw me.

However, when they look at (1b), in which the young man is the object,

1b. I saw the young man.

students conclude that "the young man" can be *either* the subject or the object of the sentence.

Students are then asked: "How can one determine if the noun is going to be the subject or object in a sentence?" Through class discussion they are guided to the conclusion that *first, one has to find the MV; then one can decide if the noun is the subject or object of the MV.* Thus, step one of the three-part test must precede step two. A noun by itself—without an associated MV—is neither a subject nor an object. Subjects or objects exist only after the MV is identified.

Exemplar 2

This exemplar demonstrates further the inductive student-driven process that leads to students' grasp of a key concept, the MV. By applying steps one and two in deciding whether fragments (2) through (5) are complete sentences, students understand that *-ing* words, past participles, and infinitives are *not* MVs. As they analyze fragments (2) through (5), the students, with guidance from the teacher, develop the following lines of argumentation leading to an operational definition for the MV.

Observation 1: -ing *words are not MVs.*

2. *We going to the cafeteria.

This is not a complete sentence because there is no MV (a violation of step one). *Going* is an *-ing* word; *-ing* words are not MVs. Sometimes *-ing* words are part of the complete verb (CV), but they are not MVs.

Through class discussion, students offer possibilities to change (2) into complete sentences; for example: *We are (were, will be) going; we have (had, will have) been going;* or, if the subject of the sentence is changed, into: *I am (was) going; you are (were) going; she is going;* and so on. For emphasis, mutable verbs are double-underlined. Students observe that **when an *-ing* word is part of the CV, some form of *be* must always go directly in front of the *-ing* word**. They observe also that *-ing* words can be changed into MVs, such as *go, goes,* and *went*.

Observation 2: Past participles are not MVs. In class discussion, students argue about and eventually determine that

3. *She spoken to him.

is not a complete sentence because it does not contain an MV. *Spoken* is a past participle; past participles are not MVs. Fragment (3) might be made into a complete sentence, as follows: *She <u>has</u> (<u>had</u>, <u>will have</u>) spoken to him;* or, if the subject is changed, as: *I <u>have</u> spoken to him.* (If, at this juncture, a student suggests a sentence such as *"I am spoken to him," it is best for the teacher to simply state that sometimes a form of *be* can be placed before a past participle when the sentence is passive, but it can't be done in this sentence. The issue of active versus passive is addressed shortly.) Students observe that **when a past participle is part of the complete verb, it is *sometimes* preceded by some form of *have* (for active sentences)**. Students also observe that the past participle form in fragment (3) can be changed into MVs, such as in *She <u>speaks</u> (<u>spoke</u>, <u>will speak</u>) to us* or *They <u>speak</u> to us.* A similar analysis takes place with fragment (4), where students discuss and determine that

4. *The book written by Ruth.

is an incomplete sentence since it lacks an MV. *Written* is a past participle. As we already know, past participles are not MVs. Possible ways to complete this sentence while maintaining the past participle are *The book <u>is</u> (<u>was</u>, <u>will be</u>) written by Ruth*; or *The books <u>are</u> written by Ruth.* Students observe that **when a past participle is part of the complete verb, *sometimes* some form of *be* is placed in front of the past participle (for passive sentences).**

Because of the complex interplay of the semantic, rhetorical, and syntactic components in the choice between *have* + past participle versus *be* + past participle, the selection of the appropriate option for active vs. passive poses a problem for many ESL students. At this juncture in the students' process, the focus should be kept on the relatively simple syntactic possibilities (of *have* + past participle or *be* + past participle) rather than on the complex semantic/rhetorical considerations governing which of the two options to choose. Students address these options later in the course, following a similar process of inducing principles from data. In addition, because students are exploring syntactic rather than semantic or rhetorical aspects of the verb system, there are no detailed accounts of verb tenses or usage at this time. Students will negotiate these once they have internalized the syntactic principles.

Observation 3: Infinitives are not MVs.

5. *We to visit India

This is a fragment because there is no MV. *To visit* is an infinitive, and infinitives are not MVs. Examples of completed sentences are: *We <u>want</u> (<u>wanted</u>, <u>will want</u>) to visit India* or *She <u>wants</u> to visit India.* Students observe that **an infinitive by itself is insufficient to make a complete verb; a mutable verb must precede it**. Students also note that infinitives can be changed into MVs, such as <u>visit</u>, <u>visits</u>, <u>will visit</u>.

At this point, the teacher asks, "What is the definition of a mutable verb?" This is a crucial question since the MV forms the crux of the verb system as well as of the sentence. The answer must be arrived at by the students, not given to them by the teacher. Students analyze the sentences examined so far and are asked to focus on the double-underlined words. Students might suggest the following as MV definitions:

S: MVs are not *-ing* words, past participles, or infinitives.

T: That's what they *aren't;* it's not what they *are.*

S: MVs show action.

T: It's true that some MVs show action, but non-MVs like *running, spoken,* and *to write* also show action.

After guided analysis of the sentences, students come up with the fact that **mutable verbs can change;** then they deduce that **MVs change according to the subject and tense.** Mutable means "able to change"; -ing words, past participles, and infinitives cannot change. For example, we cannot say **She goings home,* or **They goned home,* or **He to spoke last week.* These three types of words cannot change; however, MVs can.

In this exemplar, a cluster of well-formedness principles is built up from a set of syntactic observations, previously developed principles, and language data. By employing a variety of analytical skills, students derive from a set of simpler principles the more complex principled definition of the mutable verb. Some of the analytical thinking skills include inductive questioning of data in order to extract principles; and classification, comparison, and differentiation of both principles and data.

Exemplar 3

This exemplar represents a more advanced unit in which students apply a very early concept to more complex data. Students observe the predictive powers of this conceptual system and (hopefully) appreciate the predictive values of conceptual systems in general. In this particular case, they discover how the theories they have been developing eliminate the need for an ad hoc relative clause reduction rule. This ad hoc rule states that when a relative pronoun occurs in a complex sentence, it can be deleted only when it functions as the object of the MV in the embedded clause. Students who need this rule will learn it and apply it (not all students will need to learn it, since some already know it either consciously or unconsciously).

In the system the students have been learning, this rule need not be posited. Rather, a reiteration of the first two steps of the three-step test is all that is necessary.

6a. The man (whom we saw) is my cousin.

6b. The man (we saw) is my cousin.

7a. The man (who came here) is my cousin.

7b. *The man (came here) is my cousin.

When they arrive at this point in the semester, students already have learned from earlier units that (6a) and (7a) each consist of two clauses: an independent clause (IC) and a relative clause (within parentheses). (6b) and (7b) represent reductions of the relative clause by the elimination of the relative pronoun. In (6b), the output is acceptable; in (7b), however, the output is unacceptable. Here is the line of argumentation students employ when analyzing the relative clause in (6a). *Saw* is the MV; *we* is the subject of the MV. If we eliminate *whom,* the MV will still have its subject; therefore, we can eliminate it without violating the well-formedness principle of steps one and two (find the MV and find the subject of the MV) of the three-step test. Thus, (6b) is permissible.

Let's do the same for the relative clause in (7a). *Came* is the MV; *who* is the subject of the MV. If we eliminate *who,* the MV will no longer have a subject, which is a violation of the test. (Students would simply say that it would be "against the law.")

We can extend this argument by noting that if we eliminated *who* in (7a) to maintain the well-formedness of the embedded clause, we would need to change the form of the MV to an *-ing* word, thus making the original embedded clause into *coming here,* an adjectival phrase describing *man:*

8. The man (coming here) is my cousin.

This is an acceptable sentence, and the now-embedded *phrase* does not violate the principles that the students have learned.

Students trained to do analysis such as this will predict the possibility of (6b) and the impossibility of (7b). The application of an earlier set of principles to new language data obviates the need for the ad hoc relative clause rule. Instead, students can go back to the three-step test for a complete sentence and reinforce the principle: if we have an MV, we *must* have a subject associated with it (except for imperatives). This is a principle of syntactic well-formedness that cannot be violated.

Learning Critical Thinking Skills

As we have seen, this course uses continuing and sustained content, building from basic syntactic facts to sophisticated principles that govern grammatical operations. The set of principles students deduce, based on inspection of language data, are the conceptual tools that facilitate continued analytical inspection of language. In the process of acquiring these tools, students develop, practice, and refine the kinds of analytical skills needed to do academic work in general. The nature of this course requires that they develop these analytical tools, not just memorize them until the test is over. Essentially, students build a theory about language as they proceed.

In the previous section ("The Course Content"), we inspected exemplars, focusing on the processes students engage in while learning metacognitive principles, peripherally noting some of the analytical skills acquired in the process. In this section we look at two additional exemplars, keeping our central focus on the analytical skills students learn in each, such as inducing principles through analysis of data; classification, comparison, and differentiation of data; judgment and evaluation of principles against new data; and revising principles to accommodate new data.

Exemplar 4

Students inspect the following strings of words and begin their "line of argumentation":

9. She reads every day.

10. It is fun.

11. *Reads is fun.

In (9), *reads* is the MV and *she* is the subject of the MV. Thus, (9) is a well-formed sentence. In (10), *is* is the MV and *it* is the subject of the MV. This is also a well-formed sentence. In (11), *is* is the MV. However, *reads* cannot be the subject of the MV because (according to the principle developed in Exemplar 1) the subject must contain a noun. *Reads* is an MV (learned from Exemplar 2); *reads* is not a noun. To make (11) conform to the rule that subjects are nouns, *reads* must be changed into a noun.

Many students suggest (12) as a grammatically correct alternative to (11):

12. Reading is fun.

They reason that *is* is the MV and *reading* is the subject of the MV. Since subjects must contain nouns (from Exemplar 1), *reading* functions as a noun in this sentence. (In Exemplar 2, students discovered that *-ing* words function as part of the complete verb as well.)

The analysis continues:

13. She loves it.

14. *She loves reads.

In (13), *loves* is the MV, *she* is the subject of the MV, and *it* is the object of the MV. Subjects *and* objects must contain (pro)nouns. *She* and *it* are pronouns; therefore, (13) is well formed. In (14), *loves* is the MV and *she* is the subject of the MV, but *reads,* an MV, is functioning as an object. This is impossible because an object *must* contain a noun (Exemplar 1). To make this sentence well formed, we must change the MV into a noun. When we change *reads* to *reading*, we change an MV into a noun and produce the well-formed sentence,

15. She loves reading.

where the *-ing* word functions as a noun, in this case the object of the MV.

(Through a similar line of argumentation, students can also induce the other functions of *-ing* words as well as infinitives and past participles: *-ing* words can also function as adjectives, as in "The singing nun performed at the concert"; infinitives function as nouns and therefore as subjects and objects, as in "To swim every day is good exercise" and "I like to swim"; past participles can function, in addition to being part of the complete verb, as adjectives, as in "The broken watch was sent to the repair shop.")

In this exemplar, students judge and then extend their analysis of an earlier-developed principle (nouns function as subjects or objects of the MV) by evaluating it against a new class of data (where *-ing* words occupy noun "slots"), thereby deducing a new principle (-*ing* words can function as nouns). Students discover that words (such as -*ing* words, infinitives, and past participles)—can have multiple syntactic functions in the sentence. Additional skills employed in this analysis include using inductive questioning to extract a principle from the data; challenging data against a principle, resulting in reclassification of data to accommodate the principle (changing MVs into nouns); deductive application of a principle to new data (defining grammatical categories permissable for -*ing* words, as well as infinitives and adjectives); and using cause-and-effect reasoning (e.g., an MV *must* be changed into a noun if it occupies a noun slot).

Exemplar 5

Another example of the types of reasoning students develop appears in the unit of the course in which students learn about hierarchical constituent analysis. Students are presented with structurally ambiguous sentences whose ambiguity is based not on the different possible meanings of any of the words but on the way the speaker/student classifies and differentiates the words in his or her mind. Sentence (16) is an example of the kinds of structurally ambiguous sentences students learn to successfully analyze:

16. They are eating apples.

This sentence can have more than one meaning. Meaning (16a) signifies that what they are doing with the apples is eating them, whereas meaning (16b) indicates that the apples being referred to are those that are edible as opposed to those that are inedible.

Look at the constituent structures of (16a) and (16b):

16a. They (are eating) apples.

16b. They are (eating apples).

In class discussion, students argue that in (16a), *eating* is an -*ing* word that is part of the complete verb of the sentence and in (16b), *eating* is an adjective that, together with the noun *apples,* forms a noun phrase. In these cases, syntactic structure governs meaning.

In this activity, students categorize language data (through classification, comparison, and differentiation) according to syntactic function. Students extend earlier-developed and relatively simple principles into mastery over the more complex linguistic notion of hierarchical constituent analysis. They come to understand that structure is based not only on word order across the sentence but on the words' inclusion in constituent groupings that act as indivisible syntactic units. This is analytical thinking of a higher order, where the challenging or questioning of principles leads to the learning of new and more complex principles or "insights."

To practice this new analytical skill, students are directed to generate three separate sentences using, for example, the word *falling,* which functions as a noun (in [17]), as part of the complete verb (in [18]), and as an adjective (in [19]). Here are the sentences one group came up with:

17. (Falling) in love is beautiful.

18. I (was falling) down the stairs.

19. We watched (the falling leaves) in autumn.

In addition to focused practice exercises such as this, the bulk of skills development occurs when students edit their papers—usually their penultimate and final drafts—for grammatical correctness. They use error correction symbols and grammar logs to identify and classify their errors according to type, and they learn that inherent in each symbol (or error type) is a principled means of correcting the errors. Students also produce personalized grammar books, in which separate pages are reserved for each error type they make. Students write the sentence in which the error occurs, along with the correction of the error. Over time, as their personalized grammar books expand, they get to see the pattern of their errors and negotiate systematic means for correcting them.

By critically analyzing their writing in the editing process, students practice the principles they have developed and use them to generate and analytically evaluate future data. They apply derived rules to new data (their writings) and consciously judge the grammatical accuracy of the data through empirical means. These are the kinds of activities they would perform in any other scientific inquiry.

Evidence of Student Accomplishments

It is always a challenging task to isolate the pedagogic variables that contribute to student performance. However, a number of considerations point to the success of this method. Most notable are the very high pass rates on standardized exit exams of students using this method as opposed to other methods. A study (Camhi & Eisenstein Ebsworth, 1999) is in progress at Borough of Manhattan Community College (BMCC) of the City University of New York (CUNY) comparing, among other things, pass rates on the City University of New York Writing Assessment Test (CUNYWAT) of ESL students using this method of instruction with those not using it. The CUNYWAT consists of a timed (50-minute) writing sample in which the student responds to a prompt of an argumentative nature. Each writing sample is scored holistically and anonymously by at least two trained readers who have been "normed" immediately before scoring takes place to ensure shared understanding of the criteria for assessment. These criteria include levels of fluency, clarity of rhetorical expression, language usage, and grammatical accuracy. A total score of 8 or higher (out of a possible 12) constitutes a "passing" score. By CUNY mandate, a score of 8 or more is required to graduate from BMCC with an associate's degree. It is also a requirement at the CUNY four-year colleges. In the present study, we gathered the end-of-semester CUNYWAT scores for all ESL writing students in each advanced class. A total of 2,800 advanced-level ESL students over four semesters are currently being evaluated. (It is important to note that grammatical accuracy is by no means the only gauge by which the WAT is judged; however, it is a major challenge faced by our ESL students as well as the ESL instructors.) Our preliminary findings suggest that an important source of the very high pass rates for students using this method is their increased mastery of syntactic structure as well as their enhanced ability to employ critical thinking skills.

Descriptive data indicate a dramatically higher pass rate for those classes using this method compared with others using a range of approaches. Over the two-year period of the study, a range of 47.6 to 91.2 percent (mean = 66.3 percent) of the students who participated in this method passed the WAT, whereas a range of 9.2 to 31.6 percent (mean = 22.4 percent) of the other students passed the WAT. Of course, those ESL classes not using this method actually represent a range of teaching approaches and styles, some of which incorporate a metalinguistic component. The researchers intend to study more carefully the teaching approaches used in other classes in the future. For now, however, a comparison of the results at least allows us to evaluate the success of this method compared with the range of methods in use.

In addition to test performance, writing samples taken from students' exit exams compared with those from the same students' entrance exams demonstrate student accomplishments. The following patterns of mastery are typical of students who have taken this course. One student wrote on her entrance exam, "Permit abortion is bad." On the exit exam, the same student wrote, "Doing things well in life is necessary." In this case, the student has mastered the principle that subjects must contain nouns (or that verbs in the subject position violate well-formedness principles). Verbs in this position must be changed to nouns; *-ing* words are nouns. In her entrance essay, another student wrote sentences such as *"I am like her very much" and *"I was spoke to her often about it," in which her present tense sentences often followed the incorrect pattern of *am, is,* or *are* plus the base form of the verb and her past tense sentences often followed the incorrect pattern of *was* or *were* plus the base form of the verb. On the exit essay, this same student consistently followed the grammatically correct pattern as exemplified by sentences such as "I think she knew right from wrong" and "The children in that family followed their parents' ways." This shows mastery over the syntactic well-formedness principle of the complete verb. These are just a few of the examples possible in the space permitted that demonstrate mastery of syntactic patterns.

Additional evidence of student accomplishments comes from very high test performance on in-class exams in which students are asked to provide both passive and active evidence of mastery of syntactic principles. Students are constantly quizzed on the principles they learn in the course and can take retests (covering the same principles but different textual data) until they get 100 on all the tests. Rarely does a student fail to attain this goal. An example of passive mastery comes from this exam question:

> Inspect the following sentences: (a) We went to Bangkok. (b) They decided to visit Greece. (c) We ought to travel more. Observe that the word *to* occurs in each sentence. In which sentence does *to* function as (1) part of a modal; (2) a preposition; (3) part of the infinitive?

An example of active mastery of syntactic principles comes from successfully answering this quiz question:

Using the word *sleeping,* construct sentences in which the word functions as (1) part (or a constituent) of the complete verb; (2) an adjective; (3) the subject of the MV; (4) the object of the MV; (5) the object of the preposition.

One student's written response was

(1) I was sleeping for many hours; (2) The sleeping child was very cute; (3) Sleeping in a comfortable bed is a wonderful experience; (4) I love sleeping in a comfortable bed; (5) I don't want to write any more about sleeping.

In addition to exhibiting high test performance, many students consciensciously used their correction logs to identify their errors and correct them according to syntactic principles. As a result, many of these students demonstrated marked improvement in their ability to self-correct. Many students also formed outside study groups to go over these logs, pointing to a high level of engagement in this analytical process.

I have also found it helpful to look at student responses to the approach. During one semester, independent interviewers sampled a random group of seven students. Here are some of the comments these students made:

By going through a step-by-step process, I learned that you first have to learn to crawl, then walk before learning how to fly.

We were guided through a process, and it became easier as we progressed.

It is important to have a system of learning. Now I know my weak and strong points, and I can focus on my weak points when I do my editing.

I felt prepared and confident at the end of this course to communicate better because I was able to figure out how to correct my errors according to a system.

Students' written evaluations of the course show extremely high support. Their most frequent comments about the course included: "I noticed a lot of improvement in my grammar"; "I learned about the structure of the English verb system"; "I learned how to correct my errors using a system."

Conclusion

This chapter has examined a sustained content approach for empowering ESL/ EFL students to evaluate and analyze their own grammatical production in English writing. The means to this end involve the use of conscious metalinguistic principles that also enhance cognitive development in a more general sense. Engaging these students in the learning/thinking process described here gives them the tools to succeed in the short term by passing an important gatekeeping exam. Furthermore, students are empowered to continue with their grammatical development long after the class ends.

Of course, the total grammar of a language cannot be taught strictly by conscious attention to form (Krashen, 1992). Also needed are pedagogic environments that incorporate reading, writing, listening, and speaking activities driven by spontaneous "communicative exchange(s) of meaning" (Ellis, 1995). Clearly, a language learner benefits from both of these approaches; they are not mutually exclusive.

In this course, the consciousness-raising activities on which students focus do not conflict with the basic tenets of the whole-language approach. Indeed, students read and write essays throughout the semester, and it is through the students' communicative writing experiences that they generate the language data they need to continue analyzing their own language for grammatical correctness. As their metacognitive *awareness* of syntactic structures becomes more firmly anchored, and as their ability to use critical thinking skills increases, they become freer to focus on the more complex interplay of semantic and rhetorical aspects of syntactic structure. This course provides students with the resources they need to continue this process.

References

Azar, B. (1989). *Understanding and using English grammar*. Englewood Cliffs, NJ: Prentice-Hall Regents.

Camhi, P., & Eisenstein Ebsworth, M. (1999). *Incorporating a metalinguistic component in process writing: A two-year community college study*. Twenty-First Annual Applied Linguistics Winter of NYSTESOL, New York, NY.

Celce-Murcia, M., & Larsen-Freeman, D. (1983). *The grammar book: An ESL teacher's course*. Boston: Heinle and Heinle.

Chomsky, N. (1965). *Aspects of the theory of syntax*. Cambridge, MA: MIT Press.

Chomsky, N. (1986). *Knowledge of language: Its nature, origin and use*. New York: Praeger.

Cummins, J. (1981). The role of primary language development in promoting educational success for language minority students. In California State Department of Education (Ed.), *Schooling and language minority students*. Los Angeles: Evaluation, Dissemination, and Assessment Center.

Ellis, R. (1994). *The study of second language acquisition*. Oxford, UK: Oxford University Press.

Hovy, E. (1993). How MT works. *Byte, 8*(1), 167–176.

Krashen, S. (1982). *Principles and practices in second language acquisition*. Oxford, UK: Pergamon.

Rutherford, W. (1988). *Second language grammar: Learning and teaching*. London: Longman.

Scott, B. (1993). The five layers of ambiguity. *Byte, 8*(1), 174–175.

Sharwood Smith, M. (1981). Consciousness-raising and the second language learner. *Applied Linguistics, 2,* 159–169.

Sorace, A. (1985). Metalinguistic knowledge and language use in acquisition-poor environments. *Applied Linguistics, 6,* 239–254.

Troyka, L., & Nudelman, J. (1986). *Steps in composition*. Englewood Cliffs, NJ: Prentice-Hall.

Table of Contents

Section One: The Simple Sentence

The Seven "Parts of Speech"; Steps One and Two for a Complete Sentence; Complete Sentences vs. Fragments; Definition of the Mutable Verb (MV); Nouns Function as Subjects or Objects of the MV; The Correct Ordering of Steps One and Two; *-Ing* Words, Past Participles, and Infinitives Are Not MVs; *-Ing* Words and the Complete Verb (CV); Past Participles and the CV; Active vs. Passive Sentences; The Five Main Forms of the Verb; *-Ing* Words Can Function as Nouns and Adjectives; Infinitives Function as Nouns; Past Participles Can Function as Adjectives; Modals; The Structure of the Complete Verb; Prepositions; Prepositional Phrases; Nouns as Objects of the Preposition; Hierarchical Constituent Structure; Word Forms

Section Two: Editing Component

Error Correction Symbols; Practice Sheets; Grammar Logs; Personalized Grammar Sheets; Self-Editing as an Ongoing Process

Section Three: Sentence Combining

Step Three for a Complete Sentence; Subordinating Conjunctions; Dependent Clauses, Relative Pronouns, and Relative Clauses; Independent Clauses; Complex Sentences; Relative Pronouns; Relative Clauses as a Class of Dependent Clauses; Reduction of Relative Clauses to Phrases; Coordinating Conjunctions; Compound Sentences; Compound Phrases; Adverbial Conjunctions; Punctuation Principles of Sentence Combining; Review of Sentence Combining Principles

Chapter 8

Managing Information for Writing University Exams in American History[1]

Gayle Nelson with Jill Burns

Georgia State University

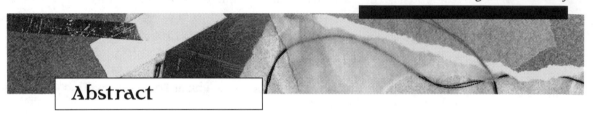

Abstract

On the basis of a three-year study of the academic literacy tasks of undergraduate courses at Georgia State University (GSU), the ESL program revised its curriculum to reflect the literacy tasks students are actually expected to perform. Curriculum goals included simulating undergraduate classes and using authentic textbook material. This chapter describes one of our courses: academic writing for university exams, in which American history is the area of sustained content. The course focuses on answering exam questions and taking reading notes. The types of exam questions (i.e., tasks) are identification, short-answer, and essay. By successfully completing the exam questions, students demonstrate their understanding of the content. Each academic task is supported by pedagogical tasks that provide the scaffolding needed for students to complete the academic tasks. Pedagogical tasks consist of student-generated answers and questions, graphic organizers, and charts for academic language structures. ■

[1]This course evolved over several years. We would like to thank the teachers who developed materials for earlier courses, materials we have adopted to American history. In particular, we are extremely grateful to Sharon Cavusgil and Debra Snell for leading the way. We also thank Marcia Pally for her helpful comments and thorough editing.

Student A: I think using U.S. history is good because it helps us prepare for regular U.S. history class.

Student B: It's good for me to learn how to write for college exams right now, so when I get to college, I won't be shocked about it.

Background

This chapter describes the development of one ESL course: academic writing for university exams. The topic of sustained content is American history. The course is the most advanced one in a three-course sequence in which the intermediate course uses earth science as the content area and the advanced intermediate course uses anthropology. The development of these three courses is part of a large-scale curriculum revision project that has been going on in the Department of Applied Linguistics and ESL at Georgia State University (GSU) for more than five years.

The seeds for the curriculum revision were planted when a faculty member, Joan Carson (see Chapter 2 of this text), was awarded a three-year grant (1990–1993) from the Department of Education's Fund for the Improvement of Post-secondary Education (FIPSE). One goal of the FIPSE grant was to study the academic demands of undergraduate courses at Georgia State University, in particular the reading, writing, and verbal demands of entry-level courses in four disciplines: American history, political science, biology, and freshman composition. For the ESL curriculum revision project, an important outcome of the FIPSE research was a description of the academic *literacy* requirements of these courses: what students were *actually* expected to do with language, not what we *thought* students were expected to do. For instance, the analysis of the FIPSE data revealed that GSU freshmen and sophomores are seldom required to write out-of-class research papers; in fact, freshman composition is virtually the only class that asks students to do extensive out-of-class writing. This dissonance between our curriculum at that time (based on ESL textbooks and the language needs we thought our students had) and the language tasks they were actually expected to perform led us to reconfigure the curriculum and, correspondingly, all courses.

This revision began during the 1993–1994 academic year. From the results of the FIPSE study, we agreed on two primary goals. The first was a curriculum built on the literacy tasks students perform in their academic classes, tasks (e.g., writing an essay exam) that students recognize as being transferable from the ESL classroom to "real" classrooms. As we began defining the academic tasks, we realized that we needed to provide scaffolding for students to be able to accomplish the university-level work. We used the term *pedagogical task* to describe this scaffolding. An example of an academic task is writing a response to an essay exam. A pedagogical task is using a graphic organizer to understand the relationships in the material on which the exam will be based. Thus, the pedagogical task is what the ESL instructor assigns and the students complete in order for students to more fully understand the material before the instructor assigns and students complete the academic task. It is by successfully completing the academic tasks that students demonstrate they have understood the material and acquired the knowledge.

The second goal of the curriculum was to simulate undergraduate entry-level university classes as much as possible; therefore, we decided to use sustained content based on authentic textbooks and materials. Perhaps not surprisingly, finding materials proved frustrating. Although there are numerous ESL textbooks on academic writing (e.g., Benesch, Rakijas, & Rorschach, 1987; Levy, 1988; Lites & Lehman, 1990), many use readings from magazines (which are seldom used in actual academic classes) and writing assignments that are personal and expressive (tasks not commonly assigned in undergraduate courses). In addition, most of the ESL writing textbooks are based on thematic units, not on sustained content. We attempted to use an ESL textbook with a focus on reading-to-write and developed a coursepack of activities to supplement the book. However, this book, *Strictly Academic: A Reading and Writing Text* (Curry & Cray, 1987), went out of print and also never met our goal of using authentic textbook material in one content area. The book consisted of eight thematic units and often used articles from magazines rather than textbooks. The process of developing the coursepack for Curry and Cray did, however, move us closer to defining the specific academic and pedagogical tasks that would eventually become the course entitled Academic Writing for University Exams.

Why Use Sustained Content?

Sustained content courses use one content area throughout the entire course. We would like to emphasize that a sustained content course focuses on the *academic needs of the students* and follows "the sequence determined by a particular subject matter in dealing with the language problems students encounter" (Brinton, Snow, & Wesche, 1989, p. 2). The content dictates the language items taught. A course using sustained content is particularly beneficial if the content is from a course that students will later be required to take as part of their academic program. As indicated by their end-of-term evaluations (described in this chapter), most students commented that studying American history in their ESL class would give them an advantage when they take the course as undergraduates. It was clear that the course content increased their motivation to learn. In addition, in sustained-content courses, topic-related vocabulary and concepts are continuously recycled. This recycling is particularly important in courses that many ESL students find difficult because they lack background knowledge. By studying one content area throughout an ESL course, students—and teachers—begin to build up a knowledge base in that discipline. However, the processes involved in learning the specific content, academic vocabulary, registers, and study skills are transferable and applicable to other courses and contexts, not merely to the content area taught. These advantages hold true for both ESL and EFL contexts. Instead of using EFL textbooks, EFL teachers and programs can also develop curricula using English-language, discipline-specific textbooks.

Why Reading-to-Write?

Reading-to-write requires students to produce their own texts. They must transform information for a specific purpose and synthesize the reading material(s) with their own knowledge (Carson & Leki, 1993). This transformation and synthesis of knowledge is the goal of critical literacy (Carson, 1993). Also, as Pally points out in Chapter 1 of this text, reading-to-write familiarizes students with the rhetorical structures of the discipline they are studying, the structures they will go on to use in their writing. In terms of schema theory, students learn both structural and content schemata (Carrell & Eisterhold, 1983). Furthermore, reading-to-write simulates university coursework. Writing in academic contexts (with the possible exception of freshman composition) is always based on reading, and reading typically has as its goal some form of writing (Carson, 1993). As freshmen and sophomores, students read textbooks and write about them, commonly by answering test questions.

Why American History?

American history, a required course, is particularly difficult for ESL students at GSU (Carson, Chase, Gibson, & Hargrove, 1992). They often know little about American history when they begin the course and therefore have little background knowledge on which to build. Because of this difficulty, we selected American history as the content area for the most advanced course in the academic writing for university exams sequence. A survey conducted by Carson, Chase, & Gibson (1992) put forth two additional reasons for selecting American history. First, the reading load in "real" American history courses averages approximately 85 pages per week. ESL students in the study found this amount of reading unexpected and intimidating; about two-thirds of them expected fewer than 60 pages a week. Their apprehension and intimidation suggest that they need strategies to manage and organize this amount of reading. The second reason is that in most American history classes, students' grades depend primarily on their performance on exams, not on projects or papers, and most of the exam items consist of identification, short-answer, and essay questions. The history textbook we selected for this course was the one used in the majority of American history classes at GSU, *America* (Tindall & Shi, 1997).

The Course: Academic Writing for University Exams

The course, taught by the two authors of this chapter, met three times a week for 1 hour and 35 minutes for 10 weeks.

Why Two Instructors?

Our goal was to develop supplementary materials (i.e., a coursepack) for the American history textbook and an instructor's manual to be used the following term in all of the advanced academic writing for university exams classes. Because of the amount of work involved, we decided to team-teach the course. Jill Burns had taught the course twice, using the "old" coursepack based on the Curry and Cray (1987) text. As an experienced teacher of the course, she had a holistic understanding of its goals that was essential to the process of developing the "new and improved" coursepack. Gayle Nelson had an understanding of the theoretical underpinnings of the course and had been involved in the years of curriculum discussions, but she had not taught this course before.

Who Were the Students?

The advanced class consisted of 19 students: 7 males and 12 females. The males had been in the United States for an average of 3.6 years, ranging from 3 to 8 years. The females averaged 4 years in the United States, ranging from 3 months to 15 years.

The students came from 13 countries, 7 from Vietnam and 1 each from Cameroon, Egypt, Ethiopia, India, Pakistan, Russia, Sudan, Taiwan, Thailand, Ukraine, Venezuela, and Zaire. They spoke nine different first languages: Arabic, French, Gujarati, Lingala, Russian, Spanish, Thai, Urdu, and Vietnamese. Their placement at this level was determined by a combination of listening, grammar, vocabulary, reading, and writing skills from a university-developed placement exam. Scores from students in this class corresponded roughly to TOEFL (Test of English as a Foreign Language) scores, ranging from 460 to 530. All students gave us written permission to use examples of their work in this chapter.

Inevitable Mistakes, or Learning as We Went

We quickly learned that the process of developing materials to support students' learning of academic material is one of trial and error. Before the course began, we developed an extensive course syllabus based on the amount of reading material we expected students to be able to cover in 10 weeks: the first 3 chapters of a 36-chapter American history book. In the end, we covered the first chapter (52 pages). Though this is not commensurate with the 85-page-per-week reading load in mainstream history classes, our ESL students progressed more slowly because the course focus was on strategies for managing content. Initially, we also thought we would each teach part of the course daily, but we soon realized that the significant amount of time needed to plan and coordinate a class while developing support materials and an accompanying instructor's manual made this option impractical. After the second week, we decided that each of us would teach a two-week unit. We selected a two-week unit because students took a test every two weeks; thus, one of us developed and taught the materials and made and corrected the tests for a full unit. This arrangement gave the other instructor time to revise materials that had just been taught, to begin developing the next unit's materials, and to write the supplementary materials for the instructor's manual.

The original syllabus also included student journals, a carryover from the former writing course. For a week we struggled with how to use student journals in a way that was consistent with our overall goal of making the course as similar to a "real" American history course as possible. The American history courses at GSU do not include any kind of journal, so we dropped the journal from the course.

Course Components

Academic Tasks

The primary academic tasks taught were writing identification (ID), short-answer, and essay questions. In weekly meetings with the instructors from the other levels of the course, we made decisions affecting the sequencing of courses to produce a coherent curriculum. For instance, we agreed on a systematic grading system, the number of tests per course, the number of points per test question, and the length of the essay questions for each of the three levels of the course. The guidelines we developed appear in Appendix A. The second academic task was taking reading notes; reading note guidelines are presented in Appendix B.

Each of the three main types of test question was clearly explained and exemplified. Students received numerous handouts, now collated into a coursepack that they buy at the university bookstore. (See Appendix C for handouts students received on the three types of test questions.) ID questions were the first type of question taught. They tend to be the shortest type of written test question, often asking for definitions of key terms or information about important people, places, or theories. ID questions are important for learning the content area's key terms, concepts, and events, and also for learning how to determine what terms, concepts, and events are important. In responding to ID questions, students also learn (and the teacher must teach) how to write definitions.

Short-answer and essay questions also require these skills, but in addition students must learn how to manage and organize larger amounts of information. To accomplish these tasks (e.g., to answer the questions), students need to learn the rhetorical structures inherent in the questions (e.g., cause and effect, comparison/contrast, description, classification). Although students learn the rhetorical conventions of a specific academic discipline, the conventions are widely applicable to other disciplines and contexts (see Appendix C for an example). In writing responses to essay questions (first short ones and later longer ones), students need to manage even more complex information and rhetorical structures. Appendix H presents a comparison/contrast essay question.

The progression from ID questions to more complex essay questions illustrates several advantages of using sustained content. By reading one content area, students become familiar with the vocabulary, grammatical structures, and rhetorical patterns of the academic discipline. In the beginning of the course, they write short answers, which gives them time to become familiar with the rhetorical conventions and background of the discipline needed for writing more complex essay questions. Without sustained content, students would not have the opportunity to gradually acquire (through reading) an in-depth understanding of the language and conventions used in one discipline—the kind of understanding that is expected of them in both academic and workplace settings.

Pedagogical Tasks

Three main pedagogical tasks were used to prepare students for the academic tasks: student-generated answers and questions, graphic organizers, and charts for academic language structures.

Student-Generated Answers and Questions After students were introduced to each question type described in Appendix C, they practiced both answering and writing each type of question. At the beginning of the course, we wrote the ID questions and students wrote the answers. Those with particularly good responses showed them to the class on the overhead projector (OHP), enabling us to point out the qualities that made the good answers good! Later, students began writing their own ID questions either on paper or on a transparency and exchanging them with a partner who answered them. Again, examples of answers were shown on the OHP and explained.

This method was valuable not only because it enabled us to point out the qualities that made up a good answer but also because it helped us assess the areas with which students were having trouble. For example, one student identified Amerigo Vespucci as "a merchant and a navigator who sailed to the New World." This example illustrates a problem that occurred repeatedly with ID questions: Students had difficulty selecting the key information from the reading. We asked the class, "What makes this person important? Is this person famous because he is a merchant and navigator or because of something else?" After questions such as these, students reread this section of the textbook and realized that Amerigo Vespucci was famous not for being a merchant or a navigator but because "America" was named after him, and also that the naming was a mistake. Working with ID questions, students became aware of the need to pinpoint what made a person or an event important (i.e., worth studying) and to state that importance in their answers.

Through formal evaluations and informal conversations, we monitored the students' reactions to this class activity. We did not use students' names, and we treated answers respectfully with comments such as "This information is correct. Amerigo Vespucci was a merchant and a navigator, but he is famous for something else." There is a danger in using not-so-good examples of student writing as examples to show to the rest of the class. Students may feel embarrassed, inadequate, and defeated, all factors that may interfere with motivation and learning.

With short-answer and essay questions, the same format was followed: pairs of students wrote and answered each other's questions and also our questions. In class discussions, the quality of the questions as well as the answers were discussed. Students were also given the self-assessment form provided in Appendix D to evaluate their own responses.

This process of identifying key information to write and answer questions reflects the link among reading, writing, and critical thinking. Students read the material; take notes on what they perceive to be key terms, concepts, people, and events; and use that information in answering test questions. To be able to identify key information, however, students must think critically. They must determine which information from the text is worthy of notetaking and studying. Both of these processes involve critical decision making: deciding what material is important and what information is needed to correctly complete the task. The process of reading, writing, and answering questions also reflects the progressive and cyclical nature of learning. In the Amerigo Vespucci example, the student had learned some information about the man, but not the most essential information. As a result of the class discussion and revisiting the text, the student learned what is most important about Amerigo Vespucci, learned the need to identify key information, and perhaps learned that the process of reading and writing is cyclical: students read, then write, and then read some more (both their own writing and the writing in the text) to determine if they have said what they want to say, understood the text, and correctly completed the task.

As students move from writing ID questions to writing essay questions, the tasks become more complicated and the need for sustained content more important. If students are faced with processing new information, vocabulary, and rhetorical conventions from numerous thematic units, as well as learning new academic tasks, the cognitive demand is extremely high. Also, learning to synthesize, compare, and contrast is problematic if the content changes from one thematic unit to another. If the content remains constant, however, new information builds on previous information, patterns of knowledge emerge (e.g., similarity among patterns of settling the colonies), and rhetorical conventions remain stable. Consequently, students learn both content and skills that they will use later.

Frank Smith's (1988) metaphor of the literacy club may be helpful here. Smith compares academic disciplines to clubs (e.g., tennis or gardening clubs). Like other clubs, the literacy club has members, rules, conventions, traditions, and membership criteria. Smith argues that for students to become a member of a particular literacy club, they must participate in the literacy of that community, which includes the community's linguistic and rhetorical practices. Similarly, Bartholomae (1988) contends that a student has "to try on the particular ways of knowing, selecting, evaluating, reporting, concluding, and arguing that define the discourse" of a particular discipline (p. 273). The kind of knowledge acquisition to which Smith and Bartholomae are referring is not possible without content; it is not possible in the abstract. To become members of Smith's literacy club and to acquire the linguistic and rhetorical skills to which Bartholomae refers, students need to study one content area in one course. They need sustained content.

Graphic Organizers Graphic organizers provide a way to record and organize information from the text as a supplement to reading notes or as an aid in studying for a test. They are more visual than traditional notetaking and clearly achieve several goals of sustained content, such as identifying key ideas in reading, recognizing the relationships among key and supporting ideas, and learning and practicing argumentation and rhetorical conventions (e.g., cause/effect, comparison/contrast). Early in the course we developed graphic organizers for students to fill out, but by the end of the course students were preparing their own graphic organizers to help them make sense of the material (see Appendices E-1 and E-2). The instructor versions of the organizers are in the instructor's manual.

Charts for Academic Language Structures The academic language structure component consists of two parts: identification of textual cues that signal a particular type of academic language in the history textbook and students' implementation of the structures in their own writing. Consistent with the goals of sustained content, the academic language charts focus on the language needed to produce the written discourse used in the discipline. We used academic language charts for structures such as definitions, exemplification, attribution, classification, cause and effect, and comparison/contrast. The academic language charts were implemented as follows. Students were provided with blank charts. Then, as a class, we defined each structure and listed words/symbols that are commonly used with each. Once the students were familiar with these types of words and symbols, we asked them to look at the text and find two or three examples of that particular academic language structure. They wrote the "clue words/symbols" in the left-hand column of their charts and the sentence from the text in the right-hand column.

For some academic language structures, such as definitions, the textbook provided useful examples that students could use in filling out academic language charts—for example, putting the word *corn* in parentheses after the word *maize* (Tindall & Shi, 1997, p. 12). The textbook was less helpful, however, for other types of structures. The textbook determined the types of test questions asked, but did not necessarily provide examples of the language structures needed to answer them. In these cases, we did not ask students to fill out the academic language charts. Instead, we distributed completed charts so they could use the appropriate academic language in writing their essays. For example, from the descriptions of the different colonizations, compare-and-contrast patterns emerged. After reading the material, taking reading notes, and filling out the graphic organizer (see Appendix E-1), students were instructed in the structure of a comparison/contrast essay question (Appendix F). Students wrote and revised an essay question comparing and contrasting the early years of Virginia and Maryland, using the academic language chart in Appendix G. Then we provided a model answer and asked students to underline the academic language of comparison/contrast and to circle other types of academic language (see Appendix H).

A Typical Unit

A typical unit began with a prereading activity to build enough background knowledge to allow students to comprehend some or most of the reading assignment. Students read a portion of the chapter and took reading notes. Although they learned from reading and taking reading notes, they came to class with questions. Given the density of the information, in the following class we discussed the content and answered students' questions. If we did not know the answers, we wrote down the questions, looked up the answers, and reported back during the next class, building our knowledge base for the next time we taught the course. The topics in the first chapter of the history book illustrate the density of the material and also its unfamiliarity to many ESL students. Topics included the indigenous populations of Latin and North America; the Spanish, British, and French explorers; early voyages to the New World; the Protestant Reformation; Henry VIII, Queen Elizabeth, and Mary Queen of Scots; the Spanish Armada; the complex differences in the settling of the colonies of the Chesapeake, New England, the Carolinas, and New York; and the colonists' relationships with the indigenous populations of North America.

After answering students' questions, we employed the pedagogical tasks described earlier in the chapter: Students wrote and answered sample test questions, filled in graphic organizers, and identified academic language structures. In grading the essay questions, all three course levels used the same criteria for 25-point essay questions: content, 10 points; restate question, 2 points; move from general to specific, 2 points; grammar (interferes with meaning), 7 points; and use academic language, 4 points.

Student Performance in Answering Test Questions

All students made a C or better in this course. We graded strictly, meaning students could not have made a C without grasping both the content and the appropriate language and conventions to express it. To illustrate question types, student responses, and student application of reading and writing strategies, we will provide examples and analyses of students' work.

An example of an ID question was "encomienda." A student who received full credit for her answer wrote,

> is a system which was transfer by the conquistadors to America where officer took control over the village. This system required tribute and set up class system.

This student utilized at least four strategies that were taught in class. First, she used a cue from the text to recognize the importance of the term; *encomienda* was italicized. Second, she employed the definition form we taught (i.e., word + class word + characteristics that distinguish it from other members of its class). Third, her information was correct. Finally, she stated the essential information (" . . . officers took control of the village. This system require tribute and set up class system"). The significance of the "encomienda" was that it "set up class system" that was a precursor to the social and political systems that followed.

One short-answer questions was: "Why didn't the French exploration in the New World have a lasting effect on Spain's control?" Again, we'll use an answer from a student who received full credit. The student wrote,

> The French exploration in the New World didn't have a lasting effect on Spain's control for many reasons. The French didn't permanently settle in the New World. They came to a certain region or river to do trade with the Indian. Moreover, they were busy battling over religion in their country. Therefore, they didn't have a lasting effect on Spain's control of the New World.

Using strategies explained in Appendix C-2, the student restated the question in the first sentence of the response. He moved from the general (e.g., "The French . . . didn't have a lasting effect") to the specific (because they "didn't permanently settle in the New World" and "were busy battling over religion in their country"). He also provided details, explaining that the French came "to do trade with the Indian" but, as directed, did not use an excessive amount of detail. The student used two academic terms taught: *moreover* and *therefore*. However, none of the above would have mattered if the student had not learned the content and anticipated the question (i.e., realized what content was important). Without the content, the form is empty.

"Why was Roger Williams important in U.S. history?" was one of the essay questions. Here was one good response:

> Roger Williams was an important person in U.S. history. In 1631 Williams arrived in the New World. He was the purest of the Puritans—a Separatist who wanted to cut off church from the state. He was unhappy because the other Separatists didn't separate completely from Church of England. His belief was that a true church could not have relationship with government or Church of England. He had job as a pastor in Salem, Massachusetts, but at the time, no one supported his beliefs and he was fired from that job. In fact, he was sent back to England, but he did not go. Some Indians helped him and he founded town called Providence in Rhode Island. This town was the first to legalize religious freedom. Although Roger Williams and his beliefs were not popular when he lived, religious freedom and separation of church and government later became important parts of American life. That is why he is important.

Like the other students, this student demonstrated an excellent grasp of the course content and the information needed to answer the question. She did not merely present random information but stated explicitly why Williams was important in American history by writing, " . . . religious freedom and separation of church and government later became important parts of American life. That is why he is important." She also followed conventions taught in class and presented in Appendix C-3: rephrasing the question, moving from general to specific information, providing details and examples to demonstrate a thorough understanding of the material, and giving correct information.

Student Course Evaluations

Eighteen students completed the end-of-term evaluation form. Two evaluation questions related to specific points of course content: students' reactions to American history as the topic of sustained content and writing for exams as the focus of writing activities. Fourteen students made positive comments about using U.S. history as the content area. Typical comments were "is good because it helps us prepare for regular history class" and "help ESL students understand U.S. history." Responses from the few students who did not like history as the area of sustained content ranged from "it's not very important" to "confusing." These comments raise important issues. For instance, what subjects are appropriate for sustained content courses? The answer to this question depends on numerous factors, such as the proficiency level of the students, the goals of the course and the department, and the needs of the students. Another important question is, Do students have to like the subject to learn from the course? As undergraduates, students are required to take courses they do not like, but they learn from them. Liking the subject of sustained content seems less important than these issues: Do students perceive the content and the tasks/skills they are learning as valuable? Does the course have face validity from the students' point of view?

All but one student supported the focus on exam writing. Typical comments were "it's what we need to know as ESL students" and "now we won't be shocked when we get to the university." It is sustained content that enables the instructor to simulate a believable content-area course with a focus on exams. One question asked what students would change about the course. Nine students made no suggestions, and most of the others made positive comments such as, "The other advanced writing class should use this book and method." Four students stated that the course should include more reading and cover more of the textbook. Thus, even though the textbook was difficult to read and cognitively demanding, students recognized the benefits of simulating a "real" course with authentic textbooks and tasks—so much so that four students wanted to read more. Students' recognition of these benefits has positive implications for their motivation.

In response to the question "What things did you like about this class?" 15 students mentioned the method or style of teaching, with 6 specifically applauding the amount of student interaction in class. One student wrote, "The teachers encouraged students to participate so it was fun and stimulating to learn." Others noted the explicitness with which the material was explained, as well as the helpful use of example test items, test answers, graphic organizers, and practice tests before real tests. Three commented that they liked the focus on university tests, and two appreciated the focus on academic language. These comments relate to simulating a "real" academic course by using sustained content. Students recognized the value of mastering authentic university-level material and demonstrating their mastery in real exam formats. Students also realized the importance of negotiating and unraveling meaning by working with other students.

In response to the question "What things didn't you like?" 12 students indicated that there was nothing they did not like. Two wanted a faster pace; two disliked using a history book; and one thought the content was too difficult to remember. The paucity of negative comments is in itself an argument for using sustained content. Even though American history was a difficult subject, only a few students mentioned that they disliked American history as a content area.

The students' comments clearly demonstrated their enthusiasm for the course and for sustained content. They recognized the value of simulating an undergraduate American history course using an authentic university-level textbook. They also recognized the value of learning how to identify and learn important information from the text and how to organize that information in writing answers to test questions. In addition, they benefited from working together and learning from one another. In Chapter 1, Marcia Pally contends that students must engage in a variety of negotiations and discussions to unravel the meaning of the material. Students clearly needed such negotiations, as illustrated by the number of positive comments on the value of student interaction and participation.

As a result of students' evaluations, we made revisions in the instructor's manual, increasing the emphasis on particular activities that the students mentioned (e.g., working together to develop and answer questions, to develop graphic organizers, and to identify academic language). Although a few students wanted to cover the material more quickly, most were pleased with the pace of the course. Though most students saw the benefits of using American history as the area of sustained content, a few did not. It may be that we need to do a better "selling" job the next time the course is taught: explaining the benefits of using sustained content and strongly emphasizing that despite the difficulty international students have with American history, it is a required course for undergraduates and also necessary for understanding America today. Students clearly saw the benefits of using university exams as the focus of writing tasks.

Challenges to Face

One objection to content-based or sustained content syllabi is that language teachers have been trained to teach language and not to teach history, biology, or psychology. One argument against this criticism is that language teachers should teach the language of the discipline and help students identify and use the vocabulary, sentence structures, rhetorical conventions, and methods of argumentation of the area of sustained content. Although this "solution" makes sense, we found that we needed a grounding in American history in order to provide students with correct information. As Pally (see Chapter 1) points out, " . . . if students are to study content in a sustained way, ESL/EFL teachers must acquire sufficient content-area expertise." In the beginning, learning the content means extra work for the teacher, but once the coursepack is created, others can teach the course, especially if it is an introductory content class. Also, if instructors teach the course repeatedly, they will build up a body of knowledge in the content area. By becoming more knowledgeable about the field, teachers can make more informed decisions about both content (what in the discipline is crucial to know) and language (what types of language are most widely practiced).

The amount of time it takes to develop the support materials for a content-area textbook is another challenge. One instructor, Gayle Nelson, was given a course release to work on the development of this course. If the sustained content course is to become part of an ongoing curriculum, giving a teacher a one-time course release to develop the course is an investment in a more effective curriculum.

Another challenge is deciding the amount of content to cover. Several of our students wanted to read more of the history textbook. In terms of our overall goal, to simulate an American history course as closely as possible, we should have covered more material. By not asking students to read more, we may have given them the idea that they needed to learn all the content thoroughly and contributed to their answering test items with memorized phrases or passages. In the future, we plan to have students read more. At the same time, however, the focus of the course is on writing, and students receive reading instruction in their reading and listening course (see Carson, Chapter 2).

Conclusion

Students responded so positively to this course and the instructors were so energized by developing and teaching the supplementary materials that we do not want to end this chapter with the challenges to be faced. Both students and instructors learned more about the early colonization of the Americans than they knew before, and also enjoyed the process of learning the content. The class was truly collaborative as students and instructors worked together to unravel the meaning of the text and learn the material. In the beginning of the course, we enthusiastically developed materials and appreciated having a partner to share the excitement of our "inventions." Later, when students were developing test questions and graphic organizers, they too experienced the pleasure of inventing creations that helped them learn. Most important, however, students learned reading and writing skills that they can apply to other disciplines and contexts.

We had the privilege of working with a partner in developing this course. However, even without a partner, one can experience the joy of creating materials, and, as teachers, we experience pleasure in our students' success. So although we worked as a team, teachers can, and more frequently do, work alone to develop the materials needed to support sustained content instruction.

References

Bartholomae, D. (1988). Inventing the university. In E. R. Kintgen, B. M. Kroll, & M. Rose (Eds.), *Perspectives on literacy* (pp. 273–285). Carbondale, IL: Southern Illinois University Press.

Benesch, S., Rakijas, M., & Rorschach, B. (1987). *Academic writing workshop*. Belmont, CA: Wadsworth.

Brinton, D. M., Snow, M. A., & Wesche, M. B. (1989). *Content-based second language instruction*. Boston: Heinle & Heinle.

Carrell, P., & Eisterhold, J. (1983). Schema theory and ESL reading pedagogy. *TESOL Quarterly, 17,* 553–573.

Carson, J. (1993). Reading for writing: Cognitive perspectives. In J. Carson & I. Leki (Eds.), *Reading in the composition classroom: Second language perspectives* (pp. 85–104). Boston: Heinle & Heinle.

Carson, J., Chase, N., & Gibson, S. (1992). *Literacy analysis of high school and university courses: Summary descriptions of selected courses*. Atlanta: Center for the Study of Adult Literacy, Georgia State University.

Carson, J., Chase, N., Gibson, S., & Hargrove, M. (1992). Literacy demands of the undergraduate curriculum. *Reading Research and Instruction, 31,* 25–50.

Carson, J., & Leki, I. (1993). *Reading in the composition classroom: Second language perspectives*. Boston: Heinle & Heinle.

Curry, P., & Cray, E. (1987). *Strictly academic: A reading and writing text*. Boston: Heinle & Heinle.

Levy, A. (1988). *Writing college English*. Washington, DC: Harcourt Brace Jovanovich.

Lites, E., & Lehman, J. (1990). Visions: *An academic writing text*. Englewood Cliffs, NJ: Prentice-Hall.

Smith, F. (1988). *Joining the literacy club*. Princeton, NJ: Princeton University Press.

Tindall, G. B., & Shi, D. E. (1997). *America*. New York: W. W. Norton.

Appendix A (for Instructors)

General Curriculum Guidelines: Condensed

1. Reading Notes

   Go over the criteria that will be used to evaluate reading notes. These criteria are provided in the instructor's manual and the student study guide. After students have taken reading notes, give them feedback (according to the criteria) and return the notes before the test. In the beginning, it is suggested that you collect the reading notes in sections (that is, don't assign the entire chapter and collect all the notes at once). When collecting in sections, students can apply the feedback offered to improve future notes and their overall notetaking skills.

2. Tests

   a. Tests are graduated. The first test counts less than the last test. One possibility is as follows: Test 1, 15%; Test 2, 20%; Test 3, 20%; Test 4, 25%; and the Final Exam, pass/fail.

   b. The final exam covers the last section studied. It is not accumulative.

   c. The first test includes ID and short-answer items; all other tests consist of about five ID questions, three to four short-answer questions, and one essay question for the intermediate class and one or two essay questions for the advanced classes.

   d. For ID questions, if the content is incorrect, students earn NO points.

   e. The essay question is graduated. In the intermediate class, the question should generate about half a page, in the advanced intermediate class a half to one page, and in the advanced class one to one-and-a-half pages. These page limits are goals to be reached by the middle to the end of the course.

   f. The three major issues in grading the short-answer and essay questions are content, format, and grammar. If format is a problem (e.g., student does not follow the correct format), then the teacher should deduct points. If grammar is a problem (e.g., it interferes with the meaning), then the teacher should deduct points. Teachers should pay particular attention to verb tenses, especially in the advanced class. If verb tenses are wrong, points should be deducted. However, focus should not be placed on grammar errors that do not generally interfere with meaning.

   g. All essay questions are worth 25 points (with the exception of the advanced class). The grading for the essay questions will be criterion-referenced; all students are evaluated according to whether or not they have the criteria in their response. The criteria are specified in the instructor's manual and the student study guide.

   h. To assist students in becoming comfortable with writing under time constraints, time limits should be given for tests.

Taking Reading Notes (for Students)

In your academic classes, there is a large amount of reading assigned to you. For example, a professor might assign 200 pages of reading the first week of classes. In order to manage this much material and be able to prepare for class discussions, writing assignments, and course exams, students must take reading notes. In addition, at the end of the term, there is no way a student can reread all assignments before the final exam. You MUST be able to rely on the accuracy, readability, and completeness of your reading notes.

Each person reads and takes notes a little differently. However, there are some basic procedures to follow whenever you take notes.

1. Date and label notes at the top of the page.

2. Use headings to help you organize the main points and ideas. Notice the font size of the headings—this will help you understand the relationship of ideas.

3. Indicate main ideas, names, and terms (with definitions) by putting them close to the left margin. Indent to show details about those main ideas. Underline or circle to show main ideas.

4. Include examples that clarify ideas. Be brief in your detail of those examples, though. Use numbers, letters, and marks to show details.

5. Use diagrams and charts to show the relationship of ideas (signal words and phrases in the reading can help you understand this relationship). Skip lines to indicate a change of ideas or different sections of the readings.

6. Include information from the charts, pictures, and graphs within the chapter.

7. Abbreviate when possible, and use phrases (not complete sentences).

8. Mark places that you don't understand, and leave space so that you can elaborate or clarify during or after class discussion and lectures.

Appendix C-1 (for Students)

Type of Test Question: IDENTIFICATION (ID)

The shortest kinds of test questions that require written responses are identification or ID questions.

- ID questions usually ask for definitions of key terms.

- They also ask for information about important people, places, or theories. Be sure to include details about their relationships to the content you are studying.

- Complete sentences are not usually necessary in your written responses. However, you may wish to use complete sentences so that your answer is as clear as it can be. To be safe, *ask your individual instructor what length is expected and if complete sentences are necessary.*

- These questions are usually worth about 2 to 5 points.

- Remember, you MUST state the significance of the term. (Why is it important?)

Sample Question and Answer

Question: Mayas

Answer: A major civilization that lived in Middle America during the pre-Columbian period. They reached their peak between AD 300 and 900. They are important because they dominated a large area of Middle America for 600 years.

Type of Test Question: SHORT-ANSWER

Short-answer questions usually ask for more information or more complex information than simple ID questions. They often require a written response of approximately four to eight sentences. Short-answer questions do the following:

- ask you to compare two concepts or to define or explain a concept and give an example
- do not ask for a lot of detail or explanation as an essay question would
- are usually 5 to 10 points each

You should begin your answer by restating the question. Then quickly provide the necessary information, moving from the general to the specific. You should also provide an appropriate example, if required. If an example is not required, you should provide one anyway or explain the idea in more detail.

Sample Short-Answer Question and Answer

Question: What were some of the foods and devices that the Indians introduced to the Europeans?

Answer: The Indians introduced the Europeans to many foods and devices. Some of the foods were corn, potatoes, and beans. When Columbus first ate corn, he didn't like it but he brought some back to Spain, and soon corn was popular in Spain. The devices the Indians introduced to the Europeans included canoes, snowshoes, hammocks, ponchos, and kayaks. The Indian influence on Europe is important because it shows the diffusion of the cultures.

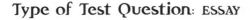

Appendix C-3 (for Students)

Type of Test Question: ESSAY

Another common form of test question is an essay question. Essay questions ask you to explain more complex ideas than ID or short-answer questions, and you need to write more sentences. Short essays should be from one to two paragraphs (or six to ten sentences) in length and longer essays from three to five paragraphs. These questions are usually worth from 15 to 30 points.

- Essay questions ask you to explain a concept, event, or procedure in detail. You should provide accurate examples to prove or support your ideas.

- Essay questions also ask you to show the relationship between two or more concepts, events, or procedures (cause/effect, compare/contrast, classification, etc.); to summarize the main ideas of or describe a theory, invention, or event; or to discuss the importance or advantages/disadvantages of an idea, invention, event, or theory.

The most important part in answering an essay question is that your information is correct. However, you must also follow the correct form in your response:

- Begin by rephrasing or repeating the question.

- Move from general statements to specific details. For instance, you define a concept and then explain its importance.

- You do not necessarily need a conclusion. However, you may need to end with a general statement that restates your main idea.

Judge the number of sentences by the number of questions in the test and the number of points for the question.

Sample Short Essay Question and Answer

Question: Provide evidence for the statement: King Henry VIII's rejection of papal authority in England occurred for political reasons.

Answer: The rejection of papal authority in England occurred for political reasons. Henry VIII wanted a son in order to maintain his family's reign in England. Because Henry VIII's wife gave birth to a daughter, he eventually asked the Pope to annul his marriage. The Pope refused Henry VIII's request, and as a result, Henry VIII severed ties with Rome and the Catholic Church. The fact that Henry VIII rejected Catholicism to keep his family in power tells us that his intentions were political.

Self-Assessment Checklist for Answers to Short-Answer and Essay Questions

After you have written your short-answer and essay responses, ask yourself these questions:

- Are my form and organization correct?
- Is my information correct?
- Did I restate the question at the beginning?
- Did I use complete sentences?
- Does my response move from the general to the specific?
- Did I provide transitions between paragraphs (if I used more than one paragraph)?
- Did I use evidence to support my major points?

Comparison/Contrast Graphic Organizer

Directions: Read pages 25–30 and fill in the graphic organizer below:

Compare and Contrast the Early Years of Virginia and Maryland	

Virginia	Maryland
Similarities	
Differences	

Completed Graphic Organizer

Compare and Contrast the Early Years of Virginia and Maryland

Virginia	Maryland
Similarities	
Founded by English	Founded by English
Founded in the early 1600s	Founded in the early 1600s
Settled on the Chesapeake	Settled on the Chesapeake
Settled by gentlemen and servants	Settled by gentlemen and servants
Eventually depended on tobacco	Eventually depended on tobacco
Differences	
Granted to a stock company	Proprietary colony (granted to an individual)
Founded for stockholders to gain wealth (e.g., gold) and for a passage to India	Founded for religious reasons—by a Catholic who wanted a safe place for other Catholics (Lord Baltimore)
Leaders appointed by company (John Smith and John Rolfe)	Governed by a charter; Lord Baltimore could make laws with the consent of the other freemen
At first, colony was controlled by company in London (company made the rules). Ex.: "Headright Policy"	The charter said that they could also grant estates

Appendix F (for Students)

Writing Comparison/Contrast Essays

- In comparison/contrast essays, the word *compare* often means writing about similarities and the word *contrast* means writing about differences.
- When you write a comparison/contrast essay, you can organize your material in several ways. Often the writer writes about the similarities first. It is more difficult to write about the differences.
- A common organizational pattern for comparison/contrast essays is given below.

Organizational Pattern

Paragraph 1:

Assertion (General Statement): (e.g., "The settlements of Virginia and Maryland were similar in several ways.")

The Specifics/Evidence: Explain the similarities between Virginia and Maryland.

Paragraph 2:

Transition Sentence: (e.g., "Although the settlements of Virginia and Maryland were similar, there were also differences.")

Assertion: (e.g., "One difference was that each colony was settled by people who had different reasons for coming to the New World.")

Specifics: For Virginia

Specifics: For Maryland

Paragraph 3:

Assertion: (e.g., "Another difference was that each colony had a different type of government.")

Specifics: For Virginia

Specifics: For Maryland

Academic Language of Comparison and Contrast

Comparison is a way to show that two or more things or ideas are similar. Sometimes, when instructors ask you to compare, they want you to look at both the similarities and the differences.

Contrast is a way to show that two or more things or ideas are different.

Showing Similarities

Coordinators	Transition Words	Subordinators	Others
and	similarly likewise also	just as	A and B *are similar* in several ways. A and B *are alike* in several ways. A *is similar to* B in several ways. A *is like* B in several ways. A *is the same as* B in several ways. *There are several similarities between* A and B. A, *like* B, . . . A, *just like* B, . . . *Not only* A *but also* B . . . *Both* A and B . . . A and B *both* . . . A *can be compared to/with* B . . . When comparing A to/and B, we can see that they are quite similar.

Showing Differences

Coordinators	Transition Words	Subordinators	Others
but	however in contrast in/by comparison on the other hand	while whereas although even though	A and B *are different/dissimilar* in many ways. A *differs from* B in many ways. A *is different from/than* B in many ways. A and B *have many differences.* A and B *differ* in many ways. *There are many differences between* A and B. *Unlike* A, B is . . . *Opposite to* A, B . . . When comparing A to/and B, we can see that they are quite different.

Source: Developed by Sharon Cavusgil and Debra Snell.

Example of Comparison/Contrast Essay Given to Students (Answer Key)

Directions: Read the essay. Underline the words that signal comparison/contrast. Circle other types of academic language.

Question: Compare and contrast the early years of Virginia and Maryland. Discuss their similarities and differences.

Answer: The early years of Virginia and Maryland were <u>both</u> <u>similar</u> and <u>different</u>. <u>One similarity</u> was that they were <u>both</u> founded by the English in the early 1600s. <u>Similarly,</u> <u>both</u> were settled by gentlemen who brought servants with them. <u>Both</u> <u>also</u> tried to grow various agricultural products but eventually depended on growing tobacco to make a living.

    <u>Although these</u> two colonies shared some <u>similarities</u>, there were <u>also</u> <u>differences</u>. (For example,) the colonization of Virginia was funded by a stock company that wanted to make money for the stockholders. The company hoped to find gold and other valuable items in the New World. It <u>also</u> hoped to still find a passage to India. <u>In contrast,</u> Maryland was a colony that was granted to an individual—Sir George Calvert, Lord Baltimore. He was a Catholic and wanted to start the colony for other Catholics who were discriminated against in England.

    A second <u>difference</u> is related to how the colonies were governed. The leaders of the Virginia Colony were appointed by the company; they were John Smith and John Rolfe. <u>Also,</u> in <u>Virginia,</u> the company made decisions about the government of the colony. (For example,) to increase the population of the colony, the company offered 50 acres to anyone who could get to Virginia. <u>In contrast,</u> Maryland had a charter that stated that Lord Baltimore could make the laws with the consent of the other landowners. <u>Likewise,</u> he could grant estates to the colonists.

    (So,) <u>although</u> these colonies were <u>both</u> British and were neighbors, Virginia was <u>more</u> tied to England and Maryland was <u>more</u> independent of England.

Chapter 9

"Film & Society"

A Course for Analyzing Readings,
Writing, and Critical Thinking[1]

Marcia Pally
New York University

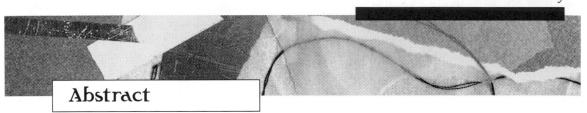

Abstract

This chapter describes a course in film and society, developed to improve the text analysis, writing, and critical thinking skills of intermediate through advanced, college-bound ESL students. It describes the content, materials, and content-skills integration. Excerpts of student discussion and portfolio writing are evaluated to assess student progress. Student responses to the course were collected in two phases: (1) in formative course evaluations and (2) from open-ended and directed interviews in five case studies. Results and excerpts from both are discussed and implications for teaching are explored. ■

[1]Portions of this chapter have appeared in *Screening English: Studying Movies for Reading, Writing and Critical Thinking,* 1997, Edina, MN: Burgess Publishing; in the May 1998 *Journal of Adolescent & Adult Literacy, 41*(8), 620–628, copyright by the International Reading Association, all rights reserved; and in the 1997 *Journal of Second Language Writing, 6*(3), 293–311.

Introduction: Text Analysis and Writing Among Non-Native Speaker (NNS) University Students

Among the skills required by academic, professional, and technical work are the accurate reading of texts and clear writing of expository/persuasive nonfiction, from university papers to quarterly reports. Text analysis includes identifying, questioning, and synthesizing the main points and argumentation of readings. Text construction includes developing original ideas or distilling a position from existing material, and expressing the idea or position using the rhetorical conventions of written expository/persuasive English, however the conventions may differ from argument and rhetoric in students' L1s (Al-Abed Al-Haq & Ahmed, 1994; Leki & Carson, 1994). As Connor (1996) writes, summarizing Leki (1992), "English-speaking readers are convinced by facts, statistics, and illustrations in arguments; they move from generalizations to specific examples and expect explicit links between main topics and subtopics; and they value originality" (p. 167; see also Johns, 1997, p. 59).

The reading and writing skills of NNS college students have been described as not so much below the standards of NS as other-standard. This may be the result of interference from first-language (L1) patterns of text organization (Mauranen, 1993; Moser & Raphan, 1993) and/or insufficient practice with English academic expository/persuasive writing (Braine, 1996). In reviewing the work of my own university-bound ESL students, I found that this other-standardness was noticeable in three areas, even when surface-level errors were negligible:

1. Text analysis—students tended to list summaries of articles rather than identify, synthesize, question key points, or use the articles to construct ideas/positions of their own; at times the summaries followed a text's paragraph order rather than its argumentation, showing a poor grasp of the distinction between key ideas and their support (for similar findings, see Connor & Kramer, 1995; Leki, 1995).

2. Paper organization—notably unclear main ideas and unclear organization of support.

3. Exemplification—insufficient examples in support of ideas, lack of concreteness in examples, confusion in matching examples with the ideas they support.

To address these difficulties, I developed a sustained content course for low-intermediate through advanced ESL classes at New York University and Fordham University. This chapter reports on seven classes, with a total of 89 students from Europe, Asia, Mexico, the Middle East, and Central and South America.

Premises for Course Development: Sustained Content Study, "Transferable Knowledge," Explicit Instruction, and Modeling

I found my way to content-based ESL—specifically to sustained content-based instruction (CBI)—in thinking about how my native speaker (NS) students acquire expertise throughout college. They learn subject matter and the critical thinking skills required for academic study in content classes, using the cyclical, synergistic relationship between content and critical thinking skills described in Chapter 1. Yet sustained CBI is not a standard strategy of ESL courses, outside sheltered or adjuncted classes, and so ESL students may not be getting the training that we afford NS. The research on sustained CBI found in second-language acquisition (SLA), immersion programs, text analysis, and genre studies, in ESL and EFL settings (Chapter 1), led me to explore sustained CBI both because it is how NS learn higher-level reading and writing and because studying one area over time (and having the skills to do so) is the kind of work that will be expected of my students once they leave ESL.

The central point in choosing the skills emphasized in the course was that they would not only address the immediate text analysis and text construction problems of my students but also apply to future content classes. I wanted to identify skills that are among the "transferable language knowledge" described by AMES (1992), Flowerdew (1993), and Widdowson (1993) and that would benefit students with wide-ranging goals.

With this objective in mind, I developed a simulated semester-long university course with film and society as course content. I chose this subject because of its wide appeal among students with varying backgrounds and goals (Stempleski, 1990, 1992), the importance of media literacy in today's screen-filled world (Karl, 1981), and because it lends itself to practicing the skills that troubled my students. Since films reflect the conflicts, myths, and assumptions of society, students often respond strongly to movies and articles about movies. These responses prompt them both to identify the key points of films and readings and to challenge them. In addition, the topic of film and society lends itself to learning academic paper organization and exemplification. Because cinema is composed of clearly marked component parts, a student who wishes to investigate the assumptions of a film can show how they are expressed in the film's script, camerawork, lighting, music, and so on—material that students can readily organize using English rhetorical conventions, including exemplification.

The Film & Society course also included **explicit instruction** in text analysis (Carrell, 1985; Davis, Lange, & Samuels, 1988) and paper organization (Cumming, 1995; Flowerdew, 1993; Hilder, 1997; Jacoby, Leech, & Holten, 1995). The explicit instruction included two kinds of **modeling:** models of text analysis and paper organization (for example, a text marked for main and supporting ideas or a model of an outline for a writing assignment) and models of strategies that students may use to analyze texts, create outlines, and so forth (Cumming, 1995; Swales & Feak, 1994). Models were included not so that students would produce mechanistic copies; rather, they served as a guide to the structure of English academic/expository texts that students would modify as they became familiar with more types of texts and developed their own "voices" in writing. Models allow students to highlight the structures of English academic/expository texts and then automate or "chunk" them (Purves & Purves, 1986), simplifying the task of composing while retaining the complexity of academic work.

Description of Course and Materials

Students began the Film & Society course by reading two types of materials: (1) articles on conflicts and assumptions in American life, such as the conflicting needs for individual freedom and community; America's need for immigrants and its suspicion of them; issues in race, gender, and class; and the role of violence in American society; (2) chapter-length essays on how these assumptions and conflicts are reflected in American movies and how to identify assumptions and conflicts in script, camera, performance, lighting, and sound. The information and vocabulary included in the essays are at the level of introductory college texts for nonmajors. Lower-level students read the same material as higher-level ones, albeit more slowly. To prompt student discussion and schema development (mental maps with which one organizes information; see Carrell, 1987, and Tobias, 1994), essays were accompanied by prereading and prewriting questions such as "Since the beginning of history, people have told stories. Why?" or "What are the sources of film sound? What does silence do in film?" (Material for the Film & Society course has since been organized into a textbook, *Screening English: Studying Movies for Reading, Writing and Critical Thinking,* 1997, Edina, MN: Burgess Press.)

The essays follow three films as examples throughout to illustrate conflicts, assumptions, and specific points about script, camera, and so on. The sample films are *The Untouchables,* about federal agent Eliot Ness's capture of organized crime leader Al Capone in Prohibition-era Chicago; *Do the Right Thing,* which explores racial and ethnic tensions in contemporary New York and challenges the use of violence to combat police brutality; and *Thelma and Louise,* which also explores the use of violence, as well as the dreams and myths underlying the American road movie and issues in gender relations. Each essay focuses on one component of filmmaking such as script or camerawork, and links that component to the conflicts and assumptions in the sample films. For example, the essay on camerawork describes how camera angles and editing affect viewers' emotional response to movies, and then illustrates the effects by describing scenes in each sample film. Students are asked questions such as these:

> In the opening scene, Al Capone is filmed with overhead shots, which are usually used for epics and grand scenery. By treating Capone like grand scenery, what does the camera tell you about him? How does this treatment set up the conflict in the movie? What colors surround Capone in this scene? What colors surround Ness? What do they tell you about these characters?

While working with the readings, students viewed, discussed, and wrote about the sample films; later they worked in groups and individually to write about films of their own choosing. Looking at immigration, for instance, *The Untouchables* proposes the "melting pot" ideal, which *Do the Right Thing* debunks. Using examples from plot, camera, dialogue, and other elements, students showed how these opposing propositions appear in each film and in "real life." Who, for example, believes in the "melting pot," and who does not? Why? What is the relationship between assimilation and economic or political success? For whom? Are there alternatives? In one group project, students compared *The Untouchables* with another film about immigration and crime during the Prohibition era, *Once Upon a Time in America*. Other students watched Arnold Schwarzenegger's *Last Action Hero* to augment class discussion of violence. Another group compared the feminist issues raised in *Thelma and Louise* with those in *The Piano* and, interestingly, *Fatal Attraction*.

These were the content goals of the course. Yet, in order to grasp this content, examine films, and write about them, students had to analyze the texts they read and express ideas of their own using the conventions of academic expository/persuasive writing—in short, develop a range of critical thinking skills appropriate to academic work.

Students practiced text analysis on the reading assignments (the articles on American life and the essays on cinema), which are themselves instances of English academic/expository writing. In other words, they got double duty out of the readings, using them both as content and as material on which to practice skills development. For each essay, I drew up an explanation and a model of a text analysis and writing task, progressing from simple to more difficult (see the appendix to this chapter). I modeled the task using the first section of an essay. Students practiced on subsequent sections of the essay, on the articles about conflicts and assumptions in American life, and on authentic-text film reviews included with each essay. Text analysis tasks include (1) drawing out and outlining the "logical skeleton" of a text's main ideas, supporting ideas, and examples (and distinguishing them from paragraph order); (2) identifying transition devices; (3) using the "skeleton" outline to develop summaries; and (4) raising questions about surprising or problematic ideas found in the readings and using those questions to formulate or support one's own ideas (for example, in "refute opposing opinion" strategies, where students identify authors who disagree with them and, by casting doubt on the opposing authors' positions, thereby strengthen their own). Activities for questioning texts include marking a text whenever students react strongly to it (even when they are not sure of the reason for their response), comparison and class discussion of marked passages, and working with a question Outline designed to help students articulate and support their reactions.

Each essay on film ends with composition assignments in which students draw on the rhetorical and organizational structures they discovered in the reading and recycle them as guides for their writing. To create models of this process, I abstracted the organizational structures of readings and applied them to the content of writing assignments. After studying these in class, students were asked to use the abstracted structures to guide the writing of their own papers.

Student Progress: Discussion and Writing

I monitored student progress through class discussions (taped and transcribed) and portfolio writing, which I read holistically with an emphasis on clarity and originality of ideas, clarity of paper organization, and sufficiency and specificity of exemplification. Though excerpts from student work are inadequate measures of it, the samples of discussions and papers that follow illustrate how students analyzed and questioned what they read and saw. (Surface errors are retained in all excerpts.)

Samples of Student Discussion:
Questioning Films, Linking Questions to Life

Among the issues that students raised during the course were ethnic and race relations, questioning the authority of texts, and the role of culture in interpreting texts. Here is an excerpt from a high-intermediate discussion of ethnic and race relations in *The Untouchables* and *Do the Right Thing*:

Sung-hee: *Untouchables* is about immigration, and *Do the Right Thing* is black people—not same thing.

Antonio: In American everybody come from another place. It's just immigrants and new immigrants. And the blacks have problems, not just whites, also with Latino and Korean. Latino are not "white" in the U.S., but they have problems with blacks.

Choong-yul: Asians also not white and have many problems with blacks and some whites too.

Antonio: Why Americans say over and over that is so many opportunity for immigrants? There is so many problem. . . .

Christiana: But compare to other places, not so many. . . .

Antonio: But I remember riot in L.A. . . .

Teacher: When do you say something over and over?

Antonio: I don't know.

Hisato: This "over and over," this is personal problem, not race problem, not immigrant problem.

Christiana: It is a personal reaction. You say over and over when you want someone to believe you. So Americans say over and over there is opportunity for immigrants. But people believe idea about opportunity for immigrants in America. Why say it . . .

Antonio: Immigrants believe, that's why we come.

Hisato: Americans don't believe . . . ?

Christiana: No?

Hisato: They believe it is a good place for immigrants, I think, but their families, every family, had also problems, and much violence till today. There is . . . , hard to get a job, competition, you know? So everybody thinks first family and then little bigger group—that is natural. I think so.

Antonio: So is idea—no, idea-l?—ideal about opportunity. We know it is ideal. Why put it in the movies?

Christiana:	It's not just ideal, compared to other places.
Hisato:	If it's not ideal, why Spike Lee showed so many problems?
Christiana:	But compared to other places . . .

This discussion led to one on the conflicting pictures of immigration in America (melting pot, welfare menace) and the socioeconomic issues that each image reflects. As the conversation about "compared to other places" suggests, students began to question not only the melting pot ideal but the American myth of easy opportunity, even as they believed in the educational and economic possibilities in the United States.

Other class discussions led to questioning the truth value of "factual" or historical works and the concepts of absolute and socially constructed truth. A high-intermediate student asked, "What about *Schindler's List?* . . . It author opinion? Hitler actually happened." Another student remarked that people have written books trying to disprove the Holocaust, and that "Japanese books about the World War Two are very difference from American books." Yet another said, "'Hitler' is not the main thing in *Schindler's List;*" rather, it is "the idea that one man can change a war, a politic can change a big army organization like Hitler. This is important idea." This comment represents a significant leap in thinking, in which the student sees that the thrust of a film (in this case, that one individual can make a difference) is not its plot or "facts" (Hitler) but must be inferred from how facts are weighted and presented.

From another discussion of "facts" in a low-intermediate class:

Takaya:	Which propositions from film we put in our composition? Which are correct?
Teacher:	Which do *you* think are correct?
Takaya:	Where do I put what I think? At the end?
Larisa:	No-o-o-o. Put opinion about proposition in beginning; whole composition is your proposition, your idea about proposition.
Machiko:	But what . . . which . . . what one are true?
Yulee:	She mean, what is fact.
Teacher:	We've been talking about the propositions that you believe are in *The Untouchables.* . . .
Takaya:	Just my opinion.
Machiko:	He mean, what are fact.
Takaya:	I can write my opinion about film, but some thing are fact.
Teacher:	Like what?
Takaya:	Like . . . like . . . example: sun in sky.
Teacher:	It is? Doesn't the earth go around the sun?
Takaya:	Okay, earth go around . . .

Larisa: Why you write so stupid composition?

Teacher: Hey, Larisa . . .

Larisa: No-o-o-o, I no mean Takaya. I mean nobody write composition about sun in sky.

Yulee: Like war. It start, it happen. It is fact.

Ming: Maybe there are fact, but book about war, I know, every book, one book say one thing, one book say a little different.

Larisa: Every author put fact different. You can't trust no one.

Machiko: No fact? Yes, yes, I know, author see war different. But what is fact? How do we know for composition?

This class decided that authors present "facts" differently depending on their views. Yet, while students seemed comfortable with author subjectivity in the abstract, they hesitated to question specific authors' claims or note when texts contradict one another. Yet these critical thinking activities—questioning and noting contradictions—are key to academic work, to developing one's own ideas and backing them up. Students' hesitations were reflected in their portfolios and are discussed in more detail in the Student Interviews section.

Classes at all levels debated the role of culture in interpreting cinema. In discussing *The Untouchables,* a low-intermediate student wrote that Eliot Ness's initial powerlessness is evident when reporters show they lack respect by crowding around him in the hallway. Yet what was disrespect to her seemed like interest to others, which led to the idea that culture colors one's image of a film. Yet other students objected, including one who said, "With the imagination, we can understand everything."

Once students began using their reactions to films to question real-world issues, they extended their questioning in their compositions. Two low-intermediate students, after studying law and outlaw in *The Untouchables,* wrote papers asking whether citizens of their home countries should obey laws—specifically tax laws—that they knew were "stupid" and "corrupt." One wrote, "Obedience to laws bring many good thing like calm, order life, and safe on street. But some time other thing get also important. Calm order is not only important part." Another student used Alfonso Arau's *Like Water for Chocolate* to discuss the role of tradition in modern life: which traditions should we keep and which, such as the subjugation of women, should we discard?

Student Portfolios: Organization, Exemplification, and Questioning Texts

Student portfolio writing showed varied progress. It consistently improved in originality of main ideas and clarity of organization. Papers began to support claims generated by students (rather than to summarize readings); main ideas became more specific and were placed so that the purposes of the papers were better defined. Supporting ideas became clearer and more closely linked to main ideas. However, students showed less improvement in exemplification and questioning printed texts.

The following excerpts illustrate how students stated their main ideas, setting up what they had to support in the remainder of their papers. The first is from a high-intermediate paper:

> Shadow is long and the movie, *Stanley & Iris* diffuses mild light which is like either dawn or dusk on the screen. People are always on the edge of giving up or starting over. There is an American myth that there are always chances to take. The movie evokes proposition that it is never too late to take a chance to success while this needs courage and deliberation. . . . [plot summary]
>
> Cox says, "Anything is possible." Why? There are chances. Why? Americans have ideas: "America newfound land and City on the Hill and Second Eden; America, land of new beginning, promised land, chosen land, sweet land of liberty, and land of the free; tabula rasa and virgin continent; America exempt from time, America outside history." (Barber, 1992, p. 53)

The student stated his main idea in paragraph one and selected the quote, extracted from an earlier reading, to support it. Later in the paper, he further supported his claims with examples from the sound, camerawork, and lighting: "The color of the movie is mostly warm yellow and orange, and sunshine is soft. . . . The light is more like dawn than dusk. . . . This evokes that there are chances."

Another excerpt, from an intermediate paper, follows:

> *Muriel's Wedding* proposes that every human being has to be authentic, just the way they are. Every human being has to be proud of who they are, regardless of society's pressures or regulations. In order to get what we want, we need to believe in ourselves, our values, and especial talents.
>
> In the movie, the director shows that beauty is a subjective concept that can't be considered as important as personality. Supporting this point, the protagonist of the movie, named Muriel, who is a young woman that lives in Australia and insists in going out with a group of "old friends" from high school days. Those women depreciate Muriel because she is fat and not "in." So they tell her that they don't like to be seen with an awkward person. But at last Muriel succeeds just being Muriel. When Muriel gets married, her husband can't stand her because he married her for professional reasons. But when he really starts to know Muriel, he falls in love with her.

Here the student reviewed the plot specifically to support her ideas about the role of individualism in the movie. Later she added evidence from the soundtrack: "Music is one of the most powerful elements in the movie because it helps to communicate positive elements about Muriel, making her an attractive and special person even though she doesn't have a sculptural figure." The student continued by describing a specific scene:

> There is a party where Muriel and her friends take the stage and start to sing. This scene is powerful for two reasons: first, Muriel is seen as a desinhibited and independent woman, free of all the rules that inted to change her way of being. Second, this scene recreates a situation that is

familiar to audiences because it is a vivid image of a video made by Abba (a famous group on the 70s and 80s). The director supports Muriel's character in a special imagery and a special moment.

Exemplification

With this improvement in clarity and originality of main ideas/positions and paper organization, problems in exemplification nevertheless remained. In the *Muriel* paper, the Abba example is a page away from the point it supports, the two sections interrupted by a section on character development. In a discussion of light in *Braveheart,* a student wrote, "the colors give a special atmosphere, the director having used blue filters" without explaining "special atmosphere" or the effect of blue filters. What feelings do blue filters give the audience, and how does this contribute to the story or conflicts of the film?

These difficulties can perhaps be seen more clearly when compared against a paper on *12 Monkeys,* in which the student (low-intermediate) makes clear links between claim and example. She begins,

> The story of *12 Monkeys* is about future and like many other films about future, it shows the fear of Orwellian society (restrained, organized and systematized society of future), and the fear of destroying nature by progress of science. This film says, not so strongly but roundabout (beneath the story), over systemized society will destroy humanity.
>
> In this film, there are four different times, 2035, 1990, 1920, and 1996. These times show Orwellian society of future, present and past. However these times can be devided for two diffrent society not accroding to time. One is the society of 2035 and of mental hospital in 1990, in which humanity is repressed by over systemizing. The other is society of 1996 in which humanity is still protected and freedom is remained. During the time travels, Cole (Bruce Willis) shows that man should live in freedom not as a controlled slave.

In her discussion of dialogue, she wrote,

> Jeffrey said to Cole, "System put us here to protect others from us because we are 'crazy.' That is system." Jeffrey is a very unique character because he is crazy but he recognizes, system which can repress humanity and progress which can destroy nature and humanity.

This student believes the film argues for freedom in the face of systematic, authoritarian repression, and she selected her quote to exemplify that claim. Later she did the same in her discussion of camerawork:

> Camera uses wide lens to make distorted pictures to show Cole's restrained situation and repressed humanity. In the scene of hospital, camera also uses wide lens and oblique angles to make distorted picture, too. It shows Cole's instable mind and confusing situation. In both scenes, shots of scientists of future and the shots of doctors of mental hospital use similar compositions because both scenes show the same things that system repress humanity.

In her first sentence, it would be useful to have a more detailed description of "distorted pictures" so readers could see how they express "restrained situation and repressed humanity." Nevertheless, she links the camerawork to the central conflicts of the movie. In her second example, she more specifically explains that the lens and angles create distortion that reflects Cole's mental state. Though her third example would be clearer had she described the "compositions," she clearly links them to systems that repress humanity, which in her view is the main point of the movie. She has begun to select and describe examples, not to summarize the plot but to support her claims about the film.

Questioning Texts

Students in all classes were comfortable with the concept of author subjectivity and the need to synthesize ideas from a variety of views. Yet they hesitated to question specific texts or use such challenges to advance their ideas or support them. (Though resistance to questioning is difficult to show without excerpting long passages of writing, similar findings appear in Ballard, 1984; Grabe, 1991; and Matalene, 1985.) The central reasons for student reluctance were "it takes too much time"; "it is difficult"; and "it might humiliate us because it sometimes show our ignorance." In the student interviews presented in the next section, concern about this "ignorance" emerged as the key factor, and students suggested ways to address it.

Student Responses to Sustained CBI: Course Evaluations and Interviews

Students in low- through high-intermediate classes completed formative course evaluations (student feedback about the class [Widdowson, 1990]) at one-month intervals through the first term of the Film & Society course. Aimed at eliciting a broad range of responses, the evaluations asked what students liked and disliked, what they found useful and not useful, and how they would improve the course. Evaluations did not prompt students to mention sustained CBI or any specific activities.

At one month, low-intermediate students were frustrated in their attempts to identify the conflicts, myths, and assumptions of films, the main points of their writing, and examples that would support them. Nevertheless, all but one wrote that they liked the course and 33 percent volunteered of their own accord that they were improving in their writing. One student wrote, "I think the movies are one of the most important part of culture in U.S.A. Therefore, we analyze those, I think maybe we could understand U.S.A." High-intermediate students did not report frustration at the first evaluation; 50 percent volunteered that their writing was improving.

In the final course evaluations, 63 percent of low-intermediate students reported that the course improved their writing; 31 percent added that it improved their "logic," which one student defined as [learning] how to think, how to organize my thoughts, how to express them in written English and also how to criticize the film which I've seen. It is helpful not only for learning English but also for living my life regardless of English. I've never had this type of class before even though my major was journalism.

In the high-intermediate final evaluations, 93 percent of students wrote that the course improved their writing, 36 percent volunteered that the course improved their "logic," and 79 percent reported that they liked learning from film.

Student Interviews

After obtaining initial feedback from student progress and course evaluations, I conducted case studies of five high-intermediates to uncover more about what students found difficult, which activities were helpful and why, why questioning texts and exemplification remained problematic, and what students believed would help them. Before coming to the United States, Carina worked as a travel agent in Sweden, Soo worked as a production assistant in a Korean film company, Patricia graduated from college in France with a major in math, Yoshio hoped to study architecture in the United States, and Pierre planned to return to France to become a writer (perhaps even of film scripts). After examining their portfolios and course evaluations, I taped and transcribed open-ended and directed interviews. Looking for the broadest range of responses, the open-ended interview asked students if they had improved during the term; if so, at what; and what helped or impeded them. It included no prompt to mention sustained CBI, film, or specific activities. In the directed interviews, students went over their papers and assignments with me; talked about specific difficulties and reasons for improvement; rated the main activities of the course; and explained what was most and least useful, what they liked and disliked, and how they would change the class.

Student Reports on What They Found Difficult

Though students showed less progress in exemplification and questioning texts, they did not single these out in interviews. Rather, they identified *all* the text analysis and writing skills of the course as difficult: "Reading analysis outline is good, but it's difficult. I can memorize the whole thing—essay—but I cannot analyze" (Yoshio). Student comments perhaps indicate that they recognized the skills they had not yet mastered (i.e., the skills were difficult), but were less certain of where they had improved. Since students still found the goals of text analysis and writing challenging, they may have known quite well how much they struggled with all of them, but sensed less accurately that they got closer to their goals in some areas than in others. It's hard to know if you have hit the target if you're not sure what it is. Students frequently attributed their difficulties to interference from L1 rhetorical conventions, as do researchers such as Bloch and Chi (1995), Kobayashi, (1992), Mauranen (1993), and Moser and Raphan (1993). Soo said,

The way of my thought is Korean. But it doesn't matter because usually I wrote my essay—just, I was born in Korea blah blah, my hobby is blah blah. But when I take this class you request make nonfiction composition with main idea. . . . I can't organize my thought in American. Usually I make my thought in Korean and then . . . I can't translate exactly and my composition is very mess.

Interestingly, these students asked for practice in analyzing more complex readings in which, for instance, there is no clear "main idea," even though they felt the Film & Society material was demanding. "We usually speak general idea," Soo said. "What is typical American? What is different thing between culture? It's too general. . . . In this class we have specific subject. It makes more difficult, so I have to find more specific word. I have to think more specifically."

Student Comments on What They Found Helpful: Sustained Content, Explicit Instruction, and Modeling

In the open-ended interviews, students reported that the central benefit of sustained CBI was the accretion of content-area expertise. It gave them more information for developing their ideas (in discussion and writing), familiarity with rhetorical conventions, and more confidence in their grasp of both. "If you read about something different every week or few weeks, you just have to force yourself to find something to write. . . . I need to read more, more back information" (Carina). The directed interviews echoed these comments. Yoshio described the effects of sustained CBI on skills development, specifically the cycle between text analysis and writing: "In the other class we just read and react: what do I think? But in this class we have to analyze the author's opinion and we feedback the analyzing to our writing. . . . I didn't like analyzing other writing, but if we cannot analyze other writing, we cannot organize our writing." This recycling of information and rhetorical forms from reading to writing occurred when students read extensively in one area. By analyzing many texts in the field, they became familiar with vocabulary, information, common arguments, and the range of rhetorical and organizational conventions. By writing several papers, they had the chance to practice them.

A secondary benefit of sustained CBI was motivation. "It's much more interesting to learn one—in this case, movies—instead of trying to study everything and in fact study nothing. . . . You read a lot of stuff, a lot of general opinion, but in the end you have nothing" (Pierre). Soo brought a different perspective:

Students are not children, so they want some useful knowledge, not just English. English and good text, specific idea. . . . So we—the students— talked about this class. It's very useful because we can study writing, we can study listening with the movie, we can study reading and also speaking—four—everything. It's good. One package—with entertainment.

The chief benefit of explicit instruction and modeling was their specificity. "There was an explanation of the structure and then a chance to practice it. All these examples are very helpful. If you don't understand the explanation, it is much more clearer through examples. Examples talk" (Pierre). Carina emphasized a similar point: "You need to see how to do it, to practice . . . working with the outlines."

Student Comments on Questioning Texts and Exemplification

Questioning Specific Texts While confirming student hesitation about questioning texts, the interviews also revealed that this hesitation, evident in discussions and writing, came not from a lack of understanding or an inability to question material but from a lack of content-area expertise. Students understood why questioning texts is important: It is "very useful to help the analysis of the text because you have to understand quite deeply the ideas—main ideas and development—to question it" (Patricia), and it is a way to "question other people's thoughts to prove your own" (Carina). Yet, consistently, the key complaint about questioning specific texts was insecurity in the content area: "It's very difficult because they are professional articles, so it's difficult to have another recommendation" (Pierre).

Commenting on the last paper of the term, which required students to question at least one text they had read, they said that the accretion of information began to provide a basis for comparing information and questioning at least some of it. Questioning texts improved toward the end of the term because "The last one was nice to write because I knew more about film. It was hard in the beginning because I didn't know anything" (Carina). These students already had explicit instruction and modeling both in questioning texts and in writing papers in which to practice, and they understood the role that challenging texts plays in academic work. Moreover, they appreciated having the command over material that questioning texts implies ("the last one was nice to write"). But comparing and questioning texts remained off-putting until students gathered enough information to do so. Questioning texts improved when students gained the confidence that comes, simply put, from knowing what you are talking about.

Questioning Texts and Critical Thinking The interviews also suggest that questioning-text activities affected a broader academic project: the development of intellectual skepticism. Patricia said,

> It was very interesting to connect American movies to American history, but I guess this is a very broad subject because there are a lot of versions of analysis about what made American culture, so I was a little confused by the idea that there are several ways to explain why Americans are individualists, etc. It's confusing that you can't rely on one explanation with certainty. You read one text, but you know this is one version, not a complete analysis.

Interview responses such as this echo class discussions about author subjectivity, truth, and the social construction of knowledge (such as the one about "what is correct for our composition?" in the previous examples of student discussion). To date, these discussions have arisen in each Film & Society class. One semester, student debate on the "truth" of historical accounts was sparked by

Schindler's List (a film about the Holocaust), another semester by *Braveheart* (about the medieval revolt of the Scots against the English), and a third semester by *Dead Man Walking* (about capital punishment). Debate about the objectivity of biological or sociological "facts" arose one semester from a discussion of *The Accused* (based on a New Hampshire gang-rape case) and another semester by *The Bird Cage* (about a middle-aged gay couple who pretend to be straight to please the conservative parents of their son's fiancée). In the Film & Society course, students extended their skepticism from films to printed texts; in the interviews, they reported that they began as well to challenge readings outside the Film & Society course, such as assignments for other classes and news stories.

Exemplification Interviews confirmed student frustration with exemplification and, as with questioning texts, suggested that improvement at least began with studying a subject over time. Students did not mention exemplification in isolation but folded it into discussion of three other areas. First, in their comments on sustained content study, students said they were best able to gather material for examples by reading extensively on a subject. "If you know more, you can write more and you are not writing the same thing all over. . . . It's hard to be tough and say something if you can't support it" (Carina). Second, in their comments on text analysis, they said that tracking an author's argumentation and examples created models for exemplification in their writing. Third, in their comments on writing, they stressed the importance of practicing collecting, sorting, and placing evidence. Yoshio complained, for instance, when paper assignments in previous classes were too simple: "The topic the teacher gave, I couldn't go the wrong way." One thing these students may be saying is that exemplification improves when they explore the ways evidence appears in authentic readings and when they must synthesize an array of information to select examples and match them to the points they wish to develop, much as students do to fulfill authentic academic writing assignments.

Taken together, the comments on questioning texts and exemplification suggest that reading and writing academic/professional work requires doing just that: analyzing complex texts, taking positions, and building argumentation by collecting, questioning, selecting, and placing information. Considering the time it takes native speakers to gather information and write in response, I suspect these students are right. The longer they practice—the more ESL classes provide these sorts of tasks—the more adept they will become.

Summary and Discussion

This project explored the effects of sustained content study, explicit instruction, and modeling on the text analysis and text construction of NNS college students. I reasoned that it would be easier for students to synthesize and question what they read if they gathered material to compare and consider over time. It would be easier to write academic expository/persuasive papers if they did enough research to generate ideas and categorize and select evidence to support them. I added explicit instruction, including modeling, to help students acquire the skills that NS learn in (good) secondary school education and when they internalize the "logic" of their culture. It is easier for ESL/EFL students to identify, synthesize, and question ideas in readings if they know how English expository/persuasive texts are organized. It is easier to use the rhetorical conventions of English expository/persuasive writing if those have been highlighted and studied.

I looked for effects of this approach in class discussion and portfolio writing, which showed improvement in text analysis and paper organization. Less improvement was found in questioning texts and in exemplification until students acquired some content-area expertise. Once they did, exemplification and questioning texts improved (though not as much as text analysis and paper organization), and their grasp of intellectual skepticism advanced. Moreover, in interviews, students reported that all skills became easier with increased knowledge of the content area. Accrued information provides a range of material from which students can develop ideas and select examples to back them up. It allows for a comparison of texts that forms a basis for questioning them.

While student interviews supported sustained CBI, explicit instruction, and modeling, it is likely that students identified these approaches as helpful because these were the ones practiced. However, this means not that the approaches were actually *un*helpful but rather that other approaches also may be useful. Nonetheless, acquiring content-area expertise appears to be central to the critical thinking skills explored in this course. Interviews suggest that expertise cannot be faked. Students know when they have read enough about a subject to compare material, challenge it, and use it as a basis for ideas of their own. Indeed, if we as ESL teachers do not provide sustained content study and yet ask that students analyze texts precisely, respond critically, and write with standard evidentiary conventions, we ask them for academic performance without giving them the tools to do it. We force them to rely on personal experience and opinion, and while these are important for academic/professional work, they are not sufficient. Formulating educated ideas, backing them up, and developing well-placed skepticism stem from extensive, precise reading and writing on a topic.

After several semesters of teaching Film & Society, I began thinking about the effects of an extended program of sustained CBI courses. How would students progress if, instead of taking a sequence of leveled courses in "Speaking & Listening" or "Grammar & Writing," they took leveled courses in "Introduction to Health" (see Bailey, Chapter 10 of this text), "Basic Concepts in Art History," or "Marketing and the Public" (see Kasper, Chapter 4), and practiced English academic skills through their accrued knowledge of these topics? How would students progress if they took a full program of sustained CBI courses throughout their ESL training?

In part to explore that question, I began to develop other sustained CBI courses, including one using contrastive rhetoric as content in which students read introductory articles in the field and wrote papers comparing English to their L1s (for similar courses, see Johns, 1990; Kutz, Groden, & Zamel, 1993; Liebman, 1988). Another course (sparked by Film & Society) looked at American history, political science, economics, and sociology to uncover the assumptions and contradictions underlying American life. Each course included the text analysis and text construction skills generated in Film & Society because those skills remain key to accurate reading and clear, developed writing in a wide range of subjects. Student progress in and responses to these classes echoed the findings reported here. Text analysis and paper organization improved early on and, with increased content-area expertise, exemplification and questioning texts followed with moderate improvement. In addition, the recycling of vocabulary and information facilitated retention and freed students to notice form (both grammatical and rhetorical). Students began noticing, to take one linguistic example among many, when to use "American life" rather than "Americans' lives"—a fairly refined distinction—and they began exploring a wide range of devices to link evidence to concepts. Students who took a sequence of sustained CBI courses progressed in ways similar to students in this study, but they improved more, advancing to greater control of text analysis and text construction. This may be a case of people improving at what they practice, but that is the point of sustained CBI: to highlight and give students practice at the skills they will need in the future.

If ESL/EFL students took a series of sustained CBI courses, they would have not one but several opportunities to practice, in settings that simulate academic/professional work, the range of academic skills—those emphasized in this course as well as listening, notetaking, library and Internet research, timed writing, exam taking, oral presentation, and group negotiations, among others. They would study not one subject and set of rhetorical conventions but several, as native speakers do. This span of disciplines would expand their vocabularies; their grasp of various forms, rhetorical conventions, and patterns of argument; and their knowledge of the world. As one student said,

> Most of the time what the teacher asks you to do is just to understand but not to organize your ideas in front of a text or an opinion. I received English courses from high school to university, but I think the analysis of the text and culture was quite superficial. This course offer a deep analysis which was very interesting for us—even if some steps are boring at the beginning—because it's a method.

References

Al-Abed Al-Haq, F., & Ahmed, A. (1994). Discourse problems in argumentative writing. *World Englishes, 13*(3), 307–323.

AMES (Adult Migrant Education Service). (1992). *Literacy for further studies. Project report.* Queensland Australia: Author.

Ballard, B. (1984). Improving student writing: An integrated approach to cultural adjustment. In R. Williams, J. Swales, & J. Kirkman (Eds.), *Common ground: Shared interests in EL and communication studies.* Oxford, UK: The British Council and Pergamon Press.

Barber, B. (1992). *An aristocracy of everyone.* New York: Oxford University Press.

Bloch, J., & Chi, L. (1995). A comparison of the use of citations in Chinese and English academic discourse. In D. Belcher & G. Braine (Eds.), *Academic writing in a second language: Essays on research and pedagogy* (pp. 231–274). Norwood, NJ: Ablex.

Braine, G. (1996). ESL students in first-year writing courses: ESL versus mainstream classes. *Journal of Second Language Writing, 5*(2), 91–107.

Carrell, P. (1985). Facilitating ESL reading by teaching text structure. *TESOL Quarterly, 19,* 727–752.

Carrell, P. (1987). Content and formal schemata in ESL reading. *TESOL Quarterly, 21*(3), 461–481.

Connor, U. (1996). Contrastive rhetoric: *Cross-cultural aspects of second-language writing.* New York: Cambridge University Press.

Connor, U., & Kramer, M. (1995). Writing from sources: Case studies of graduate students in business management. In D. Belcher & G. Braine (Eds.), *Academic writing in a second language: Essays on research and pedagogy* (pp. 155–182). Norwood, NJ: Ablex.

Cumming, A. (1995). Fostering writing expertise in ESL composition instruction: Modeling and evaluation. In D. Belcher & G. Braine (Eds.), *Academic writing in a second language: Essays on research and pedagogy* (pp. 375–397). Norwood, NJ: Ablex.

Davis, J., Lange, D., & Samuels, S. (1988). Effects on text structure instruction on foreign language readers' recall of a scientific journal article. *Journal of Reading Behavior, 20,* 203–214.

Flowerdew, J. (1993). An educational, or process, approach to the teaching of professional genres. *ELT Journal, 47,* 305–316.

Grabe, W. (1991). Current developments in second language reading research. *TESOL Quarterly, 25*(3), 375–406.

Hilder, J. (1997). Comments on Jill Sinclair Bell's "The relationship between L1 and L2 literacy: Some complicating factors." *TESOL Quarterly, 31*(1), 158–162.

Jacoby, S., Leech, D., & Holten, C. (1995). A genre-based developmental writing course for undergraduate ESL science majors. In D. Belcher & G. Braine (Eds.), *Academic writing in a second language: Essays on research and pedagogy* (pp. 351–374). Norwood, NJ: Ablex.

Johns, A. (1990). Coherence as a cultural phenomenon: Employing ethnographic principles in the academic milieu. In U. Connor & A. Johns (Eds.), *Coherence in writing: Research and pedagogical perspectives* (pp. 209–226). Alexandria, VA: TESOL.

Johns, A. (1997). *Text, role, and context: Developing academic literacies.* New York: Cambridge University Press.

Karl, H. (1981). What it means to be media competent. In C. Cooper (Ed.), *The nature and measure of competency in English* (pp. 139–164). Urbana, IL: National Council of Teachers of English.

Kobayashi, J. (1992). Helping Japanese students write good paragraphs. *The Language Teacher, 16,* 21–22.

Kutz, E., Groden, S., & Zamel, V. (1993). *The discovery of competence: Teaching and learning with diverse student writers.* Portsmouth, NH: Boynton/Cook.

Leki, I. (1992). *Understanding ESL writers: A guide for teachers.* Portsmouth, NH: Boynton/Cook.

Leki, I. (1995). Good writing: I know it when I see it. In D. Belcher & G. Braine (Eds.), *Academic writing in a second language: Essays on research and pedagogy* (pp. 23–46). Norwood, NJ: Ablex.

Leki, I., & Carson, J. (1994). Students' perceptions of EAP writing instruction and writing needs across the disciplines. *TESOL Quarterly, 28*(1), 81–101.

Liebman, J. (1988). Contrastive rhetoric: Students as ethnographers. *Journal of Basic Writing, 7,* 6–27.

Matalene, C. (1985). Contrastive rhetoric: An American writing teacher in China. *College English, 47,* 789–808.

Mauranen, A. (1993). Contrastive ESP rhetoric: Metatext in Finnish-English economic texts. *English for Specific Purposes, 12,* 3–22.

Moser, J., & Raphan, D. (1993). Russian students' writing: An adaptation of skills. *College ESL, 3,* 43–52.

Purves, A., & Purves, W. (1986). Viewpoints: Cultures, text models, and the activity of writing. *Research in the Teaching of English, 20,* 174–197.

Stempleski, S. (1990, March). *Video in U.S. classrooms: Culture in context.* Paper presented at the 16th annual international conference of the Japan Association of Language Teachers, Omiya, Japan.

Stempleski, S. (1992). Teaching communication skills with authentic video. In S. Stempleski & P. Arcario (Eds.), *Video in second language teaching: Using, selecting, and producing video for the classroom* (pp. 7–24). Alexandria, VA: TESOL.

Swales, J., & Feak, C. (1994). *Academic writing for graduate students: A course for non-native speakers of English.* Ann Arbor, MI: University of Michigan Press.

Tobias, S. (1994). Interest, prior knowledge, and learning. *Review of Educational Research, 64*(1), 37–54.

Widdowson, H. (1990). *Aspects of language teaching.* Oxford, UK: Oxford University Press.

Widdowson, H. (1993). The relevant conditions of language use and learning. In M. Krueger & F. Ryan (Eds.), *Language and content: Discipline and content-based approaches to language study* (pp. 27–36). Lexington, MA: D.C. Heath.

Sample of Explicit Instruction and Modeling for Text Analysis

At the end of the first section of an essay assigned early in the term, students read the following instructions.

Analyzing the Text

Essay Two, Part One has been divided into an introduction, middle, and final thought. The main idea of each paragraph has been bracketed [ ] and written in **bold**.

Below is an outline of the introduction, middle, and conclusion of Part One. The outline is composed of:

1. **The main idea of the whole article** or chapter (found in the introduction) contains the topic and author's opinion. It is what the author must prove in the article or chapter.

2. The **main points of the middle** (numbered I, II, III, etc.) support the main idea of the whole article or chapter. They often answer the questions **why** or **how**. They will be big, broad ideas.

3. The **supporting points of the middle** (numbered 1, 2, 3, etc.) explain and develop the main points of the middle. They will be more specific.

4. The **evidence for the main or supporting points** (a, b, c, etc.). Evidence may be examples of the supporting points, statistics, quotations, and any other material that persuades readers that the points are correct. They will be the most specific.

5. The **conclusion** or final thought restates the main idea of the article or presents a new idea or question. The conclusion of one article or section may become the main idea for a new article or section.

After reading the outline, a person who has not read the essay should be able to understand its basic ideas and organization.

Model Outline of Essay Two, Part One

Main Idea (from the introduction): Film is a juxtaposition of images in which audiences find or invent themselves.
(Topic: film. Author's opinion: it is a juxtaposition of images in which audiences find or invent themselves.)

Middle:

How?

I. Audiences find themselves directly and indirectly.
  1. directly
     a. audiences identify with the hero
  2. indirectly
     a. Westerners think film is the work of one person
     b. the movie theater itself is a fantasy world
     c. the dark gaps in the frame invite viewers to "slide" into the story (Hollander quote)

How?

II. Films are two-dimensional places where audiences live lives that are not their own.
  1. They contain characters and events that audiences try out and propositions that audiences consider.
     a. description of the cop film

How?

III. Audiences confront the fears and desires that they cannot confront in life.
     a. description of the film about Mary Queen of Scots
  1. The fears and desires shared by many people become myths.
     a. Kracauer examined German films to discover the fears and desires that led to Nazi Germany.
     b. Tyler found two kinds of fears in film that become myths: eternal fears and modern-life fears.
  2. Film offers stories and characters that do not obey time and space limitations of life, and they develop according to emotional needs.

How?

IV. The unresolved issues of each individual viewer will determine what he or she pulls out of a film—how he or she interprets a film.

Conclusion: Film is composed of the unresolved fears and desires of society, viewers, and filmmakers.

* * *

At the end of the first section of a later essay, Essay Three, students read the following:

Analyzing the Text

This class focuses on the outline structure because it is clear, frequently used in English nonfiction writing, and can help you organize your writing. However, some writers use different organizing structures. For instance, in the classic paper, the idea comes first and the examples follow. Yet in some papers, the examples come first. Some papers will not have a classic conclusion.

Essay Three, Part One is divided into an introduction, middle, and conclusion. The main ideas in each paragraph are bracketed [ ] and written in **bold**.

In some paragraphs, the order of the sentences is *not* the logical order of ideas. For example, in Essay Three, Part One, the order of the sentences is:

external conflicts
internal conflicts
abstract conflicts
examples of external, internal, and abstract conflicts

But the outline of the logical organization is:

external conflicts
    examples of external conflicts
internal conflicts
    examples of internal conflicts
abstract conflicts
    examples of abstract conflicts

When you outline an article or book, write the logical organization, even if it differs from sentence order.

Alone or with your partner or group, study and discuss this outline: *[outline follows]*

* * *

To give students practice in drawing out the "logical" skeleton of a text, they are asked to read the next section of Essay Three and complete the following assignment:

Alone or with your partner or group:

1. Circle the important point or points of each paragraph in Essay Three, Part Two (avoid transition sentences). Does Part Two have its own introduction and main idea? If it does not, go back and find the main idea of Part One. Does Part Two continue to develop this main idea?

2. Divide Essay Three, Part Two into an introduction, middle, and conclusion.

3. Find the main idea for Essay Three, Part Two.

4. Find the main points of the middle (I, II, III, etc.). What questions do the main points answer: how? why?

5. Find the supporting points of the middle (1, 2, 3, etc.). Make sure the connection between main and supporting points is clear.

6. Identify the evidence (a, b, c) (examples, quotes, statistics, etc.) that supports the main and supporting points. Make sure the connection between the supporting points and the evidence is clear.

7. Is there a conclusion in Essay Three, Part Two? Does it restate the main idea or offer a new idea?

8. Write your analysis in outline form.

Chapter 10

E Pluribus Unum

Health as Content for a Community of Learners

Nathalie Bailey

Lehman College

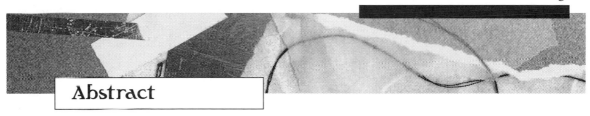

Abstract

Health, in the sense of physical, emotional, and mental wellness, is the content of this integrated-skill, high-intermediate ESL course. It starts with journalistic writing, autobiographical reading, and viewing films that focus on medical and legal issues concerning AIDS. Genres of student writing include summaries, recounts, reading responses, and descriptive, comparison/contrast, and persuasive essays, the lexicon and rhetoric for which are practiced orally. The course culminates in jigsawed, oral, and written presentations of chapters of an academic clinical psychology text, which students then synthesize on their final exam.

A community of learners is created through the integration of speaking, reading, writing, and grammar using interactive, interdisciplinary, intertextual, and intercultural methodology made possible by sustained and complex health content in an extended-hour course. Learning a second language and culture together maximizes students' motivation and collegiality, which in turn "pushes" their linguistic competence, coherence, and critical thinking. ∎

Overview of the Course

Students

Eighty-five percent of the students I teach are first-generation immigrants from the Dominican Republic; the rest are Asians, Africans, Eastern Europeans, and Latinos from other regions. They enter Lehman College of the City University of New York (CUNY), an inner-city campus serving 9,000 students in the Bronx, for four years of liberal arts education. They have not passed the university reading and writing skills placement tests, which they must prepare to retake. Nevertheless, the mission of ESL is not simply to prepare students for the CUNY reading and writing assessment tests but to help them with their language problems in extended-hour courses that focus largely on content. At the high-intermediate level, courses meet six hours weekly. Students simultaneously take two or more "sheltered" general education courses, such as humanities or origins of the modern world, while they are enrolled in ESL courses. These sheltered courses are required courses taught with sensitivity to the language needs of ESL students. Commonly these ESL students have work responsibilities to help their families financially, which makes enrollment full-time in college very difficult.

My overall goal is to help ESL students develop scholastic confidence and competence in their reading, writing, and English-language use. More specifically, my aim is to develop their critical skills to help them to analyze a text and relate it to other texts, personal experience, and prior knowledge, and to question and evaluate texts. I target these abilities throughout the course so that students can perform the academic tasks required of them in college. I have found that the key to their successful acclimatization to college work in English is to deeply engage them as learners. This is accomplished through sustained content-based instruction whose content has strong personal implications for students' personal lives and college careers.

Content

Health as a topic for sustained content in an ESL course was my students' idea. I became aware of their strong interest in health topics because of their frequent selection of articles about health when given a choice of articles from a newsmagazine. I use *Time* magazine because it is available internationally. I first became a reader of *Time* while a Peace Corps volunteer in Central America; it is equally accessible for ESL or EFL teaching situations. *Time* works well in high-intermediate ESL courses because of its wide range of articles and its international coverage. Given a choice of what they want to read, students are able to match their interest and ability levels quite easily among the magazine's many articles each week.

My students read about health issues that affect them as well as about issues that affect people they know. Women read about prostate cancer; men read about breast cancer. In the hierarchy of human values, it seems to be true, as Maslow has written, that people are concerned first with physiological and survival needs above other important needs, which he identifies as safety and security, love and belonging, and self-esteem and self-actualization. It was by following up on their interests in physical and mental health that students located both of the books that now anchor this sustained content course. Those books are *Ryan White, My Own Story* by Ryan White and Ann Marie Cunningham and *I Never Knew I Had a Choice* by Gerald and Marianne Corey. The first book was found by a student on an assignment (for another teacher) to find a book in a bookstore that she wanted to read. The use of the second book is described later in the chapter.

Physical health is the starting point of the course, but mental health is the ultimate focus. My goal in using this content is to promote students' awareness of the importance of good physical and mental health for their college education. Using Maslow's hierarchy of needs, students assess how well they and others, such as Ryan White, have achieved their own needs. Knowledge about the health rights and responsibilities of individuals in the United States is welcomed by a wide variety of students, immigrants, and refugees. I learned in my tour as a Peace Corps volunteer in El Salvador that health is not universally regarded as a right of the individual or a responsibility of the government. As a result, I came to college ESL teaching with the added incentive of creating curricula that explored such socially constructed values, especially with Latino students.

In this course, we also examine what it means to be active learners, that is, students who assume responsibility for their own learning. This is an essential college orientation for my inner-city college students, many of whom have to support themselves in several respects. Since my immigrant students are often the first ones in their families to attend college, they and their families need to learn how to adapt family responsibilities to the students' study needs, including their needs for quiet and seclusion.

Skills

My skills goals for the course are to improve students' language and literacy through the input of films and deep, broad reading—including periodical literature, autobiography, and academic text—and through the written and oral output in the form of summary/responses, recounts (retelling), expository oral and written reports, comparison/contrasts, opinion essays, and persuasive essays and speeches. I weave grammar instruction into the course in the form of mini-lessons contextualized in the reading, writing, and conversation assignments. Speaking and listening are an integral part of the course, and when adding a three-hour speech segment to my usual six-hour ESL course, I include oral work in the form of speeches to inform and persuade (by invited speakers as well as ESL students), oral periodical reading reports, and mock trials.

Integrative Rationale

Deeply engaging my students was my primary consideration in developing sustained CBI (content-based instruction) for the health curriculum. Over time the health curriculum has become complexly integrated, reflecting the engagement of both faculty and students with this material. Everybody contributes to it, sometimes students leading and sometimes teachers, creating an aura of excitement about this course. If more than one faculty member teaches the course, teachers can share ideas, experiences, and the preparation of materials. A course organized around a broad concept such as "health" can be shaped to possess stimulating attributes for ESL instruction; that is, it can be interactive, interdisciplinary, intertextual, and intercultural. Following are operational definitions for each of these attributes relative to sustained content-based instruction.

The course my students, fellow faculty, and I have worked out is *interactive* in many senses, the most important of which is that the students interact with one another, with the teacher, and with partners for writing, conversation reports, and oral presentations, thus collaborating on both content knowledge and speech and language improvement. A topic as complex as how HIV is transmitted and by whom requires collaborative learning, which entails talking to people, in class and out, and piecing together complex, controversial information by casting a wide net: conversation assignments, Internet searches, telephone hotlines, and speakers.

Health is an *interdisciplinary* topic: it includes the natural sciences, social sciences, and humanities. Sometimes an AIDS educator is invited to the class to give a talk and address scientific and sensitive issues. Discussion at these sessions is motivated by the students' personal interests and questions that the course has stimulated. Social science enters the course through AIDS-related demographic studies and later through the clinical psychology text by Corey and Corey (1997). Humanities is represented by literature and films. The route to knowing that educated people normally follow—taking information from here and there until they get whole cloth—is a privileged method of inquiry of sustained CBI and one that it shares with traditional disciplines. But an additional privilege conveyed by sustained CBI is that it frees its creators to interweave knowledge from a variety of disciplines, which greatly enlivens the learning process.

Ann Johns, in *Text, Role and Context* (1997), presents the point of view that one important characteristic of academic literacy is *intertextuality*. When students—and teachers—follow a topic across texts and contexts and find one book leading to another, they are participating in a time-honored process of literate learning. The story of the student who discovered the academic textbook we use in this course is a good example. At the time she took the course, students were making their own choices of books to read at the end of the course, guided by (but not limited to) a list of suggested readings. This student read an article in *Time* that led her to a book entitled *Emotional Intelligence.* Then she followed up that book by reading a related book, *I Never Knew I Had a Choice,* that she borrowed from her mother, who had studied it in a nursing course. What excited me about this book, aside from the student's enthusiasm for it, was that it specifically addresses college students and is divided into chapters, each covering one broad topic, that in themselves could be choices for students' reading. The topics include "Invitation to Personal Learning and Growth"; "Reviewing Your Childhood and Adolescence"; "Adulthood and Autonomy"; "Becoming the Woman or Man You Want to Be"; "Work and Leisure"; "Your Body and Wellness"; "Managing Stress"; "Love, Sexuality, Relationships"; "Loneliness and Solitude"; "Death and Loss"; and "Meaning and Values."

At first I thought this information-packed academic textbook would be too difficult for intermediate-level ESL students. But then I realized that by using the same choice methodology with this textbook that I use with newsmagazines and with whole books, students could choose which chapters they wanted to read and report on them orally and in writing to one another. Choosing a topic that interests them and for which they have background would help to control for the difficult level of the text. And that is how students have chosen—and continue to choose—their own texts for this course.

If learning in general is accomplished by talking to people (interaction) and by combining ideas (interdisciplinarity) and texts (intertextuality), language learning in particular is greatly facilitated by *interculturality.* Teaching a second language through the use of autobiographies such as that of Ryan White (a hemophiliac from the midwestern United States) and films such as *Philadelphia* (about a gay man with AIDS) can stimulate second-language development by providing learners with access to multicultural experiences. This exposure provides students with situational and attitudinal information that underlies language choices (Ervin-Tripp, 1973). For instance, *Ryan White, My Own Story* raises the issue of the right of a child with AIDS to attend school and shows how it was resolved differently in the two towns where Ryan White lived. The cultural differences between the towns are reflected in the behavior and the type of language that was used to express rejection of Ryan in one town and acceptance of him in the other. In the movie *Philadelphia,* subtle differences in the language used by the defense and the prosecution express discrimination against or solidarity with the gay lawyer stricken with AIDS who is contesting his right to work. We examine American positions on justice, freedom, and certain civil rights as part of this course in order to motivate language learning, which is embedded in the values, attitudes, relationships, and activities of the native speakers of the language (Ervin-Tripp, 1973). Students must decode and encode new language to be able to understand and express the values of the new culture, and also to question and assess those values. They are eager to do this to survive and flourish in this country. My own students, who live and study in virtual Latino ghettos in New York, find it culturally and linguistically broadening to learn about some of the relationships and issues faced by people from other parts of the United States, such as the Midwest, and other subgroups, such as the gay community.

Part One of the Course

Newsmagazine

I devote the first six weeks of the course to periodical and autobiographical reading and writing to ease students into the content and academic skills objectives of the course. I arrange for student bulk subscriptions to *Time* magazine to arrive by the first day of class, at which time students peruse the issue and recommend articles to one another. This gives them practice in skimming and scanning that will be useful in their other college courses. By the end of the first day of the course—in our case, two-and-a-half hours of instruction—the class has been divided into small groups of students who are interested in reading the same article. Having a choice of articles to read and write about helps them to recognize their language and literacy needs. Students who choose longer, more difficult articles inspire confidence (or humility) in one another. Reading one another's reports on the articles is a reality check on how well they have understood and written about what they have read compared with others.

The first writing assignment for the course is a summary/response periodical reading report that introduces students to basic compositional practices such as dividing a piece of writing into an Aristotelian beginning (introduction), a middle (body), and an end (conclusion) (see Appendix A). Summary and response writing gives students both content and rhetorical form to constrain them and a chance to develop a personal voice. To further ease their initiation into critical literacy, I have prepared a writing prompt containing a set of ten questions that gives students suggestions about appropriate content for each section of their paper (see Appendix A). For instance, at the beginning of their paper, they might want to explain why they are interested in the topic they chose to read about and what they want and expect to learn from the article. This multipart writing prompt also serves as a self-assessment tool so they can check whether they have accomplished all the objectives of the assignment. As an additional aid, I photocopy and distribute copies of student papers from previous semesters as models for students' summary/responses.

After completing this assignment, students can compare their writing with that of classmates in the small groups that have read the same article. They often ask permission (!) to rewrite these papers after they get ideas from one another about how to do the assignment. Students may also read their writing aloud, either in small groups or to the whole class, and ask questions relating to the opinions expressed. Writing in groups phases out, however, as students become more independent college readers and writers. (See Appendix D, Composition 1, for a sample completed *Time* report.)

Any number of variations of periodical reading/writing can be designed into the course. To maximize the health theme, students could be required to read articles on health only. Instead of subscribing to a newsmagazine, they could choose articles from newspapers or the Internet that they believe reflect their experiences and feelings or that address topics raised in class discussions. The teacher might want to introduce students to new, unfamiliar periodicals by giving them articles to report on to one another. This part of the course can be adjusted to the particular students in the class. My own students seem to benefit from subscribing to a magazine and reading it regularly. This permits them to follow topics over time, recycling lexicon and forms and motivating deeper analysis of content.

Autobiography

Concurrently with the newsmagazine reading and writing, students begin reading the autobiography of Ryan White. (If any students have already read this book, they can be assigned *Working on a Miracle* by Mahlon Johnson, the story of a doctor who was infected with HIV at work.) The level of the reading is not difficult for high-intermediate students because it is the story of an adolescent boy written in a very authentic voice (with the help of Ann Marie Cunningham, who provided the book with clear organization as well). Relatively short sentences and a minimum of multisyllabic words allow students to read without having to look up a lot of words in the dictionary, thereby improving their reading speed and comprehension skills such as retention of the meanings of previous portions of the text.

Writing about the autobiography begins with recounts. Some novice writers like, and get good language practice from, summarizing rather fully the content of chapters of the text. When assigned to write a book review, however, my ESL students tend to produce summaries rather than critical reviews. I have found that it is a good idea to teach them the difference between recounting (retelling) a substantial portion of a book and briefly summarizing a book at the beginning of a book review.

I segue into critical book reviewing by assigning descriptive essays on topics that permit only brief summarizing or synthesizing of text. Such topics include the role of Ryan White's mother in his life, how Ryan White got AIDS, how he handled pain, how he tried to get back into school, and what happened when he did. Students then progress to expository writing on such questions/topics as "How is HIV transmitted?" and "How did Ryan's case establish a legal precedent for the right of a child with AIDS to an education?" Finally, persuasive writing can be introduced using topics such as "Does a child with AIDS have the right to a public education?"

Another form of expository writing is the development and expansion of written summaries into oral reports on aspects of AIDS that students research with the help of documents such as those obtained from the Centers for Disease Control (CDC) in Atlanta (by calling the CDC national hotline at 1-800-342-AIDS) or those found in libraries or on the Internet. These searches are a natural extension of sustained CBI as more information is required to fully answer questions that come up in class. For instance, a particularly enterprising student used Internet texts to research the role of selenium in controlling HIV advancement.

Six weeks of recount, summary, expository, and persuasive writing culminate in an in-class midterm composition exam in which students write for 90 minutes on a topic they choose from a list of three or four. (See Appendix C for sample exam questions and Appendix D, Composition 2, for a sample midterm composition.) An in-class exam is important if students need experience with timed writing, as mine do. Students are well prepared for the questions they will encounter on this exam, not only because of all the reading, writing, and discussion they have done in their sustained CBI with its overlapping vocabulary and issues but also because of the grammar lessons embedded in that reading and writing over the first six weeks of the course. After giving the midterm, I conduct whole-class conferences using an opaque projector, choosing a sequence of papers on the same question and projecting them onto a screen. The student writers read them aloud, and classmates say what they like about them and what they think could be improved. I sequence the papers from weaker to stronger so that students will get ideas about how writing problems can be solved and language errors corrected.

Grammar in Context

In a content-based course, grammar use can be highlighted in assigned readings and practiced in speaking about, listening to, and writing about those readings. The key to the effectiveness of grammar teaching, in my opinion, is the contextualization of grammar. This comes about very naturally in sustained CBI because discussion of closely related topics recycles vocabulary and provides a touchstone of "truth." Knowing what it is they want to say "pushes" students' output (Swain, 1985), which includes their grammar acquisition, because students "further analyze the grammar of the target language" to express "appropriately and precisely their intended meaning" (p. 249). The breadth and depth of knowledge that accrue in sustained content-based instruction motivate successful communication.

In this course, I focus on a small number of complex grammar areas that high-intermediate students need help learning: past perfect; conditional; passives, gerunds, and infinitives; complex sentences; and reported speech. Editing errors are dealt with in students' writing. I assign a grammar text, to be used selectively, as a reference (students are asked to refer to the text in relation to their errors) and for grammar explanations and practice. I look for a text that includes diagnostic and summary quizzes, which I find an invaluable aid in holding students accountable for their learning. Quizzes and feedback on writing errors give my course "face validity" for ESL students who are anxious about how they will improve their English while focusing on course content. Many students come from academic settings where teaching "grammar on the board" is the norm. Providing them with some formal study of grammar satisfies their expectation and accomplishes my purpose of focusing them on form. I do not expect them to completely master the grammar they study; rather, I aim to raise their consciousness about the meaning, usage, and form of some of the more difficult areas of grammar to enable students to monitor for them in the language to which they are exposed and that they use.

I begin grammar lessons on the first day of class by introducing students to the usage of the past perfect in the prologue of the Ryan White book, which contains many authentic examples of its use. We read the prologue aloud, and I ask students if they notice any unusual verb forms. We discuss the meaning of the past perfect in the reading and then practice it in the context of their experience. Either in class or as a homework assignment, I ask students to conduct a conversation with a person in English using the past perfect. For instance, a good conversation topic would be to ask a person whether he or she had known about AIDS or known anyone with AIDS before coming to the United States. Students submit a written report on their conversation and share these conversation reports in pairs or groups, which gives them a chance to edit the reports together before submitting them to me for minimal grading (check, check minus, or check plus). Conversation reports encourage students to speak English using the grammar, vocabulary, and content information we have been studying and increase their confidence that they can understand and be understood by native speakers.

I will briefly describe some of the ways I incorporate the other grammar topics we study into the content of the course. I teach the passive in the context of a newspaper story about HIV and babies. For complex sentences, I take sentences out of Chapter 1 of *Ryan White, My Own Story,* which I make into a matching game of sentence beginnings and endings (see Appendix B). Knowing the story helps students learn the meanings of the subordinators. Gerunds and infinitives can easily be made into a team competition by using phrase completions—again based on the Ryan White story—such as "he liked _____," "he looked forward _____," "he avoided _____." Reported speech can be used in any number of recounts of the story. The conditional can be practiced by talking, writing conversation reports, or writing essays about such questions as "Would you tell people if you had AIDS?" and "What would you have done if you had been Ryan?"

Part Two of the Course

Drama

Right after the midterm, we segue to a more oral/aural segment of the course via the made-for-TV movie *The Ryan White Story,* in which the real Ryan White plays a cameo role (the film was produced by the Landsburgh Company and can be obtained by contacting the distributor, Tele-Video Entertainment, 1-800-545-4500). After viewing this film, students discuss their reactions to it. Typically they are moved by the film, but often are critical of the fact that it does not cover more of Ryan's life; it focuses mainly on Ryan's court fight to get back into school. This book-movie comparison reinforces the value of reading because of the broader and deeper understanding it can provide.

A week after I show the first film, I show a second, *Philadelphia,* which ups the ante considerably for intercultural understanding. It is the story of a gay lawyer, Andrew Beckett, who was denied the right to work when it was discovered that he had AIDS, and who took his case to court and won. This film challenges students to move from empathy with a child who has AIDS to empathy with a homosexual individual in an analogous situation. Teachers need to be prepared to work with students on the issue of homophobia.

In this second part of the course, we also work on comparison/contrast essay writing. After viewing the two movies, students are given an assignment to compare the situations of Ryan White and Andrew Beckett. Comparison/contrast writing is complex, so later students are given a second opportunity to compare and/or contrast, this time focusing on court trials in the drama segment of the course that follows when a speech component is added to the course.

Having provided models of court trials in the two movies, I set students up with guidelines for conducting mock trials themselves using Nitza Llado-Torres's (1993) *People's Court: Socio-dramas for Advanced ESL Conversation Classes.* A handout can summarize court procedures, describe who the "players" are (plaintiff, defendant, witness, prosecuting attorney, attorney for the defense, bailiff, judge), and explain the steps of a trial (opening statements, presentation of evidence, closing statements, and instructions to the jury). Llado-Torres's materials also contain brief scenarios of cases on abortion rights, surrogate motherhood, child abuse, immigration rights, and so on. (See Appendix D, Composition 3, for some scenarios for socio-dramas [mock trials] that my students chose to use. Llado-Torres's abortion rights scenario and an immigration rights scenario taken from current events are described in that composition.) These court cases are within the range of students' experience and are relatively self-explanatory, allowing students to construct their trials independently of the teacher. The planning and execution of the trials requires group collaboration, which provides students with oral language practice and problem-solving experience. Mastering court register using the modeling of the films becomes a directed listening task, as some students view the movies more than once to improve their courtroom performances.

Part Three of the Course

Academic Text

In the last part of the course, students are asked to take on their hardest reading, writing, and speaking tasks: reading and reporting on academic material in both writing and a speech. The text *I Never Knew I Had a Choice* (Corey & Corey, 1997) is both well suited to student interests and introduces them to academic writing. As the authors say in their introduction, "this book was developed for use in college courses dealing with psychology of adjustment, personality development, applied psychology, personal growth, and self-awareness." Yet the book treats its subjects in a scholarly fashion and therefore makes this course more like other college courses. Using *I Never Knew I Had a Choice* permits individual students to select, from the many topics covered in the text, one special topic tailored to their personal interests. They can do this without teacher intervention. Choosing research topics and texts to read is a college practice with which many ESL students may be unfamiliar, so being given a choice of highly relevant reading within the constraints of the chapters of one book gives students an experience of guided independence that has a high probability of success. They have the opportunity to select and explore a topic, and synthesize the new, more academic information they are acquiring with earlier information from the course and their own prior knowledge.

The first assignment students receive in this part of the course is to read Chapter 1, "Invitation to Personal Learning," which presents the thesis that there is a relationship between choice and change, and proposes Maslow's hierarchy of needs as a model of personal growth. I ask students to read those sections closely, after which we discuss how choice has led to personal growth in their own lives or in the lives of the two individuals we studied earlier: Ryan White and Andrew Beckett. Next, I give them an oral presentation about Maslow's hierarchy, which will serve as a model of how to present information to the class about the chapter they will read. (A good source of additional information about Maslow's theory of self-actualization is Chapter 3 of Maslow, 1971). I speak from an outline, shared with students in a handout, that provides a model for the outlines they will later prepare themselves. One choice of topic offered for the first writing assignment in this part of the course is an expository essay in which students apply Maslow's hierarchy either to their own lives or to the life of someone they know or have read about. Another choice is to write about themselves in relation to "self-actualization between two cultures."

The following week, I ask students to choose and read the chapter of *I Never Knew I Had a Choice* on which they would like to report. I explain that they will be required to give a speech and write a paper suitable for distributing, on request, to their classmates, who will use it to prepare for the final exam of the course. On the final, they are asked to write about what they learned that was particularly valuable from their own chapter and from the chapters reported on by two other students. To write a good final, they need to listen carefully to classmates' speeches and to read their papers. The final is given in the fifteenth week of the semester, so two weeks of preparation and one week of presentations is all that is available to them to complete this project.

Student Accomplishments and Further Challenges

Warning: The content of this course can provoke conflict among students, since they are encouraged to speak out on sensitive issues. In my classes, this has led to resentment by females of males who dominate discussion. However, with diplomacy and patience on the teacher's part, this becomes a growth experience for students. Negotiating class disputes is wonderful language practice and critical for future academic and professional work for both men and women.

In addition, the mock trial and final speech and paper are projects that require collaboration with others, which is essential for much university research and professional work. These projects are difficult for students because they are carried out independently from the teacher but interdependently with one another. In my experience, and in contrast to male-dominated class discussions, female students do better on collaborative projects than male students, which gives them confidence in taking the ground from male colleagues. But this can be a problem in the preparation of the mock trials, because their success rests on the collaboration of *all* members of a group. Teachers should be prepared to "sell" this approach to male students in particular and to support them in their efforts.

The accomplishments of students taking this course are numerous, varied, and highly rewarding to teacher and student alike. (See Appendix D for a chronological sequence of four papers, each followed by annotations about the problems and progress it represents.) I have enduring ties with students who have taken this course. They tell me that as they progress in college, they seldom find that they bring their feelings and identities into other courses as they do here. The final speeches and papers based on the chapters of *I Never Knew I Had a Choice* represent some of the most integrative, transformative work I have witnessed in my ESL teaching. The intent of critical literacy is to encourage students to make substantive changes in their thinking or in their lives as a result of their learning. The students who gave the most persuasive final speeches were appropriately self-disclosing and reported transforming some of their ideas or behavior. They chose topics that represented "unfinished business" in their lives, and they evaluated, questioned, and applied creative problem solving to it using information from the chapter they read. A student who chose the "Death and Loss" chapter, for example, had experienced deaths in her family that still weighed heavily on her and family members. She read the lengthy chapter looking for information that would help her and her family. In the process of preparing to present what she had learned to the class, she asked her family to let her practice her speech on them, thereby sharing with them what she had learned. Motivated by her personal interest and an academic assignment, she learned how to report personal experience in a register appropriate for public (academic) speaking. Another student chose the "Managing Stress" chapter and mastered the difficulty of conveying considerable technical information about his topic, while relating it to the lives of college students and his own experience as a college freshman (some of what he says in his speech was repeated in his final exam; see Appendix D, Composition 4).

Many of the speeches students presented were accompanied by outlines as handouts to the class, writing on the board, and question-and-answer sessions, and were, in short, examples of meaningful, effective public speaking. The final exams, on which students wrote a synthesis of three chapters, were focused pieces of writing in which the content, organization, and language clearly benefited from a semester of deep engagement with sustained content highly relevant to their lives. (Appendix D, Composition 4, shows how deeply engaged one student became in another student's topic, "Loneliness and Solitude.")

Conclusion

For the past few years, my colleagues and I have looked forward to teaching this health course because of the progress students make in learning English and because we find their learning—and ours—so interesting. By the end of the semester, students' writing is more coherent and correct, and students are more successful and confident in their language and literacy skills. I give much of the credit for students' progress in this course to the nature of sustained content-based instruction and the community of learning that it engenders. The high level of integration of the content leads to the integration of the class.

Because HIV/AIDS is highly stigmatized due to homophobia, the opening material of the course was highly controversial, and hence sparked much discussion. In fact, the rights of individuals who are HIV-positive or have AIDS is such a controversial issue that often the court must intervene. In my experience, controversial subjects involving sex, religion, and politics, far from being topics that are too hot for an ESL class, create the most *interaction* because they touch on personal beliefs and opinions as well as facts. This interaction is highly conducive to community building.

The *interdisciplinary* nature of health knowledge provides stimulation and variety in the materials and atmosphere of the course. Understanding HIV transmission and treatments requires technical and scientific knowledge. Students who have mastered some of this knowledge teach it to others. They do research and bring late-breaking news (all too ubiquitous) to the class. In the drama portion of the course, students need to actively learn about and use legal knowledge and procedures. The third part of the course, clinical psychology, abounds with new concepts and lexicon. Across all the disciplines or fields of knowledge addressed in the course, students are challenged to apply critical thinking processes such as abstracting, questioning, evaluating, problem solving, and relating information from one domain or discipline to another.

Intertextuality, characterized by citation, a defining characteristic of academic discourse (Johns, 1997, p. 63), and facilitated by the deliberate nesting of texts and contexts within the course, also enhance the community learning experience. The course starts with an autobiography/narrative (supplying contextualized examples), adds reports and news articles (supplying facts and figures), expands to a film story (supplying more context), and culminates in an academic text (complex information processing). Students share all of these texts with one another and together construct an understanding of them through their reading, writing, speaking, and listening. Their background knowledge, lexical knowledge, and critical thinking abilities are enhanced by the closely related textual experiences that students weave together communally.

Ultimately, however, it is the *interculturality* of the course content that is key to the course's success. Students find cultural differences on health issues real and engaging, and they need the help provided by the health curriculum to deconstruct these socially constructed values. In learning about health issues in the United States, ESL students learn about social values, attitudes, justice and injustice, the role of media in information dissemination, and so on. And in learning such essential cultural information as a culturally diverse group, students build community. On more than one occasion, students in this course have expressed their appreciation of the essential role of community in people's lives by pointing out how the class has functioned as a valuable community for them. They have learned from one another how to think critically and communicate their ideas in English in an academic setting. They have learned to trust themselves to talk and listen confidently and to participate willingly. They have learned about the wholeness of learning and the pleasure of learning together as a community. *E pluribus unum.*

References

Corey, G., & Corey, M. S. (1997). *I never knew I had a choice.* New York: Brooks/Cole.

Ervin-Tripp, S. (1973). *Language acquisition and communicative choice.* Stanford, CA: Stanford University Press.

Johns, A. (1997). *Text, role and context.* New York: Cambridge University Press.

Johnson, M. (1997). *Working on a miracle.* New York: Bantam Books.

Llado-Torres, N. (1993). *People's court: Socio-dramas for advanced ESL conversation classes.* Unpublished manuscript, El Camino College, Torrance, CA.

Maslow, A. H. (1971). *The farther reaches of human nature.* New York: Viking Press.

Swain, M. (1985). Communicative competence: Some roles of comprehensible input and comprehensible output in its development. In S. Gases & C. Madden (Eds.), *Input in second language acquisition* (pp. 235–253.). Rowley, MA: Newbury House.

White, R., & Cunningham, A. M. (1992). *Ryan White, my own story.* New York: Penguin Books.

Appendix A

Guidelines for a Periodical Reading/Writing Report

Instructions: Write one or two pages about an article of your choice. Your writing should have a beginning, middle, and end. Some suggestions about what you might want to include in each section are given below. You do not have to answer all these questions. Use your own judgment.

Beginning

1. Why did you select this article? What interests you about it?

2. What questions did you have before reading the article? What did the title, pictures, and subtitles lead you to believe the article would be about?

Middle

3. What was the article about? Summarize it in one paragraph.

4. Pick one of the parts of the article that was particularly interesting to you and tell why.

5. What did you learn that was new from this article?

6. If the article answered a question or expressed a point of view, what was the question and answer or point of view? Do you agree with the author?

End

7. How did the article make you feel?

8. How does the article relate to your own experience? What do you know about the topic?

9. How does who you are (your age, race, nationality, religion, gender, or geographical area) explain your interest in or reaction to this article?

10. What else does the article make you think about, or what does it remind you of?

Matching Parts of Connected Sentences

1. That happened to me only three days after I was born (32)
2. When the doctors couldn't stop the bleeding that first time (30)
3. Even though there are some cool things to do in Indiana, (35)
4. It was his first big movie (28)
5. If he wouldn't swing me, (27)
6. Later on, when I was three, (26)
7. Even when I had a bleed in my knee, (19)
8. But when we fought, (24)
9. We both liked things neat (34)
10. After I got AIDS, (23)
11. Even though I couldn't play baseball, (36)
12. If the weather was fine, (22)
13. I know the Cubs always find a way to lose the series (25)
14. Even though Andrea had a few pink and green water pistols, (21)
15. Whenever I was stuck there, (31)
16. I even figured that Grandpa was having a heart attack before he did (29)
17. Once it's been there long enough, (33)
18. Many people think of it as the gay disease (20)

Sentence Completions

19. I wasn't going to limp and shuffle around.
20. even though drug addicts get it too.
21. she never shot them at me.
22. we sat side by side on her stoop.
23. he always visited me in the hospital,
24. she never hurt me even when I hurt her.
25. even though they are a good team.
26. I fell in the bathroom and cut my head open.
27. I'd climb up into my favorite tree and sit on the branches for hours.

28. although Mom had already been following him on a soap opera.

29. because he was sweating something awful.

30. They rushed me to a hospital in Indianapolis.

31. I always asked a lot of questions and made sure I knew what medicine I was getting, how much, and why.

32. because no one ever expected me to have hemophilia.

33. it knocks out your immune system.

34. while Andrea was a mess.

35. I've spent a lot of time bugging my Mom to let us move to California to get away from the winter.

36. I felt like I had a pretty normal childhood.

Midterm Composition Exam Questions

1. Ryan White once advised Chad, "no pain, no gain." What did he mean by that? Did he live by that rule himself? If so, in what ways?

2. Ryan White said he was going to fight his disease and win. In what ways was he a winner?

3. What are the good and bad results of telling people that you are HIV-positive or have AIDS? In Ryan's case, what was good and bad about his going public? Would you advise people you knew who had AIDS to tell other people that they had it?

4. Why did Ryan call his moviemaking experience "some of the best days of my life"? What did the movie accomplish? What did Ryan want to do in his life?

5. Why were questions about girls the hardest questions that Ryan had to answer?

6. Ryan's advice to others was that "you have to be strong and not let people get you down." How did he demonstrate that strength on several different occasions?

7. Why was Ryan so famous? What did Ryan accomplish in his short life?

8. Why was the reaction to Ryan by the people in Cicero different from the reaction of the people of Kokomo? How do people you know react to people with AIDS? Why?

9. Compare three people from *My Own Story* and write about their relationships to Ryan during his life. In what ways are these people examples to you of good and bad ways to respond to someone in Ryan's situation?

10. How well did the movie about Ryan White represent the book and Ryan's life? Did you learn anything new from the movie? Which did you prefer, the movie or the book?

Sample Student Compositions and Commentary

The following is a sequence of four unedited compositions written during the health course by a single student showing the development of his writing over the course of the semester. The writer's typos and errors have been retained. My annotations regarding the problems and progress represented by each composition are in italics following the composition.

Composition 1: A Report on a *Time* Magazine Article, "Under the Volcano"

At the first the title "Under the Volcano" attracted my attention. Since my early childhood the awesome acts of nature have been causing the deep emotion to me. The fear I might say, yet not just that I wonder also. I wonder, how people cope with disasters and how powerful the nature is. I was just a child when a earthquake shook my hometown in Northern part of Albania. Even though the catastrophe was nothing to compare with menacing eruption of Montserrat. I know the feelings of what the people went through. The author has tried to recreate the dramatic setting of this disaster. Another thing that impresses me is that, how closely people are bounded to their place, and how far the frustration pierced into their lives shaking them emotionally and psychologically as well. Many people still don't want to leave. Some fearing they will never be able to return, cannot believe their old life is gone. Others refuse to budge until the government compensates them for their losses. Personally I agree with them, because it's hard to start a new life in a foreign country when you lose everything. I hope this people will solve their economic problems and receive what they want from the government. I attempt to summarize I could say that the article touched me, and if I ever would be able to visit Montserrat, the article will always remind me how devastating the island once was.

The first composition is insightful and promising, but brief and contains no paragraphing or other transitional aids.

Composition 2: Midterm Exam "Ryan White as a Winner"

Ryan White was a courageous kid who fought against his disease AIDS. He said "I am going to win or I am going to die trying".

Ryan White was always optimistic and courageous in his fight against his disease. Even though he had AIDS he wanted to be a normal kid and have a normal life but he was discriminated against by the people in Kokomo because of his disease. They treated him like dirt. They wouldn't even let him go back to school and he had to fight in court for his rights and won and that is one way of Ryan as a winner. Ryan made people understand that AIDS wasn't a countageous disease and couldn't be spread by casual contact.

Ryan was a winner in his life because he finally could have a normal life like everybody else even he had a terrible disease. He made AIDS a disease not a dirty word. Ryan White also helped other people like him with AIDS to fight the disease and never give up. His fight and his voice made people think differently to others with AIDS. And that wasn't easy how he said because ignorance dies hard. He was a young courageous kid who never gave up on his fight against AIDS. Ryan White will stay in the minds of people and kids as a brave and courageous kid that fought against AIDS. He also will stay in my spirit and my heart as a leader against the wrong opinion of people against others with AIDS.

In Composition 2, the student again has adequate content, and this time has organized the paper more coherently through the use of paragraphing, but still lacks transitional, relational language. The paper is brief and the syntax, while containing more complex sentences than Composition 1, has a staccato, report-like rhythm that comes from a lack of variety in sentence structure.

Composition 3: Two-Thirds Exam   "Justice"

In the socio-dramas we participated in, I learned about two men who went to court to fight for their rights: Mr. Lawrence and Mr. Collado. From each case I learned why each person went to court, what the results were and also I got to know more about the justice in the United States.

The first case was aobut why Mr. Lawrence went to court was because he was against his girlfriend's abortion. He wanted her to give birth to their child, but she wasn't prepared for birth as she said in court.

In the second case Mr. Collado was acused form a misdemeanor he committed 23 years ago. And by the new law he was subject to deportation by (INS) Immigration and Naturalization Service. In this case he was fighting for his right to stay in the United States.

In the first case of Mr, Lawrence the jury decided in the favor of his girlfriend. Because according to the law and the evidences she had the right to abort in the firsts 22 weeks and after that it was homicede. Something else that was indicated in the decision of the jury was not a well-established relationship between Mr. Lawrence and his girlfriend. She wanted to break up with him because as she said in court Mr. Lawrence was a possessive man.

For Mr. Collado the results were in his favor because some language was needed to be clarified about whether INS could detain and deport every immigrant who has committed a previous crime now punishable under the law, which is retroactive. Which means the law is effective in considering thing that happen in the past.

My opinion is that in both cases were fair the results. The jury was based in facts and also according to the law. These cases made me feel that the system of justice is fair for everone. But something that impressed me and made myself ask was. Why a certain amount of compassion it can't apply in the decisions, of the ocurt? For example, to save the life of the baby.

From taking part in these socio-dramas I gain many things: How the jury and the judge make their decisions, how the law really works and also some ideas to protect myself in life.

In Composition 3, the writer demonstrates progress in organizing his essay. He has learned to use his introduction to summarize the content of the upcoming essay. His goal was to compare and contrast two trials, which he does by describing each trial and the results of each separately and then comparing the justice achieved in each case. He reserves his personal reactions for the conclusion.

Composition 4: Final Exam

The book *I Never Knew I Had a Choice* was the most helpful book I ever read. This book gave me many helpful ideas about how to make choices in life and also prepared me for some situation I may encounter. The chapters that were most meaningful in my personality were "Lonliness and Solitude", "Managing Stress", and "Death and Loss".

The topic "Loneliness and Solitide" invited me to the experiences of loneliness and the creativity of solitude. Loneliness and solitude are different experiences and each has it's own values. Loneliness results from certain event in life like the death of someone we love, the decision of another to leave us fore someone else, a move to a new city, a long stay in hospital etc. Loneliness occurs when we feel set apart in someway from everyone around us. In solitude we make the time to be with ourselves to discover who we are and renew ourselves. And this chapter invited me on thinking of being alone is natural and valuable part of our experiences. I learned that by appreciating the aloneless I can surely enrich the experience of life.

A meaningful topic for me also was "Managing Stress" since my life involves stress and I needed to learn the ways how to cope with. Stress is an event or series of events that lead to strain, which often results in phisical or psychological stress. Therefore coping with stress is essential if we want to maintain a sence of wellness. The first essential step that I learned from this topic was recognizing the sources of stress which are environmental and psychological. Environmental stress is the stress we have on everyday lives. An example of this stress in the stress I had in the beging of the semester because it was the first semester for me and I had to arrange a schedule of classes to fit in my work. And the psychological stress which are frustration, conflicts, changes in our lives and the pressure that we have at work, school or by the family. I learned that as the result of stress we can become ill with different kinds of diseases like headaches, heart-disease, cancer, asthma etc. And the most effected people from those diseases are the people with high stress. An example is the Type A person who want to do make and more things in less and less time. They push selves to hard and they don't realize the price they are paying.

Also essential is knowing the destructive responses to stress. The destructive reactions to stress are defensive behavior, the use of drugs or alcohol and burnout. And the constructive responses are the sound of health, rest, exercise, timemanaging and also the type B personality which is the opposite of type A person. And esential message from this chapter that I learned was to listen in our selves what we hear.

From the third topic "Death and Loss" I learned how to accept the reality when we have death or lose in our lives, how to overcome those situatins by the choices that we have in life.

By reading this book I learned the many choices that I didn't know before and how to overcome the different kinds of situations when it happen to me.

In this long final composition, handwritten as a first draft in class in 90 minutes, the writer has a lively tone that conveys intellectual personal excitement about his subject matter. His organization includes well-developed paragraphs and highly effective transitions. His syntax, more complex than in previous compositions, reflects the complexity of the material he so cogently summarizes. The accuracy of his grammar is remarkable for a first draft. The major flaw of the paper is that he didn't develop his third topic, death and loss—probably because he ran out of time, having developed the first two topics so thoroughly.

Chapter 11

Reflecting on Commentary

Mind, Intellect, and a Use of Language

Rudolph W. Bernard

New York University

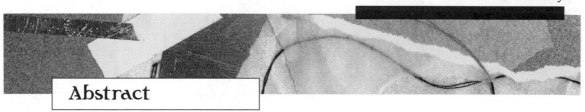

Abstract

This course is an apprenticeship in reflecting on commentary—on writing in which the author argues for taking a certain action or for understanding a subject in a new way while dealing with issues that cannot be finally resolved by reference to empirical data. For the inexperienced student, the course aims to be an introductory apprenticeship in the reflective practice; for the more experienced student, it serves as a "clarification" apprenticeship. The reflective practice is divided into two "practices" central to serious reflection: analyzing and exploring a text. The course lays out these practices in set procedures that are readily accessible to students: analysis of a text to summarize the argument and exploration of a text by questioning. Centered on a single book of commentary and other readings dealing with the themes of that book, all course activities—writing summaries, writing short comments, and seminar discussions—are directed toward developing an essay of commentary on one of the themes of the book. ■

. . . writing is an intellectual activity, not a bundle of skills. Writing proceeds from thinking. To achieve good prose styles, writers must work through intellectual issues, not merely acquire mechanical techniques. Although it is true that an ordinary intellectual activity like writing must lead to skills, and that skills visibly mark the performance, the activity does not come from the skills, nor does it consist in using them. In this way, writing is like conversation—both are linguistic activities, and so require verbal skills, but neither can be mastered by learning verbal skills. A bad conversationalist may have a very high level of verbal skills but perform poorly because he does not conceive of conversation as distinct from monologue. No further cultivation of verbal skills will remedy his problem. Conversely, a very good conversationalist may have inferior skills, but a firm grasp on concepts such as reciprocity and turn-taking that lie at the heart of the activity. Neither conversation nor writing can be learned merely by acquiring verbal skills, and any attempt to teach writing by teaching writing skills detached from underlying conceptual issues is doomed. (Thomas & Turner, 1994, pp. 3–4)

A Personal Note

Some years ago, a letter to the editor in the *New York Times* helped me to understand the extent of the inability I was addressing in my classroom. I have misplaced the clipping, but I remember the point very well. A professor at the Massachusetts Institute of Technology was responding to an op-ed article whose author claimed that high schools needed to give more attention to the teaching of math and the sciences. The MIT professor commented that he could not fault his undergraduate students' preparation in math and science. What disturbed him, he said, was that they could neither read nor write discursive prose!

Discursive prose: this was the theme of my teaching. But I had long before decided that "teaching writing" was not the way to go about it. My course, for foreign-born university students, was a course in *reading* commentary and writing a comment in response to it. Still, I was unhappy with the writing-about-reading that I was getting from most students, graduates as well as undergraduates. It was not very interesting because, I believed, it was not grounded in careful reading, even though I gave considerable class time to guiding students in close, analytical reading. So I started to design reading-by-writing activities intended to lead readers to move beyond first impressions. The question I asked myself then was how to get student readers *not* to write about first impressions. (The answer turned out to be: *Let* them. But figure out how to direct their examination of those impressions.) At other moments, I asked myself how to respond to student-readers who, when asked to write a comment about what they have read, often said things like "I agree with the author. I have nothing to say." Or "I don't know anything about this subject. I have nothing to say." Or, worse, "The author is all wrong when he says people behave in this way. I know someone who doesn't."

And so evolved what I now call *BookMarks*, subtitled *A reader's manual for thinking about a commentary—from Plato to Op Ed—understanding it, and responding to it to discover something personally significant to say about it that another reader, even someone more knowledgeable, would find worth considering.* In this chapter, however, I use *BookMarks* to designate not a manual but a concept and a practice. Over the years, I came to see the course I was teaching as centered conceptually on an act of mind: the act of ordering experience—specifically, the act of intellectual ordering. Further, I came to believe that this "doing" was the unifying concept underlying the core liberal arts curriculum in undergraduate education. My own experience with that curriculum, both as a student and as a teacher, had not been satisfying; the required courses had seemed to me—as they do to many students—if not a random grouping, then at least a collection of disparate courses. It made more sense to me to view such courses (as well as the traditional seven liberal arts of the Western medieval tradition) as embodiments of this concept of intellectual ordering—*the* liberal art, if you will.

The active form of the concept of intellectual ordering is the "reflective practice," which I divide into two "practices" central to serious reflection: analysis and exploration—analysis of a text to summarize the argument and exploration of a text by questioning. *BookMarks* lays out these practices of summarizing and questioning in set procedures that are readily accessible to students. The procedures are "rules of thumb," that, given a modicum of sustained, attentive use, can lead the student to an awareness of what it means to "think about" a discursive text.

Other practices, of course, are included in the notion of the reflective practice, such as practices normally included in courses in critical thinking, practices involved in deductive and inductive reasoning, and practices in presenting formal and informal arguments. The *BookMarks* procedures for summarizing and questioning are more holistic. I believe these holistic procedures provide the student with techniques that are more immediately useful and have wide applications in college work. Useful in themselves, they can also serve as an effective introduction to matters of logic.

Reflective procedures are, however, useful only when you need them. Pedagogically, provoking the need to reflect is essential. The need arises from two conditions: you must be intellectually engaged, and the engagement must be self-initiated. These are probably two aspects of a single moment, for genuine intellectual engagement is always self-initiated. While a teacher may choose to assign questions to talk or write about, these are useful only to the extent that they provoke a genuinely individual reaction on the student's part. I have found that my own questions often inhibit such a reaction. They are better as a follow-up to a student's question, pointing to the need for further questioning. For me the primary pedagogical aim, whatever the particular tactic, is to generate students' confidence in the merit of their own questions. (It's a confidence most students do not have. There is no such thing as a bad question, I often say to a class, as long as it's *your* question.) Authentic reflection is *initiated* by whatever emotion, reaction, or insight the individual reader has toward the text, regardless of age, intellectual sophistication, or educational background. Reflection can be *sustained* only if you have a significant personal connection with at least some element of the subject matter. Consequently, from the *BookMarks* focus on the reflective practice arises this single, key pedagogical question: *What classroom conditions might provoke inexperienced or unsophisticated readers to feel the need for a clearer, more accurate understanding of what they read—aware of the complexi-*

ties of understanding, sensitive to the tacit and the ambiguous, able and willing to test their understanding against the text to discover and rethink misconceptions? My answer: Reading commentary—and talking and writing about it.

But engaging the intellect in a serious manner can come only from reading something that has a substantive density, something that makes reading difficult, challenging, intellectually provocative, and ultimately worth the effort, and that above all is not limited to exposition, to answering the question "what is." Commentary—defined broadly as writing in which the author makes a case for "what should be," for a position about which reasonable people may disagree and where disagreement cannot be finally resolved by resorting to empirical evidence—meets those criteria and allows all readers to begin their reflection with whatever comes to mind.

Reading commentary has an additional advantage: Since skill in the reflective practice is the inevitable outcome of neither formal education nor professional or life experience, response to the same commentary can set conditions for the 20-year-old sophomores in my classes to talk with the 35-year-old lawyers about something they have in common. It enables a class of graduate and undergraduate students to move toward becoming a genuine community of inquiry, one directed by the ideal of finding a common perspective on a subject while allowing, listening to, and respecting diverse individual voices. There is no doubt that readers are excited by what goes on in their own heads and are eager to share it with others with comparable experience. While readers share this excitement, teachers can attend to guiding individual reader-writers to elaborate, question, examine, and clarify—to speak and respeak, to write and rewrite in the interest of moving closer to an acceptable meaning. Speaking and respeaking, students usually discover, as Alice did in Wonderland, that they don't know what they want to say until they say it, and then resay it, until they are, at least for the moment, satisfied.

BookMarks, then, is about the reflective practice. The *BookMarks* course aims to be an introductory apprenticeship in the practice for an inexperienced student and a "clarification" apprenticeship for the more experienced student. For both, it aims to develop an intellectual security and confidence that comes from knowing how to begin thinking about a text of commentary in English. Knowing how to start and how to go about it sets a foundation for developing more sophisticated techniques for reflection and articulating the outcomes. For myself, teaching the course has been an exploration of the notion that the reading and writing of commentary is *the* liberal art—that it is an effective apprenticeship in the practice of the art of intellectual ordering. I have chosen to make such an apprenticeship the underlying educational purpose of my classroom while serving the special interest of expanding the reading and writing abilities of foreign-born graduate and undergraduate students.

The Practice: Summarizing, Questioning, and Commenting

BookMarks presents a set of reflective procedures for summarizing, for questioning the author and discovering how the author might respond, and for writing a comment. One element of the practice is the ability to analyze a commentary in order to write a summary of the explicit argument. A second element is the ability to examine your initial responses to the major judgments in a commentary. You do this by having a dialogue with the author. The third element is the ability to present clearly and effectively a short written commentary of your own on the commentary you have read. These practices are not naturally "picked up" (by native English speakers or non-native English speakers) in working with the material of a particular field. A course is probably the most efficient means for introducing the essentials.

These essentials probably cannot be addressed in a satisfactory manner in a course whose primary concern is to "cover" a certain amount of information. A colleague once audited a graduate psychology course in which one or two students were assigned to summarize journal articles for each class. When the students could not summarize the articles coherently, the professor ended up doing it because, my colleague and I concluded, his primary concern was the information. Either he had not yet realized his students could not read discursive prose or he chose to ignore that fact. Or perhaps, as may be most likely, he assumed students would learn to do it simply by doing it without further direction—an assumption that I myself had once made and that experience compelled me to discard.

Working with a particular single subject matter is, I believe, a necessary condition for an effective course focused on reflective practices. Ideally, in some contexts, such as graduate departments, these practices can be taught in a "preparatory" course using the subject matter of the graduate field. A "single" subject matter is important, for time must be given to the *practice* of reflection—close reading, analysis, and exploration—in order for students to become aware of the elements of these procedures and to have some structured experience using them. Treating a single subject allows time for students to become familiar with the key concepts of the subject and with the reflective procedures. Changing subject matter, thereby diverting attention to new terms and concepts, precludes attending to the reflective practice in an overt, systematic, and sustained manner.

What subject a teacher might choose to read depends entirely on the particular population and institutional setting. I would opt for a single book as the central reading. A single book provides an effective pedagogical and psychological stimulus: For the student, the goal is to read this book. (An Asian student who had lived in the United States for 20 years told me at the end of the course—with a clear sense of accomplishment and satisfaction at having overcome a long-standing fear—that this was the first time she had read a whole book in English.) A single book sets a single theme, which becomes the "subject matter" of the course.

For a university "preparatory" course for students with no single academic area in common, there are two criteria for choosing that theme: First it must be of interest to you, the teacher, and second it should be of wide enough human interest to engage any student. True, there are students who say they are not interested. But even those students—if they stay with it, eventually admit that engagement in the reflective process compels interest and is worthwhile (to which a decade of student evaluations in my files attests). The teacher's role here is to provide a class with an understanding of a process that will take each member to a different outcome.

Course Description

The current teaching syllabus is for a 14-week course of 27 three-hour classes. However structured and designed, any form of this course must be thought of as an introduction, designed to give students the confidence to deal with the standard repertoire of lectures, discussions, and papers in which they are expected to write comments about the issues raised. It is not an introduction to courses that direct students to do research (understood as collecting information about events or behavior) or to develop hypotheses to explain sets of data.

Here is an excerpt from a handout distributed on the first day as an initial orientation, beginning with a brief description of the book around which the course is built:

> *A Collection of Essays on Social and Economic Affairs:*
> *E. F. Schumacher,* Small Is Beautiful *(Perennial Library Edition,*
> *Harper & Row, 1975. Reissued 1989)*

These humanistic essays on social and economic matters, written some years ago by a famous British economist, deal with issues that are still very much with us.

What is this course about? With Schumacher's book *Small Is Beautiful* as our central reading, we'll look at issues we face as we enter the next century. The general theme of the course is this: *The Planetary Interest.* Reflecting on Schumacher's book and other selections from contemporary authors, you'll attempt to answer this question, the Course Issue: What are today's most significant national problems whose resolution would be not only in the national interest but also in the planetary interest? As a partial response to this question you'll write a short essay of commentary about a position Schumacher takes relevant to the Course Issue.

Everything we do in this course is directed to writing this short essay of commentary on one of Schumacher's issues. We'll also prepare for four Class Seminars, where we'll look at our central issue and several related issues: (1) technology and policy recommendations Schumacher makes for both the developing and the developed world, (2) values underlying these recommendations, (3) several "wisdom" or value traditions that Schumacher recommends we look into when we consider what ends we want social and economic policy to serve, and (4) the concept of "the planetary interest" as one standard for evaluating such policy.

Course Structure

The basic course structure is constructed of a series of thematic "strings." The handling of these strings is reviewed and refined each term, with each term's experience being unique, provoking new pedagogical issues or variations on old ones. The "spinal" string is a sequence of readings from Schumacher's *Small Is Beautiful* and various other sources related to the central course theme. There are three additional primary strings: (1) a sequence of reflective activities for logging a text of commentary by keeping written notes of analysis and exploration, (2) a sequence of seminars and related individual and team papers, and (3) a sequence of writing activities related to developing an essay of commentary on a position of Schumacher. A fourth, subordinate sequence of activities on sentence handling is built in; this is necessary, useful, but not a central theme of the course. It consists of work on simple sentence analysis designed to clarify basic punctuation rules.

Reflection: Analysis

During the first four class meetings (two weeks), class activities are given to introduce the two basic reflective procedures: analysis and exploration. After two experiences of analyzing to summarize in class 2 and class 4, most students are comfortable with the basic terms and procedures. Classwork on analyzing to summarize will be repeated several times throughout the course, using op-ed articles and several key chapters in Schumacher. Analyzing a series of diverse examples on a single theme engenders in student-readers a growing awareness of variations on the basic English conceptual schema of "thesis and support." The work is never boring: Even if students are completely comfortable with the basic procedures, each class session is a new "puzzle" with a new twist.

Analyzing a commentary to summarize the author's explicit argument requires identifying the key features of the text. These are formulated in an acronym, DePITTSS: *design, purpose, issue, theme, thesis, support,* and *shape*. Readers need to decide what the piece is about (*theme*), what judgment the author makes about the theme (*thesis*), and what question the thesis answers (*issue*). Eventually these must be formulated to meet the ITT (issue, theme, thesis) test: The *thesis* is a statement about the *theme* that answers the *issue* question. In addition, readers must decide whether the author intends to propose some kind of action or a new kind of understanding (*purpose*). They need to identify the supporting judgments and formulate them in short, simple sentences (*support*). They need to recognize the structure the author uses to present the position: either a clear, formal distinction of thesis support or a more conversational, associative manner (*design*). And they need to identify the nature of the relationship between the thesis and the support (*shape*). *BookMarks* identifies three main "shapes." In the first and most common shape, the "T-block," the thesis has two or three explicit supporting judgments that most often answer the question *what, why,* or *how*. In the second shape, support is tacitly assumed. In the third shape, support is an explicit explanation of the subject and predicate terms in the thesis.

Preparation for class work requires completing a *Preliminary Analysis Worksheet* that asks for tentative decisions on these features, to be confirmed in class by working through the analysis in small groups. The groups work backward, first writing support sentences about subthemes, then writing a thesis sentence about the main theme, and finally identifying the question the thesis answers: the issue question. Each step along the way compels a review of previous decisions, confirming or modifying them. The final result is a *summary analysis,* a statement in outline form of issue, theme, thesis, and support.

Doing the analysis requires the reader to distinguish the *explicit* elements of the argument from important *implicit* meanings in the text, to a greater or lesser degree becoming aware of *implications* suggested by the author's judgments, *assumptions* underlying the author's argument, and possible *consequences* of the author's position. The procedure has a single aim: to make readers autonomous—able to identify the explicit position presented in the text. Implicit meanings are more elusive; many are subject to further tests of likelihood, and may ultimately be indeterminate.

Reflection: Exploration

To explore, students are guided to examine their own initial reactions to the text. An exploration begins with reviewing passages of special interest the reader has noted with check marks (or question marks or exclamation points) in the margin, passages noted because they compelled the reader to stop for a moment. From a number of passages, the reader selects to pursue further those that signal some doubt or skepticism about a judgment the author makes.

For that student who claims total agreement with the author (something occurring only occasionally), I paraphrase a line from *The Great Conversation* by Robert Hutchins (1952): "Nobody can make so clear and comprehensive and accurate a statement of the basic issues of human life as to close the discussion. Every statement calls for explanation, correction, modification, expansion, or contradiction" (p. 76). Readers who are stuck on "I agree" need to be prodded to reflect on what exactly they agree with. They can do this by "talking to themselves," telling themselves what they have understood, *without looking at the text or any notes they have taken*. While they do this, questions will inevitably arise and, as Hutchins says, they will find something about which they are skeptical. Further exploration starts from some moment of skepticism.

First, in a logbook, the reader writes a paraphrase of the questionable judgment the author makes, aiming to clarify the key concepts and ultimately formulating a question for the author in a form that reveals the reader's skepticism: "How can he possibly say that . . . ?" Then the reader examines the position as stated in the question as well as the reader's own alternative view, for each position stating reasons and identifying possible assumptions and consequences. This examination will eventually lead to the discovery of a point of difference with the author, a point not obvious prior to this examination.

Next, the reader formulates a question about the point of difference, which is most often about a tacit assumption. This question directs a rereading of the text that aims to find the author's response. If the reader discovers a likely and satisfactory response, the question is eliminated and replaced by an expanded understanding of the judgment initially perceived as questionable. If, on the other hand, the reader can find no satisfactory response, the question stands, pointing to a significant weakness in the author's position. This weakness can become the theme of a written critical comment, a comment that may also include the writer's alternative view. (See Appendix A for a sample of a moment in this process that leads to the discovery of a previously unnoticed point of difference and the formulation of a question about it.)

Essentially this exploration procedure is a procedure for formulating useful questions:

- Questions to clarify the author's concepts and key terms.

- Questions that reveal the reader's own skepticism.

- Questions to direct rereading to discover how the author might respond to skeptical comment, often resulting in a new understanding of the author's meaning that removes the initial skepticism.

- Questions that seem particularly significant in that the reader cannot imagine how the author might respond satisfactorily without modifying the position presented in the text in some significant way. The discovery of a "significant question" becomes the basis for a critique of the author's position and, perhaps, the urging of an amendment or alternative.

Considerable time is given to class activities that present different questions about a text and how they can be used to "explore" it. The primary purpose of exploration is to understand the reasonableness of positions the reader questions. Nonetheless, it will eventually and inevitably lead to a critical evaluation of one of the author's positions, providing the basis for a comment on the text.

Seminars

Students prepare individual papers and team papers for discussion in four seminars relating to key themes.

The *Seminar on Technology* aims to clarify a key concept in Schumacher's work, the notion of intermediate or appropriate technology. The main preparation for the seminar is a team paper (composed by three to four students), for which students receive these instructions:

> *Prepare the Team Paper [answering the questions noted below]*
> Assign one member of your team to present your team's response to each point. Since the team paper is limited to one page, the team members may explain and expand the written response in their oral presentations in the seminar.

- *The problem of the "dual economy":* What is it? Why is it bad? How can it be eliminated?

- *Schumacher's criticism of the goal of universal prosperity:* What's wrong with the goal of "universal prosperity" in the sense of unlimited economic growth?

- *Basic guideline for developing countries:* What is the basic recommendation for the economic development of developing countries with a majority population that is poor and has little or no education?

- *Intermediate technology:* Describe the concept of intermediate technology for someone who has not read Schumacher.

The *Seminar on Values,* using similar questions for which each student prepares answers (there is no paper for this seminar), aims to identify the standards underlying Schumacher's judgments. The usual outcome of the discussion is that although Schumacher's specific proposals provoke intense skepticism among the class members, the values that underlie them are generally acceptable to all—a realization that comes as something of a surprise. Such a realization encourages readers to reconsider their first impressions and reactions.

The *Seminar on Wisdom Traditions* also sometimes provokes reconsideration of initial reactions. It is based on selected chapters in Huston Smith's *The World's Religions* (1991). Teams present the moral and spiritual values carried within certain traditions as elaborated in Smith's book (for example, Hinduism, Buddhism, Taoism, Confucianism—Schumacher refers often to Eastern traditions). The goal is to make sense of Schumacher's recommendation in his epilogue that we should each "work to put [our] own inner house in order."

In preparation for the Wisdom Traditions seminar, students first prepare, in accordance with assigned models, individual papers on the tradition assigned to their teams and then a team paper, which is an abstract of the team's oral presentation for the seminar. Here is the model for an individual paper. (Sample responses, such as the two on Buddhism inserted here in parentheses, are not included in the model.)

> Select one recommendation—moral or spiritual—that is a necessary element in putting your inner house in order. (Here are simple definitions: a *moral principle*—a recommendation on how to behave toward others; a *spiritual principle*—a recommendation on how to treat yourself.)
>
> > RECOMMENDATION: Formulate a sentence beginning with "We should . . .". (Here is a sample sentence: *Since the cause of life's dislocations is self-ish craving, we should aim to overcome the narrow limits of such craving.*)
> >
> > CHANGE REQUIRED: Explain what changes in behavior or attitude are required in order to follow this recommendation.
> >
> > MY PERSONAL INTEREST: Explain why this recommendation is of special personal interest to you.
> >
> > HOW TO BRING ABOUT THE CHANGE: Explain how you think the change may be accomplished.
> >
> > POSSIBILITY OF CHANGE: Consider the likelihood of an individual's ability to change. You will probably conclude it is extremely difficult, if not impossible. Then, in this section, comment on what value such a recommendation has if it is almost impossible for most people to realize.

Here is the model for the team paper:

Part 1: Summary

> Write a brief overview of how your tradition would describe a person whose inner house is in order. Include an introduction to the key elements that will be described by other team members. The summary should be a brief description of the whole picture.

Part 2: Key Elements

> Identify the element in a word or short phrase. (Sample elements: the Four Noble Truths; the Eightfold Path; Buddha; Dharma; Nirvana)

Write a short paragraph about each key element that will be explained in the seminar. State it and write a brief explanation that includes the main points that you will explain in more detail in your oral presentation.

Finally, the *Seminar on the Planetary Interest* focuses specifically on the issue laid down at the outset of the course and aims to bring the various thematic threads of the course together: technology, values, wisdom traditions, and contemporary national and global issues. The seminar asks this question: What are today's most significant national problems whose resolution would be not only in the national interest but also in the planetary interest? For this seminar, the assigned reading is a monograph on "the planetary interest" (Graham, 1995). Students prepare individual and team papers using Graham's definitions of these four concepts: the vital and the normative planetary interest, and a legitimate and an illegitimate national interest. In their individual papers, students identify two national goals, policies, or programs that are legitimate national interests and two that are illegitimate. The team paper presents, for each country represented on the team, the team's judgment of the two most important national problems—relating respectively to the vital and to the normative planetary interest. The seminar discussion explores the difficulties that the countries face in developing national policies to address these problems.

The Essay of Commentary on a Position Presented in Schumacher

The basic task is to consider Schumacher's positions in light of a much-discussed national, regional, or global problem. The essay is a critique of one position, demonstrating why it is an inadequate, inappropriate, or impractical approach to that problem and offering an alternative proposal or an amendment to Schumacher's position. The essay is strictly structured: It starts with a preface that presents the problem and that ends with the writer's issue question about it. Six paragraphs follow, commenting on a recommendation Schumacher makes bearing on the problem:

- a paragraph summarizing Schumacher's recommendation
- a preview paragraph stating what Schumacher says or implies that troubles the writer and why, and ending with the writer's alternative view (thesis) or a statement pointing to it
- three middle paragraphs moving from "I understand why Schumacher says . . ." to "But I'm skeptical because . . ." to "So I'd propose . . ."
- a short concluding paragraph

The paragraphs themselves are structured. The middle paragraphs must be a T-block shape (thesis-support); individual guidelines are given for structuring the preface, preview, and conclusion. The whole is limited to 5½ pages, typed double-spaced. (A reduced version of a student essay appears in Appendix B.)

The sequence of activities that guide students through developing the essay goes like this (in a 14-week term, this process stretches out over 12 weeks). First is a series of four worksheets, discussed with teams in four class workshops. Worksheet 1, assigned for class 4 in the second week, asks students to identify a controversial national or global problem. Although they have not yet read much of Schumacher, identifying such a problem encourages them to relate what they read to real-world problems they are familiar with. Worksheet 2, asking for a critical comment on a judgment Schumacher makes, comes in the fifth week, after students have read at least the four key chapters in Schumacher's book. In worksheets 3 and 4, prepared over a period of two weeks, students begin to shape the essay, laying out a critical judgment of a position of Schumacher (paragraph 4 of their essay) and offering an amendment or alternative (paragraph 5). It is usually at this point that most students finally come to grips with the problems of formulating and shaping a comment.

In the second half of the term, over a period of five weeks, students work through three drafts. Draft 1 is read and evaluated by three student-editors over two class periods. Draft 2 is evaluated by two student-editors in one class period. These editors use an eight-page *Editor's Comment Sheet*. For drafts 1 and 2, writers and editors meet for 20 minutes to discuss and clarify the judgments. Then editors summarize their evaluations on a short form that is turned in to me (see Appendix C). Draft 3 is not discussed in class, but every student reads the essays of all members of the class and completes a brief evaluation for the writer (with a copy to me).

To ensure an intelligible presentation, I insist that the presentation be in accordance with instructions about the content of each paragraph and with the thesis-support form that is key to any English presentation of a comment. A good paper complies with the formal instructions and does not rest its argument on a misunderstanding or on an incomplete understanding. Whether draft 1 is a highly wrought piece of work (which is occasionally the case) or a very rough skeleton outline, drafts 2 and 3 are always better, and more clearly structured.

I myself read only drafts 2 and 3. Apart from annotating unnatural locutions and syntactical inaccuracies, my comments are limited to completion of a series of evaluation forms similar to those students complete on reading one another's papers. The forms embody comments on both form and content. This entire process, from worksheet 1 through the evaluation of draft 3, has a twofold purpose. One is for reader-writers to have a structured experience of developing a responsible comment on a text of commentary—an experience in which they are both doing and observing themselves doing. The second is for reader-editors to demonstrate their ability to evaluate and revise in accordance with the standards for both form and content that are embodied in the instructional guides for developing the essay.

Evaluation of Work

Many kinds of reading and writing take place in this course. Apart from the logging activities students do in their own logbooks and in class logging activities, students (1) write summary analyses and turn them into summary paragraphs, with a brief comment presenting a question for the author; (2) complete worksheets and three drafts of the essay; and (3) write individual and team seminar papers as well as reports on team meetings.

Standards for papers are presented at the outset of the course. Some assignments require revisions; for others, revisions are optional. Here is an excerpt from a handout on standards:

> An excellent paper, even though short, (1) will reveal extensive preparatory log work, (2) will do what is asked for, (3) will have few or no basic errors of mechanics (grammar, punctuation, spelling), and (4) will be neatly presented in accordance with format instructions.
>
> A paper is judged unsatisfactory if it is severely lacking in one or more of these areas: (1) It treats its subject in a way that reveals inadequate preparatory log work. (2) It demonstrates little or no attempt to do what is asked for in the assignment, or it neglects or handles unsuccessfully specific requirements of the assignment. (3) It contains excessive errors in grammar, punctuation, spelling, or intelligible usage. (4) It ignores the format instructions.

In my end-of-term evaluation of a student's performance, three areas are foremost: (1) the ability to use the language intelligibly in both writing and talking about the course reading, (2) an acceptable ability to use the basic *Book-Marks* acts of analysis to summarize and of exploration to discover questions, and (3) the final draft of the essay.

Coda

I take it as a given that a teacher must aim to set conditions that are intellectually challenging while establishing an open, personal connection with a class as a group and with the individuals within it. That said, I must admit to an inevitable limitation: Since I am who I am, I cannot reach everyone in equal measure. But what I can do, over time, is to learn to extend my reach.

My pedagogical choices reflect (as do any teacher's) my nature, my nurture, and my institutional world. Some readers may find here a clear echo of their own experience; others may not. But all teachers make pedagogical choices—I refer not to materials but to decisions about what to teach and why. All such choices are more or less tentative, debatable, subject to modification. What has been important to me is coming to the point where my pedagogical choices are made consciously, knowingly, and, I would add, reflectively—the outcome of continually reviewing the extent to which the most recent term's experience challenges them.

These reflections are often provoked by the eight-page *Quick-Comment on the Course* that students complete when it's all over. Extracts from some representative comments follow. A common initial reaction students report is puzzlement, about what they are doing and why. I do give a series of statements over the first weeks explaining the what and why. But most students lack the experience of giving concentrated and sustained attention to the reflective practice itself. Doing the essay—an activity stretching over the entire term and requiring a lot of rewriting and talking with team members—is ultimately the single activity that makes sense of all the others. It's interesting, one student says, *because* of its difficulty and challenge. (Occasionally a comment will reveal a wistful wish that we had read a story or two as a respite!) The outcome for most students is a clear sense of having learned how to use the language in certain very specific ways, accompanied not unexpectedly by a sense of confidence that they know how to go about reading and reflecting on a commentary in order to write a comment about it. And they have had an experience of learning "involuntarily," as one student put it, meaning learning without doing exercises. For my part, I read this student's comment as evidence that he learned because he was genuinely engaged—which, I take it, is a necessary condition for learning anything.

Graduate Student (Italy)

I didn't expect this kind of course. In the first days I didn't understand the meaning of what and why we were doing what we were doing. With time I realized the meaning and found it more useful than any other kind of course I could have taken. . . . I can take away [from this course] how to start to read an English book, how to write clearly, and how to explain my thoughts to make them comprehensible to someone else. And if I didn't learn them completely, I can keep going on practicing in the future. I'm sure I'll do that! . . . Now at the end of the term I'm happy I took this course for three reasons: (1) I learned how to write clearly. (2) I learned how to explore a text and find out the main flow. (3) I practice my English. Comparing this English course with others I took before I think there is no comparison. This is the most useful course! I'm sure I learned something. In the others I'm not so sure.

Undergraduate (India)

I liked the fact that the course had an interesting theme so that along with learning the language I learned a lot about the problems that the world is facing today. I gained increased confidence from the seminars. . . . I also learned that when I write English it is possible that sometimes I might construct a sentence according to my native language. I had never noticed this before.

Graduate Student (Lebanon)

Since this course has made reading English texts easier for me, I think that I will be able to "teach" myself English by further reading. . . . I think this course is very useful because it is based on simple methods to accomplish difficult tasks. . . . Writing a summary or an essay are difficult tasks. . . .

Businessman (Uruguay)

The most interesting was to learn the English writing structures, not only to identify them while reading, but also to use them when writing. I gained a lot of confidence to write (because now I'm sure that an American can understand what I'm saying). . . . With the first draft [of the essay] everything came together. I glued everything I learned and produced something with that. . . . Everything [in this course I can use to teach myself English] from skimming to exploring. I've learned procedures to improve my reading. And in terms of understanding the author's position, I believe that to be capable of discovering the elements of [the author's argument] is a great step in my English studies. Now I can read better, understand better, and comment better. . . . To me this wasn't an easy course because the things I've learned have some great differences with Spanish writing. Nevertheless, I think I've recognized and absorbed these differences, improving my knowledge and ability to use English. I'm really satisfied with the results of this course.

Graduate Student (Russia)

I found the elements of the essay—worksheets, drafts—the most interesting and useful because it was the most challenging and difficult for me. I think I became familiar with the English way of thinking and writing. But I consider it a beginning. I am looking forward to improving it. I consider this course one of the best I have ever experienced.

Graduate Student (Korea)

The most interesting: the essay and summary paragraphs. It was a valuable moment to write and think of something in an English way. I really enjoyed writing something, even though it took lots of time. I learned a lot from writing and reading. So I think the more chances to read and write, the more helpful the class is. You gave many chances to write and read. The speed of my writing and thinking in an English way increased through this class.

Graduate Student (Korea)

Team meetings and Seminars were more challenging and useful to me. I was at once puzzled, and didn't know what to say because I had had little experience. I tried to find my role as a team member, and to think about our topic as much as possible. As a result, I think I have improved myself. . . . I learned how I could find issue, theme and thesis—author's position—through it. I think I learned how to read correctly. . . . I will always keep in mind the useful methods of this course—summarizing, paraphrasing, commenting, questioning and identifying [the features of a text]. I think they are very useful whenever I try to know what the author is talking about, and to comment on it.

Undergraduate (Italy)

I think that I have learned a lot from this course. The course is an "involuntary learning." You don't know that you are learning because you are not studying grammar and making exercises. But at the end you have really something in your mind. You know how to write a paper, and how to read, and how to analyze an English text. I think that's a lot.

References

Graham, K. (1995). *The planetary interest*. (Occasional Paper No. 7). Cambridge, UK: Global Security Programme, University of Cambridge.

Hutchins, R. M. (1952). The great conversation: The substance of liberal education. In R. M. Hutchins & M. J. Adler (Eds.), *Great books of the western world: Vol. 1*. Chicago: Encyclopedia Britannica.

Schumacher, E. F. (1975/1989). *Small is beautiful*. New York: Harper & Row.

Smith, H. (1991). *The world's religions*. San Francisco: Harper.

Thomas, F. N., & Turner, M. (1994). *Clear and simple as the truth*. Princeton, NJ: Princeton University Press.

Appendix A

A Sample of Reflective Questioning Based on the Essay "Buddhist Economics" from E. F. Schumacher, *Small Is Beautiful*

Student 1

1. A short paraphrase presenting a skeptical reaction:

   Schumacher says people in Buddhist economies are self-sufficient, which in his opinion is the best way for us to conserve our resources. I disagree with him: we already have a technology and a fully developed transportation system that helps us to lead a better life, providing lots of opportunities to exchange resources with others living far from us. Is it really possible to transform our modern economy into a Buddhist economy?

2. The next step is to formulate the assertion the writer takes to be the author's (Schumacher's) position: Schumacher believes it is possible to transform our modern economy into a Buddhist economy. Once this position was formulated in a direct statement, neither the writer nor any other member of the class was willing to hold that this was, in fact, Schumacher's position. So the examination of this reaction ended right there.

Student 2

1. A paraphrase:

   Schumacher says that a Buddhist economy, which gives priority to people over goods, is better than our modern economy. However, I don't think that it gives a better result because it is not efficient and it is not realistic to go back to the old way. I'd like to ask this question: Given the fact that we have developed our technology to get better results, how can we really believe that the old way will bring us better results?

   The question assumes this to be Schumacher's position: Schumacher believes that a return to the old way will have better results than our modern way.

2. Here too neither the writer nor others were willing to hold that this was Schumacher's position. So the examination of this reaction, at least as formulated in this question, ended right there.

Student 3

1. A paraphrase:

   > Schumacher says that the attempt to reduce the workload by mechanization has destroyed the joy of work. But I think the reduction of workload allows us to focus on more creative work, giving us many benefits. Should we really stop mechanization, which gives us more benefits than harm?

2. Schumacher's position? Schumacher believes we should stop mechanization. Again, everyone rejected this as an inaccurate statement of Schumacher's meaning.

   So in these first three cases, simply formulating the author's position (as stated in the question) led the writers to reject their own formulations as inaccurate. The discovery and identification of a point of difference occurred during the next exchange.

Student 4

1. A paraphrase:

   > Schumacher said a Buddhist economy is less harmful than the Western economy because it emphasizes people more than machines and stresses the need for less consumption to conserve natural resources. I don't agree with him because religious ideas don't have much to do with the economy. Each religion has an ideal philosophy but people can't realize it so easily. Does Schumacher really believe that our problems will be closer to solution if people understand Buddhist thinking?

2. Here is the essence of the exchange between teacher and student. (This exchange, although conversational, models what *BookMarks* calls "logging the text" or "talking to yourself," which a reader can do alone, writing in a log book.)

T: I don't quite see the connection between "Buddhist thinking" in your question and the notion of "religious ideas."

S: They're the same.

T: What does your question imply about Schumacher's position?

We settled on this formulation of Schumacher's position, using somewhat different language: Schumacher believes that applying Buddhist thinking to economic issues will lead to a resolution of those issues. Then we proceeded to try to discover a point of difference between the reader and the author:

T: What reasons or explanation does Schumacher give?

S: Buddhists give priority to people over goods. And Buddhists have a greater respect for nature; they're concerned about the waste of natural resources.

The fact that these points are neither clear reasons nor an explanation of the position stated is not relevant in this "logging" process. What *is* important is for the writer to just keep the ideas flowing.

T: And it's your position, isn't it, that applying Buddhist thinking to economic issues will not lead to their resolution? OK. So what are your reasons? What explanation can you give for your position?

S: Buddhism asks people to be faithful to their heritage; it does not ask them to develop or improve their living conditions.

There was a moment of silence at this response: The connection between this "explanation" and the writer's position was not apparent. Suddenly, the writer leaned forward in a movement that unmistakably revealed a moment of discovery—the *Aha!* moment:

S: My real point is that Buddhism supports a society that's not egalitarian!

It's this kind of *Aha!* discovery that reveals the real point of difference between the reader and the author. What was discovered in this moment is something that had not been explicit in the earlier formulations of difference or in the reasons given. But it will normally be a point that the writer is tacitly assuming. There is no way to predict when this moment of discovery will occur. It arises out of "talking to yourself," usually entailing formulating and reformulating the differences with the author.

This reader-writer now knows what to ask: What is the Buddhist attitude toward egalitarianism or social mobility? A summary report of the reflection that led to the discovery of this question can be presented in a formal written statement, such as this short (four-paragraph) paper:

> Schumacher said a Buddhist economy is less harmful than the Western economy because it emphasizes people more than machines and stresses the need for less consumption to conserve natural resources. For a Buddhist economist, Schumacher says, the quality of human life is more important than the production of goods. Unlimited production and unlimited consumption can only lead to abuse—of people and of nature.
>
> Can Schumacher really believe that our problems will be closer to solution if people understand Buddhist thinking?
>
> Schumacher seems to believe that Buddhist thinking can direct social policy toward reducing poverty. Buddhism, he says, gives priority to people over goods and to using natural resources conservatively. But I don't think Buddhist thinking can lead to reducing poverty. Buddhism asks people to accept their condition, not to improve their lot in life. So the point of difference between us seems to be our view of the Buddhist attitude toward social mobility.
>
> My question is about Schumacher's understanding of the Buddhist attitude toward the possibility for people to improve their social and economic positions. Can a Buddhist view encourage social mobility?

Sample Student Essay (Excerpted)

Here is a greatly reduced version of a student essay, with extracts from the preface, which presents the issue question, and from the following six paragraphs: summary, preview, understanding paragraph, critical paragraph, proposal paragraph, conclusion.

Technology and Economic Development in India

As we celebrate the 50th anniversary of our independence from British rule, a lot of discussion is going on in India as well as abroad. While journalists in the democratic west are applauding the survival of democracy in India, experts in India cannot ignore the fact that 350 million people are still living below the poverty line. What went wrong? Was Jawarharlal Nehru wrong in bringing modern technology to India instead of developing the indigenous arts and crafts of our villages as Mahatma Gandhi wanted us to do? . . . In any case where do we go from here? . . . Obviously we have to create more wealth; this means we need to create more jobs. Which technology is better for us?

When the British left in 1947, India was poor and undeveloped. The government invited the well-known economist E. F. Schumacher to advise them. He came up with the idea of an intermediate technology—something between the modern technology used in western countries and the traditional technology used in India at the time. In his book *Small Is Beautiful* he explains this concept: Such a technology would have to be labor intensive, affordable, small-scale, and friendly to the environment.

I think his concept makes a lot of sense. I am however skeptical of Schumacher's assertion that such a technology should be small-scale and should not necessarily employ the most advanced science. I feel putting too many constraints on the development of technology will divert it from the primary goal for India today—the creation of jobs. India needs a technology that will help her accomplish that goal.

It's easy to understand why Schumacher came up with the idea of intermediate technology. He realized that modern, western technology would not be sufficient to fulfill the development needs of the east.

However attractive it may sound, I feel intermediate technology is not appropriate for India today because it is less advanced and it is small-scale. . . . In order to survive against international competition, India will have to use modern technology in some form. At the same time, in the interest of an economics of permanence, she will have to incorporate some elements of an intermediate technology.

India today needs to create a modern-intermediate technology. . . . Such a technology will have to be large-scale in order to create immediate employment opportunities for the millions of unemployed. . . . And it will have to be labor intensive. Abundant manpower is India's biggest resource. We need a technology that will make the best use of this resource. . . .

Modern-intermediate technology is the best option for the fast economic development of India today. Some might question how such a technology would be able to fulfill the development needs of an agricultural country where 70% of the people live in villages. Precisely for this reason. For too long many Indians have depended for their livelihood on farms that are too small to support them. Wherever necessary we will have to equip the farmers with the tools necessary for efficient farming. But there is also a desperate need to take away the number of people dependent on these farms and engage them in gainful employment elsewhere. Many cities in India boast of engineering colleges and design institutions modeled after similar institutions in the west. It is now up to the students of these institutes to use their knowledge to fulfill the needs of their country. They are, after all, in the best position to develop the modern-intermediate technology.

Appendix C

Editor Evaluation Form

The student-editor uses this form (Editor Evaluation of Draft 2) to summarize the recommendations made for draft 3 of the essay. The comments are similar to those on forms designed for the instructor's comments.

Part 1: Recommended to Improve Clarity of the Presentation

Issue, Theme, Thesis
- ☐ Revise to meet the Triangle Test: The *proposal thesis* and the *author's position* criticized in ¶4 should both answer the *issue question*.
- ☐ Revise to meet the ITT Test: The *thesis* must be a statement about the *theme* that answers the *issue question*.

Thesis Statement Needs Attention

- ☐ New formulation needed
- ☐ Needs to be restated in locations as instructed

Paragraph Shape
- ☐ Revise to clarify T-block (thesis-support) shape:
  ¶1 Summary   ¶3 Understanding   ¶4 Critical   ¶5 Proposal
- ☐ Revise in accordance with specific guidelines:
  Preface   ¶2 Preview   ¶6 Conclusion

Support Sentences in Paragraphs   ¶1?   ¶3?   ¶4?   ¶5?

- ☐ Signal words/phrases are needed
- ☐ Revise to make parallel in form and concept
- ☐ Backup missing

Part 2: Consider to Improve Effectiveness of the Argument

(Circle all that apply, and explain your response)

1. What you say catches my attention. It makes me stop and say, "Yes, you have a point. You suggest a way of looking at the issue I had not seriously considered."

2. An interesting paper, but it could be more effective. Perhaps you could anticipate the question/reaction, which I've noted in my comment below.

3. I am struck by a weakness in your paper that blurs your point. As a result,

the case you make for your point isn't as strong as it could be.

☐ The case you make does not hold my attention or provoke me to think about it.

☐ Your critical paragraph is based on an apparent misreading OR misunderstanding OR incomplete understanding of the author's position.

☐ Your backup doesn't anticipate a reader's possible questions.

☐ There is too little backup, not enough to involve the reader in your argument. You have just presented a skeleton outline of your case.

4. It is difficult to follow your argument because the presentation is not clear.

☐ You have not met the formal requirements of the assignment.

☐ Your sentences are difficult to understand.

Chapter 12

Linking Assessment to the
Content-Based Curriculum

Leila May-Landy

Columbia University

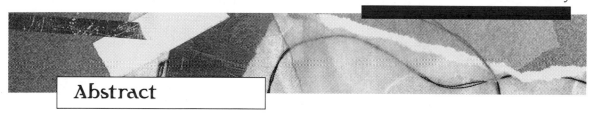

Abstract

Assessment can play a constructive role in content-based instruction by providing opportunities for teachers and students to observe and reflect on performance. Assessment tasks should reflect the underlying theories of language learning and teaching that guide the design of the content-based curriculum and should provide a way to verify that goals and standards have been internalized and mastered. When congruence between theory and practice exists, the formative role of assessment is placed in the foreground and the gap between theory and practice can be narrowed. In this model, the challenge teachers face is to design assessment tasks that properly reflect a constructivist view of language learning, which entails the ability to produce sustained discourse in the content area. The tasks most suitable for this type of assessment are open-ended response items that assess students' ability to handle both content and language in authentic communication. ■

This chapter explores the positive role assessment can play in content-based instruction as a tool to optimize teaching and learning and to further the search for greater consistency between the curriculum and its theoretical roots.

In the course of this discussion, the reader needs to bear in mind that *assessment* is a very general term that can apply to many opportunities for evaluating knowledge and skills. Too often, however, it is associated with discrete-point testing, which is a fundamental component of the psychometrically rigorous instruments that are designed for standardized testing and are often far removed from our classroom practices. As ESL instructors and curriculum developers, our goal should be to design assessment tasks that reflect our beliefs about teaching and learning in a bottom-up approach to educational testing rather than the top-down approach we have long been subjected to. The *what* (content) and *how* (method) of the assessment task should mirror the *what* and *how* of the curriculum. In its constructive and formative role, assessment should be a method that allows students and teachers to observe and reflect on performance and to evaluate progress and skills by focusing on both curricular goals and the processes involved in achieving them. As an observational and reflective tool, assessment can be an integral part of the learning process in which descriptive rather than quantitative feedback is generated and shared to facilitate the learning process. In this light, assessment will have a natural place in our classroom practice.

The Role of Assessment

Teachers in all disciplines and pedagogical models engage in some sort of evaluative process. The nature of the assessment and evaluation will vary from context to context, but the purpose is the same: Assessment is an essential tool for verifying that educational goals have been met and modifying instruction by providing teachers and students with the feedback they need to gauge progress and improve teaching and learning. As one of the ways a curriculum is articulated, assessment should depend on the curricular goals of a specific course within a particular program. This involves the conscious planning of opportunities in which teachers will provide students with feedback on the achievement of goals as the curriculum unfolds. Decisions on the nature of the assessment therefore depend on priorities set by the teacher within his or her curriculum and reflect the theory of language learning that supports this curriculum and links it to programwide goals. Problems with the concept of assessment arise when assessment is imposed by administrators who are removed form the teaching context, and teachers are left with little freedom to choose which aspects of instruction to assess, how to assess, and when to assess. The most frequent result is negative washback, which is manifest in an incongruity between theories of learning and classroom practice because teachers are forced to comply with external standards and goals. Simply put, positive washback occurs when assessment procedures are based on what is actually taught in courses and when teachers and administrators collaborate to design a coherent programwide assessment plan.

The role of assessment can also be discussed in terms of accountability. As Bachman (1990) states, accountability and feedback are "essential mechanisms

Chapter 12   Linking Assessment to the Content-Based Curriculum for the continued effectiveness of any educational program" (p. 55). Used constructively, accountability can function in similar fashion to a learning contract in which students' willingness and motivation to follow the curriculum involve an implicit acceptance of their role as active participants. When assessment is used to ensure that teachers and students carry out and meet instructional goals, it confirms that the learning contract has been satisfied (Knowles, 1986). Without clear indications that curricular goals have been met, teachers' decisions will be based on impressionistic data and students will be left feeling that evaluations of their progress and abilities are ambiguous and highly subjective, and therefore unfair and ultimately useless.

Authentic Assessment

Achieving congruence between theory and practice is the goal of all authentic assessment. It occurs when the tasks and processes students engage in while preparing for and taking the "test" are analogous to the tasks and processes described by the theory of language learning on which the curriculum is constructed. Inauthenticity occurs when a mismatch exists among assessment tasks, classroom practices, and their underlying theories of learning. To ensure assessment authenticity, the same question should be asked of both classroom practices and assessment practices: "Do these tasks reflect the theories of language learning (and teaching) I subscribe to and the goals I have set for this course?" If the answer is no, something is amiss. By narrowing the gap between assessment and teaching practices, the formative rather than summative (the assignment of a final grade) goal of assessment becomes the primary focus. The challenge for teachers and students alike is to see results constructively as indications of areas they need to focus on and develop. It is equally important to recognize that each assessment task is a "snapshot" of a complex process that is constantly emerging. It is limited by the context (the topic, task type, subjectivity of the observer, and affective influences on the subject) and is only one view of a learner's multifaceted abilities. Variation in performance is to be expected. Each assessment will yield different results, and if the assessment task is closely linked to classroom practices, gains can be expected in future assessments.

In sustained-content curricula, this means that instead of focusing on one or two summative evaluations (a midterm and final exam), students should be held accountable at regular intervals throughout the semester for the aspects of classroom practice that the teacher has set as learning priorities in his or her curriculum. If, for example, one's goal is to develop the ability to summarize or critique an author's position, students should have opportunities to perform these tasks at various points in the semester. After they complete the first task, students should be given appropriate feedback that they can incorporate when carrying out subsequent tasks. The resulting profile of a student's performance would be based on his or her ability to incorporate feedback and to reach the standards set for successful completion of the task.

From this description, you might conclude that the entire class would be consumed by assessment tasks. In some respect, this is true. If assessment is an integral aspect of learning, it should be an essential and regular feature of classroom practice and will vary in intensity and format depending on the teaching context: class size and length (number of hours per week and number of weeks in the semester) and whether the course is theme based, adjunct, or sheltered. In accepting these guidelines, we are moving away from the hit-or-miss model of assessment, which is based on one or two exams to determine a student's final grade and, in this summative role, offers little or no opportunity for learning to take place (Stiggins, 1994). What we are moving *toward* is an assessment practice that sends the message that the processes of participating in all aspects of the curriculum and of acquiring skills and achieving goals are important elements in evaluating student outcomes. In this way, the formative role of assessment as a teaching and learning tool can be placed in the foreground.

Authentic Assessment and Cognitive Theory

The movement toward authentic assessment is closely linked to cognitive learning theories. These theories rely heavily on schema theory, which views learning as "an ongoing process during which students are continually receiving information, interpreting it, connecting it to what they already know and have experienced (their prior knowledge), and reorganizing and revising their internal conceptions of the world, which are called 'mental models,' 'knowledge structures,' or 'schema'" (Herman, Aschbacher, & Winters, 1992, p. 14). Schema theory is a key underpinning of sustained-content ESL, where the unfolding of the curriculum should be an interactive and creative process in which the teacher and students collaborate in the construction of knowledge (schema) and critiquing of ideas. In this "constructivist" view, "all individuals are thought to learn by constructing information about the world and by using active mental and dynamic processes" (O'Malley & Valdez Pierce, 1996, p. 10).

This model therefore goes beyond the traditional view of classroom practices that focus on the teacher as "transmitter" and the student as "receptor" of the knowledge (Freire, 1968). The skills required of the student are no longer solely grounded on the comprehension, storage, and retrieval of facts but demand the exercise of higher-order thinking, which involves the ability to apply, analyze, synthesize, and evaluate information from multiple sources (Bloom, Engelhart, Furst, Hill, & Krathwohl, 1956) and cannot be easily evaluated with closed-ended, single-answer response items. Bloom, Madaus, and Hastings' (1981) discussion of convergent thinking, in which "the correct answer to the question can be known in advance" (p. 265), and divergent thinking, in which "the answer to the problem cannot be fixed in advance" (p. 265), has direct implications for sustained-content teaching and assessment practices. Since tasks based on lower-order thinking skills are cognitively undemanding, less will be gained from them. In this light, the focus of any authentic assessment would be a performance-based task, in which the learner is called on to construct a unique response that is the product of the personal process she or he has undergone. Once again, Bloom, Madaus, and Hastings (1981) summarize these principles in their discussion of synthesis:

Chapter 12   Linking Assessment to the Content-Based Curriculum

Synthesis, however, appears to be a type of divergent thinking in that it is unlikely that the right solution to a problem can be set in advance. In synthesis each student may provide a unique response to the questions or problems posed, and it is the task of the evaluator to determine the merits of the response in terms of the process exhibited, the quality of the product, or the quality of evidence and arguments supporting the synthetic work. (p. 265)

In content-based instruction, the involvement of higher-order thinking skills is central to the language-learning process. Content-based pedagogy involves the ability to maintain sustained coherent discourse on both concrete and abstract topics in which the speaker responds to ideas presented in multiple sources. It is by nature a dialogic and exploratory process in which language and ideas are closely linked. The greater the sophistication of the ideas expressed, the greater the sophistication of the language necessary to express these ideas. Thus, in content-based classes, intellectual engagement is key to language acquisition. It is precisely in the individual and creative process of exploring a topic (which involves handling information and ideas as well as elements of language) and formulating unique, complex responses that language learning takes place.

Assessment in Content-Based Instruction: Cognitive Learning Theory and the Constructivist Model

As we have seen, the theoretical foundations of content-based instruction have been strengthened by cognitive learning theory and the constructivist model of learning, and many of their principles have become fundamental components of content-based curriculum design. Nevertheless, regardless of which type of content-based instructional model we are working within—theme based, sheltered, or adjunct—the gap between theory and practice has been difficult to close. Old paradigms are difficult to cast off, and, under the banner of the new approach, teaching and testing practices are frequently based on the principles of models previously dismissed. In the adoption of a content-based approach, often greater gains have been made in curriculum design and teaching practices than in assessment. Assessment is sometimes confused with testing, which is perceived as a necessary evil detached from teaching. This easily leads to "fast and dirty" methods of assessing students that bear little or no relationship to methodology or curricular goals. Tests frequently include discrete-point items, which do not involve even sentence-level language production. Vocabulary, grammar, reading, listening, writing, and speaking are assessed as "autonomous" facets of language rather than as one of the many threads in the fabric of language proficiency.

Language testing which does not take into account propositional and illocutionary development beyond the sentence level, as well as the intention between language and behavior and real-world phenomena, is at best getting at only a part of communicative competence. Small wonder that we find that a student's success at second-language classroom exercises and tests appears to bear little relationship to his or her ability to use the language effectively in a real-world situation. (Wesche, 1981, pp. 552–553)

The problem would not be so great if it were possible to disconnect assessment from methodology and curriculum and the theories of learning and language acquisition that support them. But this would hardly be the purpose of any thoughtful assessment plan. The tests we employ are perceived as direct indications of our curricular goals and the expectations we have for student performance. If the gap between assessment and methodology is wide, content-based instruction will be seen as another way of arriving at narrower language-learning goals: acquiring the ability to complete synonym-matching vocabulary items, fill-in-the-blank grammar items, and multiple-choice or true/false reading and listening comprehension questions, all of which are based on the acquisition of cognitively undemanding passive language skills and are disconnected from the content focus of the course. (In many instances, speaking is not regularly assessed.) In other words, the ability to fill in a blank with the correct verb or word form does not indicate whether or not the student is able to actually use those forms in his or her own communication. The importance of content-based instruction, as with all new models, is that the methodology entails an entirely different process of language learning that should be reflected in our assessment practices.

When the focus is on the contextualized and "constructed" use of language, a quandary arises as to what aspect of performance the teacher should assess: the handling of the topic or the accuracy of the language. Brinton, Snow, and Wesche (1989) give an unequivocal response to this quandary:

> Is it possible for language instructors to avoid considering content knowledge in these [theme-based, sheltered, and adjunct] courses and to evaluate only second language capabilities? The answer is no for at least two reasons. One is that learning the subject matter itself is an objective in this type of approach. . . . The second reason content cannot be ignored is that language-learning objectives of content-based courses are performance-based: Students aim not only to improve knowledge of the language but to learn how to use this knowledge to perform tasks in an academic setting. (p. 182)

The reverse is also true for Brinton, Snow, and Wesche: language cannot be overlooked when assessing content. Within a content-based model, it is therefore important to address the dual focus of learning outcomes—the development of language skills and the acquisition of content knowledge. An implicit goal of content-based instruction is to increase the sophistication and complexity of the learner's language repertoire (use of sophisticated vocabulary, complex syntactic structures, transitional devices, and rhetorical techniques) while involving the student in higher-order thinking skills. As language ability improves, discourse should move from short, simple, isolated phrases to the long, complex, sustained discourse involved in analytic thought. Consequently, students need feedback on both the form and the content of their discourse. Feedback on form should focus on linguistic features that are salient to the handling of the topic and on errors that impede communication. Accuracy should, however, be seen as a means to an end and not the primary goal in effective communication (Wiggins, 1993, p. 58).

In sum, the constructivist model of knowledge has particular relevance to language learning in content-based instruction. In the constructivist model, students are given a central role in the development of the curriculum. They are called on to engage with the topic in an active and meaningful way by contributing relevant information from their own knowledge and experience, being responsible for the presentation and evaluation of information and ideas in the syllabus, and furthering their investigation of the topic through individual (or group) research. It is in this active exploration of the content area and the ensuing rich exposure to language—in which students have the opportunity to summarize, compare, apply, and challenge information and ideas, and formulate their own opinions—that language learning takes place. In its formative role, assessment in content-based instruction therefore should focus on the processes involved in handling the content material as well as on specific final products (term papers, essay exams, group projects). Recognition and credit should be given for all of the processes relevant to completing the task to make it a truly formative evaluation. In practical terms, there are numerous ways to assess this active participation and to give feedback on it, and the decision of what and how to assess will vary depending on the broader curricular goals of the course (see the section "Assessment in Practice" and Appendix A).

The Role of Feedback and Peer and Self-Assessment

One of the many reasons assessment has been seen in a negative light is that it is most often divorced from its most essential component: feedback. Wiggins (1993) aptly defines feedback as "information designed to enable students to accurately self-assess and self-correct so that assessment becomes 'an episode of learning'" (p. 183). In ideal circumstances, feedback should be an accounting of how the student has performed in reference to the objectives and standards established in the course (Wiggins, 1993). When curricular objectives and standards have been clearly articulated, students are able to know what is expected of them and how to assess their own performance. In concrete terms, this entails a well-designed syllabus that indicates when and how students will be assessed, as well as the standards that will be used to evaluate their performance. This can take the form of guidelines for successful completion of the task, descriptors of various levels of performance, and models of successful task completion. When commenting on the student's performance, the teacher should provide feedback on the ways in which the student met the standards and the ways in which he or she did not. The goal is for the student to be able to use the feedback, along with the guidelines and descriptors, to make adjustments and improve performance.

This short description does not do justice to the complexity of the task at hand. In practice, students are frequently called on to meet vague objectives and standards or brief directions or guidelines on how to complete a task. Directions for essay assignments often request that students delve deeply into the topic, use sophisticated language, and organize their ideas well. Unless these features have been explicitly taught, students will not have a clear idea of what is expected of them. Articulating our goals and standards may be an arduous process, but it is a necessary step in demystifying assessment. Without this clarity, it is difficult, if not impossible, for students to become self-directed learners. As international students in an unfamiliar sociolinguistic environment, our students are particularly ill equipped to second-guess what our objectives and standards are.

The role of giving feedback and of assessing performance should not, however, remain entirely in the hands of the teacher. Self-assessment is a vital aspect of all learning.

> Researchers who have studied the reading process have shown us that individuals, whether children or adults, who cannot monitor their own reading comprehension and adjust reading strategies when they sense that they are not "getting it," cannot become competent readers. Those who cannot self-assess cannot read (Valencia & Pearson, 1987). On another front, we now know that writers who cannot monitor the quality and effectiveness of their own written communication, and know how to fix it when it isn't "working" cannot become competent writers. Self-assessment is the very heart of the writing process (Hillocks, 1986). (Stiggins, 1994, p. 33)

It is precisely this type of concurrent feedback, focusing on the learning process itself, that is relevant to content-based instruction. Internalizing the strategies and standards necessary to judge and complete a task is an essential step in self-directed learning.

In addition, students should be encouraged to respond to information and ideas presented by their peers. Ultimately, the message should be sent that the teacher is not the only one who knows how to correct an error, nor is she or he the only one able to contribute information or respond to statements made by other students. Too often what is called a "discussion" is in fact a dialogue between the teacher and one student while other students simply do not attend to or respond to what their peers have said. In this format, everyone waits for their turn to present their ideas to the teacher. When the focus is shifted away from the teacher in the volley of ideas, students will be forced to engage in more meaningful exchanges in which they must articulate and support their assertions and understandings, respond to the contributions others have made, and work to clarify their statements for peers, that is, those who don't already "know" the answer.

This shift of focus away from the teacher's response should be carried over to more "formal" contexts, namely when a student is making an oral presentation to the class or to a small group. A common procedure in this circumstance is for the teacher to fill out a form that evaluates various aspects of the student's performance: overall structure, clarity of the presentation, grammatical accuracy, and pronunciation. However, to encourage both peer and self-assessment, it would be more appropriate for the presenter and listeners to respond to the presentation. The presenter would then receive feedback not only from the teacher but also from his or her "true" audience (a group of peers who are exploring the topic on equal footing), and the teacher would receive the presenter's reflection on his or her own presentation.

I have elaborated on this procedure because little attention has been given to providing feedback on speaking, while peer and self-assessment in writing has become a more common feature of our practice. These opportunities to focus on spoken language during oral presentations give students the opportunity to rehearse ideas and improve the effectiveness of their communication with restatements, summaries, and clarifications based on the concurrent feedback given by the teacher and their peers. The challenge facing teachers in all content-based programs is not to focus exclusively on grammatical accuracy but to provide feedback on the appropriateness and complexity of the handling of the topic. In a sheltered or adjunct course, it may be tempting to provide feedback on the assimilation of the actual content while overlooking the linguistic accuracy of student performance. Although the emphasis may vary in different classes, as Wesche, Brinton, and Snow (1989) have indicated, neither aspect can be neglected.

Assessment in Practice

Since ESL instructors are frequently called on to prepare students for the discrete-point tests used in some academic courses, it is necessary to clarify the limitations of discrete-point exercises and tests in content-based instruction. On a very elementary level, contextualized synonym-matching or fill-in-the-blank grammar exercises can be somewhat useful in verifying that students know the meaning of a word or the appropriate form and, to a certain extent, the use of a particular grammatical structure. What we need to recognize, as Wesche (1981) pointed out, is that the ability to complete these exercises does not teach students how to use these semantic and syntactic features appropriately and effectively in communication, nor are they good indicators of this ability. In addition to this fundamental lack of validity, most teacher-made discrete-point classroom quizzes or tests are full of flaws and have a low level of reliability (Genesee & Upshur, 1996). Although these instruments are easy to correct, discrete-point test items that are both reliable and truly contextualized are time consuming to prepare. Furthermore, the time spent in class discussing alternate responses to ambiguous fill-in-the-blank items or multiple keys to selected-response items tends to be unproductive. In replacing discrete-point items with open-ended response items, the trade-off is quite simple. Open-ended response items take little time to compose (though more time to "correct") and provide information about a student's ability and progress that is more relevant to language proficiency in content based instruction. In short, an open-ended short-answer question assesses both content and the student's use of appropriate language with an authentic communicative task—that is, the effort to explain what you know.

In practical terms, discrete-point items could easily be replaced with open-ended, integrative items that require the student to use vocabulary or features of grammar creatively in connected discourse. A simple example would be a prompt requiring the student to use specific vocabulary items to summarize or critique an author's point of view or to present his or her own opinion. The same can be done with grammar: Prompts related to the topic that require the use of a particular grammatical structure can be used to elicit connected discourse on the topic (see Nelson, Chapter 8). Grammar can be targeted by asking students to complete such tasks as hypothesizing about the present or future events (conditionals), making conjectures about the past (past unreal conditionals, modal perfects), stating recommendations or opinions forcefully (uninflected forms, negative inversion), summarizing an author's position (reported speech), explaining a step-by-step process (passive voice, use of transitional devices), and describing a character in a play or story (adjective clauses, word forms). At the very least, sentence completion items can be used to a limited extent as well to force students to use certain structures while integrating information from the content area.

Appendix A lists more global assessment tasks that reflect the dialogic nature of discourse in the academic community and the inquiry-based approach of content-based instruction. The feedback on each task will vary. Reading and listening logs can be used as dialogue journals between teacher and students or among the students themselves. Excerpts from these logs can also be used in class for further discussion. The feedback given in response to a longer or more substantive written or oral assignment, such as weekly essays and oral presentations, should be a descriptive summary of the ways in which the objectives of the task were met and the changes needed for improvement. When scores or grades are assigned, they should be based on analytic rather than holistic scoring techniques. When used with an appropriate scoring rubric (see ACTFL, 1986; Cushing Weigle & Jensen, 1997; Jacobs, Zinkgraf, Wormuth, Hartfiel, & Hughey, 1981), analytic evaluations will provide detailed information about areas to improve by breaking down the feedback into categories such as content, organization, and accuracy.

The listing of tasks in Appendix A by the main skill area should not be taken as an indication that the skills are taught separately, since each task requires multiple skills. Because assessment is dependent on the teaching context, I have intentionally limited my list to two or three tasks per area. Hopefully these will provide a stimulus for brainstorming your own possibilities and for working with colleagues to design programwide assessment procedures.

The criteria for determining the final grade should be clearly outlined for students as in Appendix B. The weighting of each task depends on the level and focus of the class and should be coordinated among the faculty in a department to ensure that the standards and criteria used for assigning proficiency levels and grades and for determining readiness for academic study are consistent throughout a language program. Although it is necessary to assign one composite (summative) grade to each student at the end of the semester, departments can keep their own final grade reports that include a more complete profile of a student's strengths and weaknesses in the various skill areas (see Appendix C).

Conclusion

In the adoption of authentic assessment practices, some might fear that we are advocating a lax system of classroom assessment in which our standards are slackened and the reliability of our "tests" is sacrificed. What we need to acknowledge is that standardized tests and classroom tests based on discrete-point items or closed-ended responses give little information about the communicative language proficiency and gains in content knowledge that we have set as our curricular goals in content-based instruction. Narrowing the gap between our classroom practices and the measures we use to gauge student progress ensures that we are assessing our students' engagement in the learning process as well as the final outcomes of this process. In maintaining the validity of the measures we employ, we are respecting the unique process each learner undergoes, the multifaceted nature of language proficiency, and the complexity of the skills required to explore a content area in an inquiry-based model. Although open-ended response items, oral presentations, logs, research projects, surveys, essays, and portfolios may not yield results that can easily be averaged to attain a final grade (e.g., numerical scores or letter grades), they offer the opportunity to gather the information necessary to give constructive descriptive feedback on student performance. Our challenge is to improve the reliability of our assessment practices by setting clear standards, establishing departmental norming sessions, assessing students at regular intervals in a variety of contexts, and using a variety of assessment tasks. In this way, assessment can be a vital and natural part of our classroom practice.

References

American Council on the Teaching of Foreign Languages. (1986). *ACTFL proficiency guidelines*. New York: American Council on the Teaching of Foreign Languages.

Bachman, L. F. (1990). *Fundamental considerations in language testing*. Oxford, UK: Oxford University Press.

Bachman, L. F., & Palmer, A. S. (1996). *Language testing in practice*. Oxford, UK: Oxford University Press.

Bloom, B. S., Engelhart, M. D., Furst, E. J., Hill, W. H., & Krathwohl, D. R. (Eds.) (1956). *Taxonomy of educational objectives: The classification of educational goals, Handbook I: Cognitive domain*. New York: David McKay.

Bloom, B. S., Madaus, G. F., & Hastings, J. T. (1981). *Evaluation to improve learning*. New York: McGraw-Hill.

Brinton, D., Snow, M., & Wesche, M. (1989). *Content-based second language instruction*. Boston: Heinle & Heinle.

Carroll, B. J. (1980). *Testing communicative performance: An interim study*. Oxford, UK: Pergamon Press.

Chamot, A. U., & O'Malley, J. M. (1987). The cognitive academic language learning approach: A bridge to the mainstream. *TESOL Quarterly, 21*(2), 227–249.

Chamot, A. U., & O'Malley, J. M. (1994). *The CALLA handbook: Implementing the cognitive academic language learning approach*. Reading, MA: Addison-Wesley.

Cummins, J. (1980). The construct of proficiency in bilingual education. In J. E. Alatis (Ed.), *Georgetown University Round Table on Language and Linguistics*. Washington, DC: Georgetown University Press.

Cummins, J. (1981). The role of primary language development in promoting educational success for language minority students. In *Schooling and language minority students: A theoretical framework* (pp. 3–49). Los Angeles: California State University, National Evaluation and Assessment Center.

Cummins, J. (1983). Academic achievement and language proficiency. In J. W. Oller (Ed.), *Issues in language testing research* (pp. 108–129). Rowley, MA: Newbury House.

Cushing Weigle, S., & Jensen, L. (1997). Issues in assessment for content-based instruction. In M. Snow & D. Brinton (Eds.), *The content-based classroom: Perspectives on integrating language and content* (pp. 201–212). White Plains, NY: Addison Wesley Longman.

Fischer, C. F., & King, R. M. *Authentic assessment: A guide to implementation*. Alexandria, VA: Association for Supervision and Curriculum Development.

Freire, P. (1968). *Pedagogy of the oppressed*. New York: Seabury.

Gantzer, J. (1996). Do reading tests match reading theory? *College ESL, 6*(1), 29–48.

Genesee, F., & Upshur, J. A. (1996). *Classroom-based evaluation in second language education*. Cambridge, UK: Cambridge University Press.

Grabe, W., & Stoller, F. (1997). Content-based instruction: Research foundations. In M. Snow & D. Brinton (Eds.), *The content-based classroom: Perspectives on integrating language and content* (pp. 5–21). White Plains, NY: Addison Wesley Longman.

Herman, J. L., Aschbacher, P. R., & Winters, L. (1992). *A practical guide to alternative assessment*. Alexandria, VA: Association for Supervision and Curriculum Development.

Hillocks, G. (1986). *Research on written composition: New directions for teaching*. Urbana, IL: ERIC Clearinghouse on Reading and Communications Skills.

Jacobs, H. L., Zinkgraf, S. A., Wormuth, D. R., Hartfiel, V. F., & Hughey, J. B. (1981). *Testing ESL composition: A practical approach*. Rowley, MA: Newbury House.

Knowles, M. S. (1986). *Using learning contracts: Approaches to individualizing and structuring learning*. San Francisco: Jossey-Bass.

Leki, I. (1995). Good writing: I know it when I see it. In D. Belcher & G. Braine (Eds.), *Academic writing in a second language: Essays on research and pedagogy* (pp. 23–46). Norwood, NJ: Ablex.

Lightbown, P. B., & Spada, N. (1990). Focus-on-form and corrective feedback in communicative language teaching: Effects on second language learning. *Studies in Second Language Acquisition, 12,* 429–448.

Lynch, B. K., & Davidson, F. (1994). Criterion-referenced language test development: Linking curricula, teachers, and tests. *TESOL Quarterly, 28*(4), 727–743.

Marzano, R. J., Pickering, D., & McTighe, J. (1993). *Assessing student outcomes: Performance assessment using the dimensions of learning model*. Alexandria, VA: Association for Supervision and Curriculum Development.

Mohan, B. (1986). *Language and content*. Reading, MA: Addison-Wesley.

Oller, J. W. (1979). *Language tests at school: A pragmatic approach*. New York: Longman.

Omaggio Hadley, A. (1993). *Teaching language in context*. Boston: Heinle & Heinle.

O'Malley, J. M., & Valdez Pierce, L. (1996). *Authentic assessment for English language learners: Practical approaches for teachers*. Reading, MA: Addison-Wesley.

Shohamy, E. (1993). *The power of tests: The impact of language tests on teaching and learning*. Washington, DC: The National Foreign Language Center.

Short, D. (1993). Assessing integrated language and content instruction. *TESOL Quarterly, 27*(4), 627–656.

Snow, M. A., Met, M., & Genesee, F. (1989). A conceptual framework for the integration of language and content in second/foreign language instruction. *TESOL Quarterly, 23*(2), 201–217.

Stiggins, R. J. (1994). *Student-centered classroom assessment*. New York: Macmillan College Publishing.

Swain, M. (1985). Communicative competence: Some roles of comprehensible input and comprehensible output in its development. In S. Gass & C. Madden (Eds.), *Input in second language acquisition* (pp. 235–253). Rowley, MA: Newbury House.

Swain, M. (1996). Integrating language and content in immersion classrooms: Research perspectives. *Canadian Modern Language Review, 52*(4) 529–548.

Tobias, S. (1994). Interest, prior knowledge, and learning. *Review of Educational Research, 64*(1), 37–54.

Turner, J. (1997). Creating content-based language tests: Guidelines for teachers. In M. Snow & D. Brinton (Eds.), *The content-based classroom: Perspectives on integrating language and content* (pp. 187–200). White Plains, NY: Addison Wesley Longman.

Valencia, S. W., & Pearson, P. D. (1987). Reading assessment: Time for a change. *The Reading Teacher, 40*(8), 726–32.

Wesche, M. B. (1981). Communicative testing in a second language. *Canadian Modern Language Review, 37,* 551–571.

Wiggins, G. P. (1989a). A true test: Toward more authentic and equitable assessment. *Phi Delta Kappan, 70,* 703–713.

Wiggins, G. P. (1989b). Teaching to the authentic test. *Educational Leadership, 46,* 41–47.

Wiggins, G. P. (1992). Creating tests worth taking. *Educational Leadership, 49,* 26–33.

Wiggins, G. P. (1993). *Assessing student performance: Exploring the purpose and limits of testing.* San Francisco: Jossey-Bass.

Zamel, V. (1993). Questioning academic discourse. *College ESL, 3*(1), 28–39.

Appendix A

Sample Assessment Tasks

Reading

1. *Reading logs with teacher responses* (on a daily or weekly basis or at the completion of a unit). Logs can be an open-ended or a structured response to questions. (Short excerpts from student logs can be read aloud to the class; longer excerpts can be copied and distributed in class. These can then be the basis for further analysis of the reading.)

2. *Oral reports on reading assignments.* Alternating students can be assigned to summarize and lead a discussion on an article assigned for the whole class or on articles related to the topic that none of the other students has read. The teacher can provide this article, or the student can be asked to do further research on the topic to find an article that offers an opposing view or a related perspective on the topic. Listeners can be asked to make an entry in their reading logs that responds to some of the elements the speaker brought up.

Listening

1. *Notetaking on lectures, in-class student reports, audio- and videotaped materials.* Students review notes in pairs or small groups to fill in gaps in comprehension, highlight major points, and compare information and ideas to those of other sources. (In the case of audio- or videotapes, the tape can be replayed for students multiple times.)

2. *Listening logs with teacher responses.* Logs can be based on lectures, audio- and videotapes, or class reports or discussions. (As with reading logs, excerpts from these logs can be used in class for further discussion.)

Oral Presentations

1. *Reports based on independent or small-group library-based research.* Library research can be an option for providing further information on an aspect of a topic dealt with in the syllabus or the foundation for a longer term paper on a topic of the student's (or students') own choice. In addition to the oral report, students can prepare annotated bibliographies, summaries, or critiques.

2. *Reports based on independent or small-group community-based surveys.* As an additional way to research and report on a topic, students can interview specific groups of individuals (elderly persons, immigrants from a particular country, students) or conduct an opinion poll on a topic discussed in class or on the focus of their term paper.

Writing

1. *Essays.* At home or in class, students can write their own essay questions from which the teacher or the class chooses two or three to be the focus of a longer writing. In contrast to traditional in-class essays, students can be allowed to refer to notes, books, and dictionaries. Students can be given take-home essay exams that require either one long essay or two or three shorter responses to questions.

2. *Portfolios.* Students can keep a portfolio of their writing to review with the teacher during mid-semester and end-of-semester conferences.

Sample Assessment Tasks for a 12-Week Intensive Theme-Based Course

Final grades will be based on the following areas:

1. Participation in class

2. Reading

   a. Completion of weekly reading logs

   b. Preparation of questions for class discussion

3. Oral reports

   a. Short report related to the topic studied in class (given in the first half of the semester)

   b. Long report based on individual research project that includes both library research and field interviews (given in the second half of the semester)

4. Writing

   a. Weekly at-home essays with revisions

   b. Term paper (on the same topic as the oral presentation)

5. In-class midterm and final exam based on a theme

   a. Reading: Article with accompanying open-ended comprehension, grammar, and vocabulary questions

   b. Listening: Audio- or videotape with accompanying open-ended comprehension, grammar, and vocabulary questions

   c. Essay: Topics related to the information and ideas presented in the article and tape

Sample Final Grade Report Form

Final Grades   Fall 98   Level _____
Date: Instructors:

EPT   Promo. | 98-f-pt- |

Final Level Fall 98 ☐   Final Grade Fall 98 ☐   # of Classes Missed_____
alp
                            Grade for Effort (Class) ☐   Grade for Effort (HW) ☐

Oral/Aural Skills ☐   Listening _____   Fluency _____

                          Pronunciation _____   Gramm. Accuracy _____

Writing Skills ☐   Content _____   Gramm. in Writing _____

Comments

Academic literacy/discourse, 24, 55, 99, 133, 137, 154–155, 182, 188–189
  charts for, 139–140
  graphic organizers for, 139, 152
  role of speech in, 75–78
Academic needs of ESL/EFL students, 2–4, 9–10, 22, 58, 60, 63, 98, 132–134
  Open Doors, 58, 60, 63
Academic writing. *See* Writing skills
Academic Writing for University Exams course, 135–144
  course components, 137–140
  curriculum guidelines, 146
  evaluations of class, 142–144
  instructors, 135–136
  mistakes, 136
  students, 136, 141–142
  test questions, 141–142
  units, 140–141
Accused, The, 172
Active learning, 181
Adjunct model of CBI, 7, 8, 99, 227, 231
Adverb (ADV), 38
AIDS as a topic, 179–199
American history, 132–157, 135
Argumentation, 2–4. *See also* Rhetoric
  cultural variance, 2–4
  definition of, 2
Assessment, 223–239
  accountability, 224–225
  cognitive learning theories and, 226–227
  congruence between theory and practice, 225
  criteria for final grades, 232, 239
  discrete-point tests versus open-ended response, 231–232
  feedback, 229–231
  methodology and, 228
  negative washback versus positive washback, 224
  peer, 229–231
  at regular intervals, 225
  role of, 224–225
  sample, 236–238
  self, 229–231
  standards for papers, 212
Assignments
  autobiography project, 47–52
  directions for essay assignments, 230
  in-class versus out-of-class, 23, 40, 133
Autobiography project, 47–52

Bakhtin, M., 5
Bird Cage, The, 172
Bookmarks course, 201–222
  course description, 205
  course structure, 205–206
Book reviews, 27, 185
Braveheart, 172
Business course, 60–63
  Internet search, 61–63
  prereading activity, 60–61
  reading activity, 61
  synthesis of concepts through writing, 61

CALLA. *See* Cognitive Academic Language Learning Approach (CALLA)
CALPs. *See* Cognitive academic learning proficiency (CALPs)
Calvin and Hobbes, 79–92
Canadian immersion programs, 5, 10
Categories, 89
Cazden, C., 5
CBI. *See* Content-based instruction (CBI)
Centers for Disease Control (CDC), 185
Charts for academic language structures, 139–140
Chunks, 82
City University of New York (CUNY) Writing Assessment Test (WAT), 127–128
Claim-and-support strategies, 10
Clause (C), 38, 44, 46–47, 123–124
  analysis chart, 47
Clause structure, 39
  clause reduction, 39
  constituent clause, 39, 40
Cognitive Academic Language Learning Approach (CALLA), 7

Cognitive academic learning proficiency (CALPs), 9, 120
Cognitive psychology
  assessment and, 226–227
  Cognitive Academic Language Learning Approach (CALLA), 7
  cognitive learning theory, 227–229
  critical skills and, 3, 9
Cohesion, 39
Collaboration, 182, 184, 189
Comic books, 78–92
Commentary course. *See Bookmarks*
Communicative approaches to language teaching, 5, 10
Communicative competence, 5
Comparison and contrast skills, 140, 152, 154–155, 156, 157, 162, 187
Complete verbs (CV), 121
Comprehension skills, 29–30
  questions for *Old Man and the Sea*, 42
Constructivist model, 227–229
Content
  accessing knowledge of, 21–22
  acquiring knowledge of, 21–22
  American history content, 132–157
  business content, 60–63
  choosing appropriate content, 12–13
  commentary, 201–222
  discipline-specific language, 13, 27
  displaying knowledge of, 21, 22–23
  engineering content, 96–116
  environmental science content, 63–67
  film and society content, 158–178
  grammar and, 36–53
  health content, 179–199
  in-depth treatment of, 10–11
  metalinguistics, 120–127
  Old Man and the Sea as content, 35–53
  psychology content, 26–27
  rhetoric conventions and, 13
  role of in ESL teaching, 2, 31
  skills for expertise in, 9, 103, 144
  technical information and, 13, 103
  textbooks as, 26–27, 103–104, 134, 182
  universal donors of, 13
Content-based instruction (CBI), 2. *See also* Sustained content-based instruction
  assessment and, 223–239
  first programs of, 4–5
  inter-faculty relations and, 6
  linguistic benefits of, 5–6

pedagogical benefits of, 6
psychological benefits of, 6
rationale for, 5–6
research findings about, 7–9
speech and, 74–94
types of, 6–7, 227
Corpus, Concordance, Collocation (Sinclair), 36
Corpus-based course, definition of term, 35
Critical literacy, 135
Critical thinking, 2–4, 9, 191
  analysis, 105–106, 226. *See also* Text analysis
  convergent versus divergent thinking, 226
  definition, 97
  for engineering students, 96–116
  evaluation, 106, 226
  exploration and, 207–208
  intellectual ordering, 202
  intellectual skepticism and, 173, 207
  metalinguistics and, 118, 124–129
  questioning texts and, 162, 168, 171–172, 202, 203–204, 208, 216–218
  synthesizing, 9, 23, 61, 64–65, 106, 134, 226–227
  synthetic reasoning, 9
Cross-cultural variation
  awareness of, 4
  of rhetorical conventions, 2–3, 173

Data-driven course, definition of term, 35
Dead Man Walking, 172
DePITTSS, 206
Dictation, 40
Discipline-specific language, 13
Discourse analysis, 13, 57. *See also* Text analysis
Discussion, 41, 162–165, 230
  seminars, 208–210
Display tasks, 21–23, 24, 27
Do the Right Thing, 161
Drama, 187–188

EAP. *See* English for Academic Purposes
Eastern Michigan University's Language and International Business Program
  EFL study, 8
Editing, 186, 211, 219–220. *See also* Error analysis
Elemental forms, 13
Emotional Intelligence, 182
Engineering, 96–116
English for Academic Purposes (EAP)
  corpus-based, 35–53
  critical skills and, 3, 9
  data-driven, 35–53

first programs of, 4
  grammar and reading, 35–53
  reading and writing, 19–34
  task-based, 19–34
English for Academic Purposes (ESP), 97
English for Intellectual Purposes, 97
English for Professional Communication (EPC), 97
English for Science and Technology (EST), 4, 97
English for Specific Purposes (ESP), 100–103
English for vocational training, 4
English language
  Black English, 4
  descriptions of spoken English, 77
  gatekeeper role of, 3
  group membership and, 4
  misconceptions about English speech, 76–78
  power issues and, 3–4
  standard English, 4
  variation in, 94
Environmental science, 63–67
  Internet search, 64, 65–67
  prereading activity, 64
  reading activity, 64
  synthesizing, 64–65
  writing activity, 64–65
Error analysis, 127, 129
ESL/EFL students
  academic needs of, 2–4, 9–10, 22, 58, 60, 63, 98,
    132–134
  accomplishments of, 67, 127–129, 189–190
  feedback from, 67–68, 92–94, 103, 142–144,
    168–172, 212–214
  fields of study of, 58, 60, 63
  power issues and, 3–4
ESL/EFL teachers, 135–136. *See also* Pedagogy
  skills for expertise in content, 9, 103, 144
Essays, 21, 61, 237. *See also* Writing skills
  of commentary, 210–211
  comparison/contrast essay questions, 140, 152,
    154–155, 156, 157, 187
  directions for essay assignments, 230
  essay exams, 132–157
  on film, 162
  sample student essays, 196–199, 221–222
EST. *See* English for Science and Technology
  (EST)
Explicit instruction, 160, 170–171, 176

Face validity, 20, 186
Faculty. *See* ESL/EFL teachers
Fatal Attraction, 162

Film and Society course, 158–178
  description of course, 158–178
  discussion, 163–165
Final-year engineering project reports (FYPs), 99,
    100–103
Fluency, 76
Focus discipline groups, 56
Foreign language immersion programs, 5
Frames, 82
Frameworks, 74–95
  applying, 86–88
  attitudinal, 84, 86, 87
  discourse, 83, 85
  emotional, 80–82
  lexical, 82
  referential, 82–83, 84
Functional literacy, 55
Fund for the Improvement of Post-secondary Education (FIPSE), 133

GAP, 77
Genre analysis
  generic commonalities, 13
  linear analysis, 2
  studies, 11–12
Georgia State University, 20–34
  academic writing for university exams, 132–157
  core courses, 25–26
  principles and parameters of EAP curriculum, 23–25
Grammar
  analytical tasks, 41–47
  content and, 36–53, 186–187
  definitions, 118
  discourse–level, 24
  in-class verus out-of-class errors, 21
  matching parts of connected sentences, 193–194
  metalinguistics and, 118–124
  reading and, 40–53
  well-formedness principles, 119
Graphic organizers, 139, 152
Great Conversation, The (Hutchins), 207
Grice's maxims, 77

Health course, 179–199
  autobiography, 184–185
  choice methodology, 182–183, 188, 189
  drama, 187–188
  grammar in context and, 186–187
  interactivity of, 182
  interdisciplinary nature of, 182, 190
  newsmagazine, 183–184

Hierarchical constituent analysis, 126–127
Homework. *See* Assignments
Homophobia, 187
Hong Kong, ESL study in, 98
Hostos Community College, 8

Idioms, 82
Induction, 74, 88–92
I Never Knew I Had a Choice (Corey), 181, 182,
    188–189
Inference, 32–33, 37–38, 105
Infinitives, 122
-ing words, 121, 126
Input in language learning, 5, 10, 21, 26–32
Intensifiers, 93
Interculturality, 183, 191
Interdisciplinary English (Kasper), 60
Internet, 54–73
    evaluating sites, 59
    hyperlinks, 59
    meta-sites, 59
    Online Writing Labs (OWL), 59
    reading skills and, 57
    searches, 59
    student research and, 56, 58–59, 61–63, 65–67
    using for business research, 61–63
    using for environmental science, 64, 65–67
    writing skills and, 57–58
Intertextuality, 182, 191
Introductions, 111, 116

Joint (J), 38, 39, 40, 46

Krashen, S., 5

Language learning. *See also specific issues*
    academic register, 24
    assessment issues and, 227–229
    discourse analysis and, 13
    input in language learning, 5, 10, 21, 26–32
    integrated, 21
    marking language, 90–91
    output in language learning, 10, 12, 27
    pedagogical language versus task-based language,
        24
    problem solving and, 52
    register, 24, 76–77, 92, 190
    transferable language knowledge, 13
    types of critical skills needed for, 3
Langue versus *parole*, 5
Last Action Hero, 162

Lectures, 31. *See also* Notetaking
Left-Dislocation, 77
Lehman College of the City University of New York
    (CUNY), 180
Linguistic competence, 108
Listening skills, 10, 236
    as input skill, 26–32
    integrated with other skills, 21
Literacy, 55, 133. *See also* Academic literacy/
    discourse
    critical literacy, 135
    media literacy, 160
Llado-Torres, Nitza, 187

Macalaster College, 7–8
Magazines. *See* Periodical reading
Maslow's hierarchy of needs, 181, 188–189
Media literacy, 160
Metacognitive ability, 119, 124–127
Metacognitive awareness, 119, 124–127
Metalinguistic course
    content, 120–127
    student population, 119–120
    table of contents for, 131
    whole language and, 130
Metalinguistics, 117–131
    principles of, 119
Mitigators, 93
Modals, 108
Modeling, 160, 170–171
Muriel's Wedding, 166
Mutable verbs (MV), 120–125
    definition of, 123

Notetaking, 21–22, 23, 30–32, 137, 147
Noun phrase (NP), 38, 42–44
    analysis chart, 43, 45
Nouns, 120–121

Old Man and the Sea, 35–53
    comprehension questions for, 42
Once Upon a Time in America, 162
Online Writing Labs (OWL), 59
Ottawa, Canada, 8
Outlining, 104–106, 112, 114–115, 162
Output in language learning, 10, 27, 106–107, 186
    comprehensible output, 10
    pushed output, 10, 12

Paraphrasing, 25, 207
Participial phrase (PP), 38, 39, 40, 46

Passive voice, 4, 187
Past participles, 121–122
Past perfect verb tense, 186
Pedagogy
    benefits of content-based instruction (CBI), 6, 9
    comic book use and, 79
    critical pedagogy, 3, 9
    critical skills and, 3, 9
    metalinguistic principles and, 119
    pedagogical choice, 212
    pedagogical language versus task-based language,
        24
    pedagogical tasks, 23, 24, 27, 133, 137–140
    tranformative pedagogy, 3, 9
*People's Court: Socio-dramas for Advanced ESL Con-
    versation Classes*, 187–188
Periodical reading, 180, 182, 183–184, 192
Philadelphia, 183, 187
Piano, The, 162
Political issues. *See* Power issues
Portfolio writing, 165–167, 237
Power issues, 3–4, 12
Pragmatic mapping, 90, 93
Prepositions
    with literal extension, 82–83
    with metaphoric extension, 82–83
Presentation skills, 10. *See also* Speaking skills; Writ-
    ing skills
    claim-and-support strategies, 10
Private speech, 6
Problem solving, 52, 100
Processing, 74–75
PROP, 77
Proposition, 77
Psychology content, 26–27
Punctuation, 39
Purdue OWL, 59

Reading skills, 10
    clause structure, 39
    cohesion, 39
    connecting to writing, 20, 134–135, 201–202
    functional shifts, 38–39
    grammar and, 40–53
    inference, 37–38
    as input skill, 26–32, 103–104
    integrated with other skills, 21
    Internet and, 57
    log books, 207, 211, 236
    prereading activity, 60–61, 64
    reading activity, 61, 64

reading aloud, 41
reading strategies, 29–30
REF, 77
Reference words, minimal, 83
Referent tracing, 46
    exercise, 48
Reflection, 202–203, 206–208. *See also* Critical
    thinking
Register, 24, 76–77, 92, 190
Relative clause, 124
Relevance theory, 77
Research, ESL
    EFL studies, 8–9
    ESL studies, 7–8
    findings on CBI, 7–9
    findings on sustained CBI, 11–12, 160
    Open Doors, 58, 60, 63
Research, student
    data collection, 101–102
    engineering, 100–103, 113, 116
    in-depth, 56, 185
    Internet, 56, 58–59, 61–63, 65–67, 185
Rhetoric
    content and, 13
    contrastive rhetoric, 2, 173
    cultural variance of rhetorical conventions, 2–3
    linear analysis, 2
    modes of, 57–58, 108, 137
    socio-political uses of, 3
Right-Dislocation, 77
Ryan White, My Own Story, 181
Ryan White Story, The, 187

Saussure, F. de, 5
Scaffolding, 6, 12, 133
Scanning, 29–30
Schema theory, 5, 135
Schindler's List, 172
Second-language acquisition. *See* Language
    learning
Seminars, 208–210
    on planetary interest, 210
    on technology, 208
    on values, 208–209
    on Wisdom Traditions, 208–209
Sequence skills, 88, 90
Sheltered courses of CBI, 7, 8, 227, 231
Sinclair, John, 36
Skimming, 29–30
Small Is Beautiful (Schumacher), 205–206, 210–211,
    216–218

Speaking skills, 10
    frames of reference, 74–94
    integrated with other skills, 21
    intonation, 81
    lexical expletives, 80
    nonlexical sounds, 80
    oral reports, 185, 236
    reactions, 80
    reading aloud, 41
    stress, 81
    suprasegmentals, 81
Speech. *See* English language; Speaking skills
Stanley and Iris, 166
Students. *See* ESL/EFL students
Study skills, 29–32. *See also specific skills*
Substitute (SUB), 38, 39, 46
Summaries, 21, 184, 185, 202, 203–204, 206
Sustained content-based instruction, 2. *See also*
        Content
    advantages of, 23, 134
    background knowledge and, 23
    comprehension development, 10
    cumulative knowledge and, 23
    Internet and, 54–73
    need for, 9–10
    research and, 11–12, 56, 160
    support for, 10–11
    syntactic awareness and, 23
    theory development by students, 11
    vocabulary development, 10–11, 23
Syllabus, 229
Synthesizing skills, 9, 23, 61, 64–65, 106, 134,
        226–227

Taboo words, 81
Task-based CBI, 7
Teachers. *See* ESL/EFL teachers
"Telling increment," 77
Temple University (Japan), 8
Term papers, 11
Testing, 25, 141–142, 195. *See also* Assessment
Test-taking skills, 20, 21
    application questions, 32
    comparison/contrast essay questions, 140, 152,
        154–155, 156, 157
    essay exams, 132–157
    ID questions, 137, 148
    inference questions, 32–33
    literal questions, 32

short answer questions, 137, 149, 151
    student-generated answers and questions,
        137–139
Text analysis, 176–178, 206–207
    assumptions, 207
    commentary, 203–222
    consequences, 207
    definition, 159
    film, 162
    grammatical analysis of *The Old Man and the Sea*,
        37–53
    implications, 207
    implicit versus explicit meanings, 207
    other-standardness and, 159
    studies, 11
Textbook content, 26–27, 103–104, 134, 182. *See also*
        Content
    language structure and, 140
Text construction, definition of, 159
"Text responsible" papers, 11, 12
"That," function analysis, 49
Thelma and Louise, 161, 162
Theme-based CBI, 6–7, 227
(THEME) CORE (TAIL) unit, 77
Time, 180, 182
Transferability of skills, 20
Transferable language knowledge, 13, 159–160
Transition devices, 162

Universal donors of content, 13
University of California at Los Angeles (UCLA), 7
University of Rhode Island
    EFL study, 8
    job placement program, 8
University of Texas, 9
Untouchables, The, 161, 162, 165

Verb phrase (VP), 38, 44
    analysis chart, 38, 44, 46
Verbs, general, 82
Vocabulary
    academic, 27–28
    affixes, 28
    in context, 28–29, 38
    discipline-specific language, 13, 27
    functional shifts, 38–39
    inference, 37–38
    for production, 27
    for recognition, 28
    stems, 28

sustained content-based instruction and, 10–11, 23, 27–29

Vygotsky, L., 6

Well-formedness principles, 119

Working on a Miracle (Johnson), 184

World's Religions, The (Smith), 209

Writing competence, 108

Writing skills, 10, 106, 107. *See also* Essays; Text analysis

    autobiography project, 47–52

    commentary, 203–204

    connecting to reading, 10, 134–135, 201–206

    for engineering students, 96–116

    error analysis, 127, 129

    essay exams, 132–157, 237

    exemplification, 159, 165, 167–168, 171–172

    explicit instruction, 160, 170–171, 176

    group writing, 184

    integrated with other skills, 21

    modeling, 160

    paper organization, 159, 160

    portfolio writing, 165–167, 237

    questioning texts, 168. *See also* Critical thinking

    sample compositions, 121–122, 196–199

    standards for papers, 212

    synthesis of concepts, 61, 64–65, 134–135

    term papers, 11

    "text responsible" papers, 11, 12

    voice in writing, 160

    writing with time constraints, 23, 140, 152, 154–155, 156, 157